Lady De Lancey at Waterloo

A Story of Duty and Devotion

To my wife, Mary, with much love and with heartfelt
thanks for her endless patience.

LADY DE LANCEY
AT
WATERLOO

A STORY OF DUTY AND DEVOTION

by

David Miller

Foreword by Sir Douglas Hall Bt, KCMG

SPELLMOUNT
Staplehurst

British Library Cataloguing in Publication Data:
A catalogue record for this book is available
from the British Library

Copyright © David Miller 2000
Foreword copyright © Sir Douglas Hall Bt 2000

ISBN 1-86227-082-1

First published in the UK in 2000 by
Spellmount Limited
The Old Rectory
Staplehurst
Kent TN12 0AZ

Tel: 01580 893730
Fax: 01580 893731
E-mail: enquiries@spellmount.com
Website: www.spellmount.com

1 3 5 7 9 8 6 4 2

Typeset in Palatino by MATS, Southend-on-Sea, Essex
Printed in Great Britain by
TJ International Ltd, Padstow, Cornwall

Contents

List of Maps

Acknowledgements

No book of this nature would be possible without the cooperation of many other people and I have been most fortunate, since those I consulted have been exceptionally helpful and knowledgeable.

Hall Family
My thanks are due to many members of the various branches of the Hall family who have endured an outsider's probing into their family history with great tolerance and good humour. In particular, I wish to record my gratitude to Sir Douglas Hall, 14th Baronet, who not only answered a great number of questions, but has also written the Foreword to this book. His son, John, has also been of immense help and, despite having a very busy job, has never failed to find the time to provide answers or to listen to my progress reports. Other members of the family who have helped include Mrs Sally Anslow-Wilson, Dr Hugo Breitmeyer, Nick Fuller-Sessions, who carried out his first research assignments most ably, Dorothy, Lady Hall, widow of the 13th Baronet, Mrs Barbara Rich, Martin Whitlock, and many others.

Harvey, Reynolds and Davies Families
My researches into the history of the descendants of Henry and Magdalene Harvey involved fewer people, but those whom I did contact proved as helpful as the Halls. These included Mrs Mary Birch Reynardson and Lieutenant-Colonel Frank Groves of the Irish Guards. I am particularly grateful to Philip Reynolds Davies, whose generosity, enthusiasm and readiness to help enabled me to fill in many areas which would otherwise have remained unexplained or unexplored.

De Lancey Family
I had greater difficulty in making contacts with the De Lancey family, but those whom I did manage to reach in Canada included VW De Lancey Esq., who was most helpful, while others who helped with information were Donna Lee Butler of Granville Ferry and Linda Davison-Landymore of Kings-Edgehill School, Windsor, both of Nova Scotia. My special thanks also go to James B Lamb of Baddeck, Nova Scotia, author of the novel about the De Lanceys, *In Love and War*, who provided early help on

the subject and without whose letter to the magazine, *This England*, I would never have found Magdalene's grave. In England, I am indebted to Martin De Lancey of Westbury-on-Trym and to Hugh Westerley, who found Cornelia De Lancey's memorial plaque in Colchester.

Local Historians

One of the great unsung resources of this country is the large number of local historians, who devote so much of their 'free' time to researching the history and people of their local area, and who are most ready to share their knowledge with serious enquirers. It is my invariable experience that they have a vast store of knowledge at their fingertips, and on the few occasions when they do not know an answer they almost always know someone who does. Among those who have helped me with this book are NJ Carr, Churchwarden of St Stephen's, Little Bookham, Mrs Pamela Gooding of Holt, Wiltshire, and DPD Stafford Esq. of St Audrie's, Somerset. I am deeply grateful to Berna Moody of Beverley, Yorkshire and to Sally Smith of Cockburnspath, Berwickshire, Scotland, both of whom gave freely of their unparalleled knowledge of their area. Sally also carried out research in Edinburgh on my behalf and the fruits of her researches have recently been published in her own book, *Cockburnspath: A History of a People and a Place* (Dunglass Mill Press, 1999), which is unhesitatingly recommended as a wonderful example of what can be achieved by a private publisher.

Other Help

Others whose help is gratefully acknowledged include Mrs Audrey Clerk, Gale Hawkes of Washington, USA, who gave considerable help on the subject of medals, Dr Jean Jones of Edinburgh, who answered many queries on the subject of the Scottish Enlightenment and Major Anthony Cullen of Manaton, Devon.

Libraries

Many librarians and their staffs provided immense help, including Gayle Barklay, The Huntington Library, San Diego, California, USA, Pam Bendall, Joint Command & Staff College, Bracknell, Nicola Best, Royal Society of Chemistry, London, Sarah Dodgson at the Athenaeum, London, Rita Gibbs, Harrow School, Mrs Penelope Hatfield, Eton College, Mrs Christine Leighton, Cheltenham College, and Tim Ward, Prince Consort's Library, Aldershot. I also thank the staff of my local library at Newton Abbot, Devon, who never failed to find an obscure reference, and the London Library who, as always, gave so freely of their expertise. Finally, my thanks to the staffs of the Public Record Office, Kew, and the new British Library, two institutions whose resources are matched by the friendliness, knowledge and expertise of their staffs.

ACKNOWLEDGEMENTS

The Peninsular and Waterloo Campaigns
The Marquess of Anglesey and Philip Haythornthwaite, both authors of much greater repute than mine, have given considerable help and encouragement on matters relating to the Peninsular and Waterloo campaigns. I am also particularly grateful to John Hussey, who provided a great deal of very helpful advice and generously drew my attention to a number of sources which I would otherwise have missed.

Photographs
Two contemporary photographers' work appear in this book. The excellent pictures of the two portraits of Lady De Lancey and of her personal copy of the *Narrative* were taken by David Garner of Exmouth, Devon. The pictures of Sir William De Lancey's grave in Brussels were taken by Lieutenant-Colonel Lynn Relph, Royal Signals, who was stationed nearby and very kindly took the pictures, thus saving me an expensive and time-consuming trip to Belgium.

Archivists
A number of archivists provided most generous help, including Mrs Virginia Murray, the librarian/archivist at John Murray, the publisher, while Dr CM Woolgar, the Archivist and Head of Special Collections at the Hartley Library, University of Southampton, gave me ready access to the huge collection of Wellington documents there. I am also grateful to the Hon. Georgina Stonor, OStJ, archivist to the Duke of Wellington, who very kindly provided information on the copy of *Lady De Lancey's Narrative* in the Duke's collection. Others included Dr Alastair Massie at the National Army Museum, Dr John Rhodes at the Royal Engineers' Museum, Chatham, and Dr Eric Anderson of Lincoln College, Oxford who advised on various matters relating to Sir Walter Scott.

Researcher
At some stages, I needed the help of a professional researcher and could not have done better than with Pauline Eismark, who provided support above and beyond the call of duty. Her great expertise provided many invaluable leads, which helped to solve some apparently insoluble problems.

Magdalene Hall's Portraits
The attribution of the two portraits of Magdalene Hall proved to be a challenge, but, again, help was at hand. I greatly appreciated the advice and expertise of Caroline Worthington of the Royal Albert Museum in Exeter, Devon, who started me on what turned out to be a long trail, which culminated at the Victoria and Albert Museum, London. There Sarah North of the Department of Textiles and Katherine Coombs of the

Department of Paintings examined the different aspects of the miniatures with great enthusiasm and made their expertise freely available to me.

Responsibility
While I gratefully ackowledge all this help and advice, any opinions expressed in this book are mine alone, as is the responsibility for any errors or omissions.

PERMISSION TO PUBLISH
Finally, I wish to acknowledge permission to publish extracts from copyright documents, as follows:

- Extracts from the letters of Captain Basil Hall, RN to Charles Dickens are reproduced by permission of The Huntington Library, San Marino, California, USA.
- Extracts from Crown Copyright documents are published by permission of the relevant custodians: the Curator of the Public Record Office, Kew, the Director of the British Library, and the Librarian, the Hartley Library of the University of Southampton.
- Extracts from Peter Hofschröer's book *1815 The Waterloo Campaign; Wellington, his German Allies and the Battles of Ligny and Quatre Bras* are published by permission of Lionel Leventhal, Esq., of Greenhill Books, London.

Foreword

by Sir Douglas Hall, 14th Baronet Hall of Dunglass, KCMG

This book is concerned with the lives of two remarkable young people who were very close to each other for a tragically short time during 1815. In many ways the Battle of Waterloo seems a very long time ago, but Magdalene Hall was my great-great-aunt, only three generations before mine.

The first part deals with Magdalene's husband, William De Lancey, and consists of a vivid description of him, and of activities in which he was involved, culminating in the Battle of Waterloo. The historical part is of great interest, and as the story gets closer to Waterloo the book takes on the character of a thriller, which I found impossible to put down.

Various pieces of history come through strongly. Particularly, perhaps, the birth of proper training for staff officers, who, following their education at the newly established 'First Department' (later the Staff College), developed a high degree of professionalism in the Peninsular and Waterloo campaigns and who, despite their youth, enjoyed a remarkable degree of responsibility. Also very striking are the improvements which have taken place since then in the care of the wounded, although these are more than counter-balanced by the severity of the wars.

Of more particular note is the splendid character of William, and of the shoddy way he was treated, taking into account what he had done as a young army officer. Official excuses seem very weak.

Part Two is concerned with some of the history of the Hall family, with specific reference to Magdalene. Not surprisingly I found this very interesting, and have learned a number of new facts which David Miller has discovered about the family.

As to Part Three, a few, like myself, will have read this before in the form of *A Week at Waterloo* edited by Major BR Ward, RE and published in 1906. This is such a poignant narrative, I feel it would be almost sacrilegious to make any comment. It so clearly speaks for itself.

The last part of the book is in some respects the most interesting of all, as it brings to light descendants of Magdalene, through her second marriage, who will never previously have been the subject of deep research. This very interesting finale probably involved the author in more detective work than any other part of the book, so it is especially good to read his acknowledgements of the splendid help he received from members of the family living today.

David Miller has recorded a most useful period of history in the form of a very readable book. Well done!

Roughes Hull

Introduction

My principal end is always to observe the
spirit of the times, since it is that which
directs the great events of the world.

Voltaire

Famous commanders are remembered by statues, but there are no such memorials for staff officers, who served out of public view and who, in many cases, made their commander's victories possible. One such is Colonel Sir William Howe De Lancey, the first truly professional staff officer in the British Army, who served the great Duke of Wellington devotedly throughout his campaigns in the Peninsula and at Waterloo, where he suffered the wound from which he died ten days later. He has just two plain memorial stones both in obscure places but, uniquely among his kind, he has another memorial which will endure, unchanged and without decay, for centuries and long after the statues of the others have been worn away or quietly removed.

The Peninsular War and the Waterloo campaign are remembered by a huge treasury of literature, ranging from official correspondence, such as Wellington's *Dispatches*, through the personal records in diaries, journals, and letters home, to the seemingly endless personal reminiscences of the Duke of Wellington. Some of these accounts were written on the day of the event or a few days later and these remain as fresh as the day on which they were written by people such as Seymour Larpent, Wellington's Judge-Advocate-General in the Peninsula or Lieutenant-Colonel Sir Augustus Frazer, who commanded the Royal Horse Artillery at Waterloo. Then there are the personal reminiscences written by the participants but some time after the event, such as those by General von Müffling, the Prussian, Captain Hay, the cavalryman, the dashing Harry Smith of the Rifles, Moyle Shearer, the educated infantryman, Basil Jackson, the staff officer, and many, many others.

Some of these books are well known, while others sit on some long-forgotten shelf, gathering dust in a specialist library. One document which is occasionally quoted in modern works is *Lady De Lancey's Narrative*, in which the writer describes how, having been married barely a month, she accompanied her husband to Brussels, was parted from him by the brief

Waterloo campaign, found him afterwards wounded, and then nursed him for ten days until he died. A few copies of the original were made and were eagerly read by men such as Wellington, Sir Walter Scott and, somewhat later, Charles Dickens; all were deeply moved by its purity of tone, its transparent honesty, the frank portrayal of emotion and, above all, by its literary merit. The work has been published three times: in abridged form in an English magazine in 1888, in full in an American magazine in 1906 and again in full, but with additional notes and commentary, in book form in England, also in 1906.

Sir William and Lady Magdalene De Lancey were almost the complete opposites of each other. He was a hardened professional soldier, whose youth and entire adult life were spent in the Army, fighting in the Netherlands, off the French coast, in the Cape of Good Hope, in India, and in both Peninsular campaigns, first with Moore and then with Wellington. He was a brilliantly successful staff officer, who was personally responsible for choosing the position which the Allies defended so splendidly at Waterloo and who, according to Wellington (and who would have known better?), would have gone on to much greater things had he lived.

Magdalene Hall was the child of two most enlightened, sophisticated and intellectual Scottish parents; a beautiful and gentle young woman, who would have been totally at home in a Jane Austen novel. These two met, wooed, married and lost each other in the space of six months, their life together culminating in a tragedy in which both demonstrated love and nobility of character rarely seen, let alone recorded.

Sir William was killed in the prime of life and did not have the opportunity to write his memoirs. Like the vast majority of his fellow officers, he must have written letters home, but to whom and whether any still exist cannot be discovered. Such few documents of his that do survive are of an official nature and closely associated with his military career, so that any personal glimpses of minor incidents or chance meetings lie in the records of his contemporaries.

It is certain that Magdalene wrote many letters, of which some forty are known to have survived. She only attempted one piece of serious writing – her *Narrative* but that is sufficient, since that short document ensures that her beloved husband and their love for each other remain alive for ever. The *Narrative* was, however, written for friends and assumes that the reader will already be fully acquainted with the two main characters, and this book seeks to enable the modern reader to appreciate it properly by examining their families and their totally contrasting backgrounds, tracing their lives until they reach a common climax at the Battle of Waterloo.

I have used a number of conventions throughout this book, which are explained here to avoid excessive explanatory notes.

Field Marshal the Duke of Wellington, KG, GCB, etc. earned a large number of British and foreign titles during his military career, many of which changed his correct form of address. In his early days he was plain Arthur Wellesley (or Wesley, according to the signatures on some of his letters), but during the Peninsular campaign he was, in turn, Sir Arthur Wellesley, Marquis of Douro, Marquis of Wellesley, Earl of Wellington, Viscount Wellington of Talavera and of Wellington, and, finally, Duke of Wellington. Within the Peninsular army he was generally known to the troops as 'Douro', but among the headquarters staff he was referred to, first as 'The Marquis' then as 'The Peer'. Later, following his dukedom, he became generally known as 'Wellington' and that is how he is referred to throughout this book. If an authority is required, then let it be the well-authenticated Peninsular story which relates how, when riding unobserved past a group of young officers, he overheard one of them proudly tell the others that he had been invited to 'dine with Wellington'. 'Give me at least the prefix of Mr before my name,' came the dry interjection, to which the unabashed and quick-witted young officer immediately replied: 'My Lord, we do not speak of Mr Caesar, or Mr Alexander, so why should I speak of Mr Wellington?'[1]

Where several different nations or a number of people are mentioned together, they are listed in alphabetical order according to the initial letter of their English names. Thus, the order gives no indication of relative size, importance, or the author's preferences.

Rather than place 'sic' after curious spellings or antiquated syntax, of which there are many examples in this book, it is stated here that all quotes are taken verbatim from the original source. Thus, any mistakes of fact, mis-spellings or curious grammatical constructions in such quotes come direct from the original, with two exceptions. Many names are spelt in a variety of ways in contemporary sources, particularly the family name of one of the two central characters, which is spelt as de Lancey, De Lancey or Delancy, and the Christian name of the heroine, which is spelt Magdalen, Magdaline or Magdalene. I have adopted the spellings used by these two people themselves – De Lancey and Magdalene, respectively – even in quotes where the original uses a different spelling.

Contemporary prices appear frequently throughout the book, at times ranging from the late seventeenth century to the early twentieth century. In order to give the reader a feel for the modern value of such figures, the 'then' price is given first, followed immediately by the equivalent value on 1 January 2000 in brackets and rounded off to the nearest £1,000.[2]

I have not followed the usual convention of indicating a character's future rank or status, e.g. Lieutenant-Colonel Fitzroy Somerset (later Field Marshal Lord Raglan). Without intending any disrespect to the people concerned, what is important is who and what they were at the time these events took place and that is how they appear in this book.

NOTES

1. *Waterloo Roll Call*, page 9.
2. These figures have been derived using the computer programme 'Value of the Pound Sterling (£) 1600–1998'.

Preface

Following the defeat of the French by the Allied armies on the evening of Sunday 18 June 1815, the British 12th Light Dragoons headed southwards from Waterloo in pursuit of the demoralised and disorganised French. Excited by the victory and the ensuing chase, Captain William Hay, a dashing young Scotsman, was most dismayed when, early the following morning, his commanding officer instructed him to take charge of a small detail and return northwards to look for the regiment's wounded men and horses. Hay expressed some reluctance, whereupon his commanding officer left him in no doubt as to where his duty lay, and the crestfallen young officer duly set off. When he reached the battlefield Hay was appalled by what he saw:

> The day was extremely hot, and the dead bodies, already offensive, were shocking to look at. Many wounded were among them, so disabled as not to have the power to extricate themselves. On gaining the road it was with difficulty my horse could pick his way or keep his footing as it was literally paved with steel, the cuirasses were so numerous, shining and glittering in the midday sun of June, making it quite dazzling to the eyesight. The ditches on each side of the road were lined with our wounded officers and soldiers, who had been borne there to be removed in some measure from the great thoroughfare, amongst whom I recognized several acquaintances. If I had felt sad and in low spirits before, this did not improve my mood. I remained some half hour offering what consolation I could to the sufferers I knew . . .[1]

Captain Hay continued on his way, passing through the hamlet of Mont St Jean, the village of Waterloo and the Forêt de Soignes until he reached Brussels. There he met a cousin, who was trying to verify reports that his brother, Cornet Alexander Hay of the 16th Light Dragoons, had been killed. Having done as his commanding officer ordered, William Hay, now joined by his cousin and by some troopers of the 12th Light Dragoons, set off, once again, for the battlefield and whilst there, Hay was told of a family friend who was nearby and in some distress. As a result, he made his way back to Mont St Jean, where:

The first, and certainly one of the most unpleasant visits I ever paid, was to a wretched little cottage at the end of the village, which was pointed out to me as the place where Colonel De Lancey was lying, mortally wounded. Conceive my feelings when I state that only a few months before, in December 1814, when at my happy home, I had been in the constant habit of meeting him whilst staying with our near neighbours and intimate friends – his wife's family (the Halls) living at Dunglass. Painful as it was, it was my imperative duty to call and enquire for her and offer my poor services.

How wholly shocked I was, on entering, to find her seated on the only broken chair the hovel contained by the side of her dying husband! An amiable, kind, and beautiful young woman, I had so recently left in the midst of her own delightful family, surrounded by every luxury, at that most trying moment in want of every comfort, and plunged in the deepest distress.

I made myself known, she grasped me by the hand and pointed to poor De Lancey, covered with his coat, just a spark of life left. Offering consolation would have been an insult and hypocrisy at such a moment; but imagine to yourself the kindhearted and high-minded young woman, in the midst of her own deep affliction, looking earnestly into my face, pale from long fatigue, and covered with dust from my already long ride in the heat, she rose, and beckoned me out of the room as if she thought it too much for me; and, returning herself, brought me some wine in an old broken teacup – the only article of that description in the house. I bade her farewell and proceeded some little distance farther into the village . . .[2]

To discover who this badly wounded officer was, how it came about that he was dying in this peasant's hovel, and why his beautiful and devoted wife was on the spot to nurse him, we must turn, first, to the husband. One of Wellington's closest friends, he was sometimes referred to as 'the American', but due to his position he was one of the most influential and highly respected officers in the army, being known as 'the gallant De Lancey'.

NOTES

1. Hay, William, *Reminiscences 1808–1815 Under Wellington*, pp 202–204
2. Hay, *op cit*

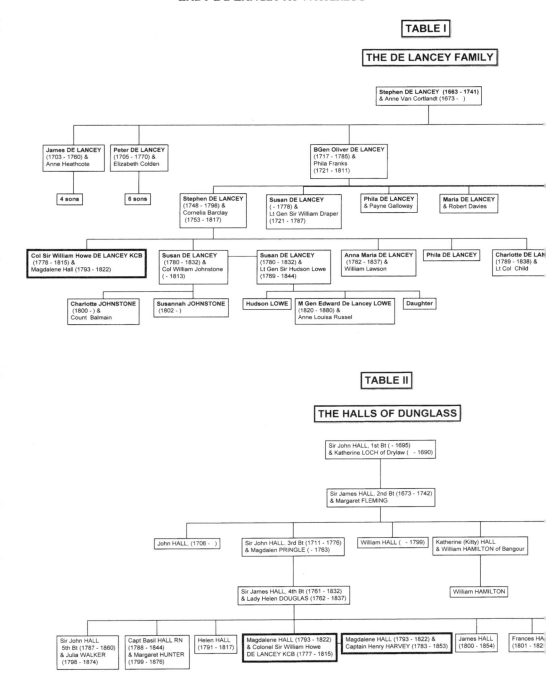

TABLE I

THE DE LANCEY FAMILY

Stephen DE LANCEY (1663 - 1741)
& Anne Van Cortlandt (1673 -)

James DE LANCEY (1703 - 1760) & Anne Heathcote

Peter DE LANCEY (1705 - 1770) & Elizabeth Colden

BGen Oliver DE LANCEY (1717 - 1785) & Phila Franks (1721 - 1811)

4 sons

6 sons

Stephen DE LANCEY (1748 - 1798) & Cornelia Barclay (1753 - 1817)

Susan DE LANCEY (- 1778) & Lt Gen Sir William Draper (1721 - 1787)

Phila DE LANCEY & Payne Galloway

Maria DE LANCEY & Robert Davies

Col Sir William Howe DE LANCEY KCB (1778 - 1815) & Magdalene Hall (1793 - 1822)

Susan DE LANCEY (1780 - 1832) & Col William Johnstone (- 1813)

Susan DE LANCEY (1780 - 1832) & Lt Gen Sir Hudson Lowe (1769 - 1844)

Anna Maria DE LANCEY (1782 - 1837) & William Lawson

Phila DE LANCEY

Charlotte DE LAN (1789 - 1838) & Lt Col Child

Charlotte JOHNSTONE (1800 -) & Count Balmain

Susannah JOHNSTONE (1802 -)

Hudson LOWE

M Gen Edward De Lancey LOWE (1820 - 1880) & Anne Louisa Russel

Daughter

TABLE II

THE HALLS OF DUNGLASS

Sir John HALL, 1st Bt (- 1695) & Katherine LOCH of Drylaw (- 1690)

Sir James HALL, 2nd Bt (1673 - 1742) & Margaret FLEMING

John HALL, (1706 -)

Sir John HALL, 3rd Bt (1711 - 1776) & Magdalen PRINGLE (- 1763)

William HALL (- 1799)

Katherine (Kitty) HALL & William HAMILTON of Bangour

Sir James HALL, 4th Bt (1761 - 1832) & Lady Helen DOUGLAS (1762 - 1837)

William HAMILTON

Sir John HALL 5th Bt (1787 - 1860) & Julia WALKER (1798 - 1874)

Capt Basil HALL RN (1788 - 1844) & Margaret HUNTER (1799 - 1876)

Helen HALL (1791 - 1817)

Magdalene HALL (1793 - 1822) & Colonel Sir William Howe DE LANCEY KCB (1777 - 1815)

Magdalene HALL (1793 - 1822) & Captain Henry HARVEY (1783 - 1853)

James HALL (1800 - 1854)

Frances HA (1801 - 182

FAMILY TREES

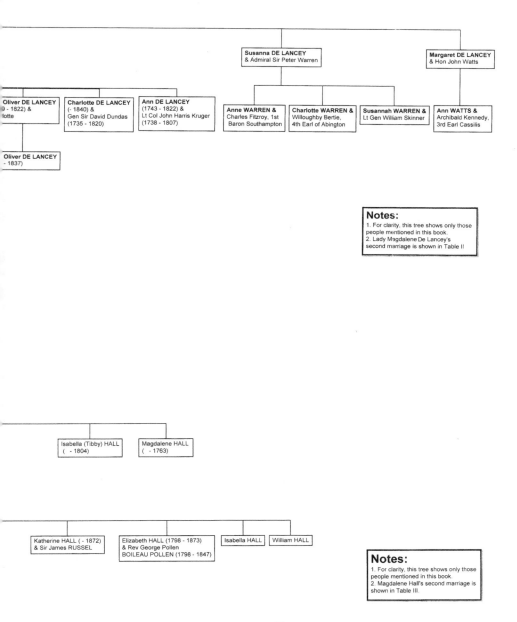

Susanna DE LANCEY
& Admiral Sir Peter Warren

Margaret DE LANCEY
& Hon John Watts

Oliver DE LANCEY
9 - 1822) &
lotte

Charlotte DE LANCEY
(- 1840) &
Gen Sir David Dundas
(1735 - 1820)

Ann DE LANCEY
(1743 - 1822) &
Lt Col John Harris Kruger
(1738 - 1807)

Anne WARREN &
Charles Fitzroy, 1st
Baron Southampton

Charlotte WARREN &
Willoughby Bertie,
4th Earl of Abington

Susannah WARREN &
Lt Gen William Skinner

Ann WATTS &
Archibald Kennedy,
3rd Earl Cassilis

Oliver DE LANCEY
- 1837)

Notes:
1. For clarity, this tree shows only those
people mentioned in this book.
2. Lady Magdalene De Lancey's
second marriage is shown in Table II

Isabella (Tibby) HALL
(- 1804)

Magdalene HALL
(- 1763)

Katherine HALL (- 1872)
& Sir James RUSSEL

Elizabeth HALL (1798 - 1873)
& Rev George Pollen
BOILEAU POLLEN (1798 - 1847)

Isabella HALL

William HALL

Notes:
1. For clarity, this tree shows only those
people mentioned in this book.
2. Magdalene Hall's second marriage is
shown in Table III.

TABLE III

THE HARVEY FAMILY

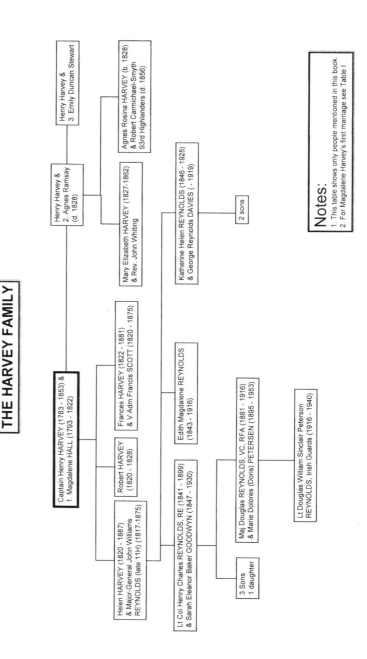

Henry Harvey &
2. Agnes Ramsay
(d. 1828)

Henry Harvey &
3. Emily Duncan Stewart

Captain Henry HARVEY (1783 - 1853) &
1. Magdalene HALL (1793 - 1822)

Agnes Rosina HARVEY (b. 1828)
& Robert Carmichael-Smyth
93rd Highlanders (d. 1856)

Mary Elizabeth HARVEY (1827-1862)
& Rev. John Whiting

Frances HARVEY (1822 - 1881)
& V Adm Francis SCOTT (1820 - 1875)

Robert HARVEY
(1820 - 1828)

Helen HARVEY (1820 - 1887)
& Major-General John Williams
REYNOLDS (late 11H) (1817-1875)

Katherine Helen REYNOLDS (1846 - 1925)
& George Reynolds DAVIES (- 1919)

2 sons

Edith Magdalene REYNOLDS
(1843 - 1916)

Lt Col Henry Charles REYNOLDS, RE (1841 - 1899)
& Sarah Eleanor Baker GOODWYN (1847 - 1930)

Maj Douglas REYNOLDS, VC, RFA (1881 - 1916)
& Marie Dolores (Doris) PETERSEN (1895 - 1953)

Lt Douglas William Sinclair Peterson
REYNOLDS, Irish Guards (1916 - 1940)

3 Sons
1 daughter

Notes:
1. This table shows only people mentioned in this book.
2. For Magdalene Harvey's first marriage see Table I

The De Lancey coat-of-arms consists of a red shield, divided into three by two silver bars, with three silver cinquefoils in the upper third. The crest is a half leopard supporting an anchor. (Michael Heywood)

PART ONE

Sir William Howe De Lancey

CHAPTER I
The De Lancey Family

The British De Lanceys were descended from a French Huguenot and owed much to the British Crown that had provided them with a haven from persecution which gave them the freedom and opportunity to make a vast fortune. The De Lanceys responded to this with a loyalty so complete that it brought them to total ruin in the American Revolution, but, undeterred, and without any noticeable bitterness, they picked up the pieces and continued to serve the Crown, none with greater distinction than Colonel Sir William De Lancey, Knight Commander of the Bath (KCB), one of Wellington's closest colleagues, the longest serving of his staff officers in the Peninsula, and his chief-of-staff at the Battle of Waterloo.

The De Lancey family is believed to have derived its name from the village of Lancie, which today lies in western Switzerland, but in the fifteenth century was part of France. The family adopted the Protestant faith at the time of the Reformation and played its full part in the religious wars which culminated in what proved to be a temporary peace brought about by the Edict of Nantes (13 April 1598).

By the middle of the seventeenth century Seigneur Jacques De Lancey was living in Caen, in northern France, where a son, Etienne, was born in 1663. The return of religious persecution in the early 1680s led to the formal revocation of the Edict of Nantes in 1685, as a result of which large numbers of Huguenots fled the country. The De Lancey parents appear to have remained in Caen, but Etienne and his sister escaped across the Channel to England, where both were granted citizenship, and, while leaving his surname unchanged, Etienne anglicised his Christian name to Stephen. Fortunately, before he left France, Stephen's mother had given him some jewels, which he sold in England to realise the then princely sum of £300 sterling (£27,000). With this small fortune in their pockets, brother and sister emigrated to the English colony of North America, arriving in New York City in 1686. There, through a combination of hard work and business acumen – characteristics shared by many Huguenots – Stephen amassed a fortune of some £100,000 (approximately £9 million), becoming one of the wealthiest men in his adopted country.

Such wealth enabled Stephen to fit easily into New York society and he married a wealthy heiress of Dutch stock, Anne Van Cortlandt, by whom he had five sons, at least three of whom were sent to England for their education, and three daughters (see Table I). He also played a major role in New York affairs, serving as an alderman (1691–1693) and assembly-man (1702–1715 and 1726–1737), and was also something of a philan-thropist, donating the first town clock and the first fire engine to his new home. He did not, however, overlook his origins and provided shelter and encouragement for newly arrived Huguenots who needed help in adjusting to their new lives.

The Second Generation
Stephen's eldest son, James, was born in 1703 and received his early education in New York before going to England to attend Cambridge University, where he was known as 'The Handsome American'. He then read law at the Inner Temple, was called to the Bar at the age of 21 and returned to New York in 1725, where he established a very successful law practice. In 1728 he married Anne Heathcote, daughter of the Mayor of New York, who brought a large dowry from her wealthy father, thus adding to the De Lancey fortune. In 1731 James was appointed a judge and only two years later became a very youthful chief justice, a post he retained until his death. Like his father he played an increasingly impor-tant role in the political life of the colony, although his progress was impeded by the British Governor, Admiral Clinton, who took such a strong dislike to James, that when the latter was appointed Lieutenant Governor in 1747, Clinton declined to hand over the Royal Commission formalising the appointment. The Governor resisted all local pressure, but was eventually forced to give in by a direct order from London in 1753. On Clinton's departure in 1754, James De Lancey became the acting Gover-nor, in which role he became President of the first Congress to be held in North America in 1754 and in 1755 he was a member of the Colonial Council, consisting of all the governors of the various British colonies in North America, which was held in Alexandria, Virginia. Thus, James De Lancey, the second generation immigrant, was the leading figure in New York until his sudden death in 1760.

The other important member of the second generation was Stephen De Lancey's youngest son, Oliver (1717–1785), who cooperated with his eldest brother in building up the De Lancey fortune and also became a politician, sitting in the Assembly for many years. Oliver also had military leanings and during the French War (1754–1760) he raised troops, mainly at his own expense, took part in the Crown Point expedition in August-September 1755 and then served as 'colonel-in-chief' of New York State under General Abercrombie for the remainder of the war, activities which earned him a formal motion of thanks from the New York Assembly in 1758.

When the American Revolution broke out in 1775, virtually all the De

Lanceys sided with the Crown. Oliver De Lancey raised a force of some 1,500 Loyalists, again largely at his own expense, which were organised into three 'De Lancey Battalions'. One of these battalions served with the British Army in the south under Lieutenant-Colonel John Kruger (1738–1807), who had married Oliver's daughter, Ann, while the two others remained in Queen's County. Oliver became a brigadier-general, making him the highest ranking Loyalist officer, serving under General William Howe as military commander of Long Island throughout the war.

On the British defeat Oliver De Lancey was named by the newly created US Congress in the Bill of Attainder, as a result of which his huge properties were seized and he went to England where, along with a number of other Loyalists, he settled in Beverley, Yorkshire. When the British government eventually settled the Loyalists' claims he received $125,000 on a claim of $390,000 loss and died in Beverley in 1785.

Numerous British naval and army officers sent to the North American colonies found brides there, and two of Stephen's daughters made particularly advantageous matches. The eldest of the three married Captain Peter Warren, Royal Navy, in 1743, whose ship, HMS *Launceston*, was refitting in a New York shipyard. Warren came from a relatively poor Irish family, but was one of the most fortunate officers in the Royal Navy where prize money from captured enemy ships was concerned, being so successful that towards the end of his life he was recognised as one of the wealthiest commoners in England. He thus proved a suitable husband for Susanna De Lancey, who was reported to have brought her husband 'a pretty fortune' as a marriage settlement. Also at the time of his marriage, Warren took the opportunity to purchase a 300-acre farm on Manhattan Island, a property whose value today could scarcely be computed, but his heirs disposed of it shortly after his death.

Admiral Sir Peter and Susannah Warren's wealth and position helped their three daughters to marry very well. Anne, the eldest, married Charles Fitzroy, 1st Baron Southampton; Charlotte married Willoughby Bertie, 4th Earl of Abington; and Susannah, the youngest, married Colonel William Skinner, who subsequently rose to the rank of lieutenant-general.

Stephen De Lancey's youngest daughter, Margaret, also did well, marrying the Honourable John Watts, a Justice of the Supreme Court. Their only daughter, Ann, married Captain Archibald Kennedy, 3rd Earl Cassilis, whose son became the 1st Marquess of Ailsa.

The Third Generation
In the third generation, the bulk of the family wealth passed to Chief Justice James De Lancey's eldest son, James (1732–1800), who had been educated in England, first at Eton College and then at Cambridge University. He was commissioned into the army and rose to the rank of captain, but was forced to leave when his father died in 1760, since he was

5

required to assume his responsibilities for the family estates and businesses. Like his father and grandfather, he entered politics and quickly established a dominant position in New York affairs. He tried very hard to get the British government in London to see sense in the lead-up to the Revolution, but when the rift came he maintained his loyalty to the Crown and departed for England in 1775. His property was seized in 1779, but he became a leading light in the fight for compensation, eventually obtaining $160,000 on a claim of $284,000, the third highest sum to be paid out by the British government. He never returned to America and died in Bath, England in April 1800.[1] His two sons died without heirs and, with that, this particular branch of the family became extinct.

Stephen De Lancey

Stephen De Lancey (1748–1798), Brigadier-General Oliver De Lancey's eldest son and father of the future Colonel Sir William Howe De Lancey, was born in New York City and was educated in England before returning to New York, where he practised law. Like most of the family he was a strong supporter of the Crown during the American Revolution, serving as the lieutenant-colonel commanding the second of the three De Lancey Battalions, but then, when the Crown admitted defeat, the De Lancey property was sequestrated and the family dispersed. A few remained in the newly created United States, but played no further part in political affairs; most went direct to England and a few travelled north with other Loyalists to Canada. Stephen and his brother-in-law, John Harris Kruger, both spent several years in Canada, and from 1781 to 1784 were employed as 'Inspectors of Loyalists', each being responsible for the welfare of the poorer Loyalists in a specific area.[2] Other De Lanceys took up farming in Nova Scotia and their descendants remain in Canada to this day.

The greatest number of Loyalists went to England, the country they had all supported but which few had seen before and, not surprisingly, on their arrival they tended to settle in clusters for mutual support. A number of the De Lanceys and their friends formed one such group in southern Yorkshire, with Brigadier-General Oliver De Lancey and his wife settling in the ancient city of Beverley, where they were joined a few years later by their son-in-law, Lieutenant-Colonel John Kruger. Stephen and his wife Cornelia and their children also moved to England, where they lived for a short period in the village of Wellton on the north bank of the River Humber, before they, too, moved to Beverley.[3] Their stay there was not particularly long, however, as by 1789 they were resident in Green Street, near Grosvenor Square in London.[4]

Having seen his family safely settled, Stephen managed to secure two successive appointments in British government service, the first of which was as Chief Justice of the Bahama Islands in the early 1790s. The second was as Captain-General, Commander-in-Chief and Governor of the Colony of Tobago, which he reached aboard HMS *Roebuck* on 18 July 1797, formally assuming the post on the following day.[5]

In the years prior to Stephen De Lancey's arrival, Tobago had been administered in turn by the Spanish, Dutch, British, French and then the British again, and the previous decade had been a most unhappy period in the island's history. The French forces on the island mutinied in 1789, a hurricane devastated it in 1790, the French governor was so unpopular that he had to be removed in 1792, and the island was invaded and repossessed by the British in 1793. Then the first of the new series of British governors stayed less than a year (1794–1795) before being moved to a more important governorship in Barbados and the next governor, William Lindsay, died on the island shortly after taking up the appointment in 1796.[6]

With such a turbulent recent history, it is not surprising that Stephen De Lancey encountered problems, particularly with the Assembly and Militia, many of the officers of the latter being members of the former. Matters reached such a state that the Assembly despatched a formal complaint to the Secretary-of-State for the Colonies, while the Militia sent another, on a separate issue, to the Commander-in-Chief in the West Indies. These differences seem, however, to have been overcome and De Lancey was able to report in April 1798 that harmony had been restored, although by that time he was suffering from an increasingly severe illness, which on 11 September 1798 forced him to obtain a certificate from his doctor who formally informed the Council that '. . . I am of the Opinion, It is absolutely necessary for him to go from this, to a Cold Climate for the Re-establishment of his Health.' The Council duly authorised the Governor to take leave for the sake of his health, extended its best wishes for a speedy recovery and voted him the princely sum of £1,000 (£58,000) to help.[7]

Governor Stephen De Lancey left the island on 16 October aboard the merchantman, *Amelia*, which was heading for the United States, from where he intended to rejoin his family in England. He arrived in Portsmouth, New Hampshire on 4 December 1798 and had the reward of a final few hours in the land of his birth before dying that very night. He was buried in St John's church in Portsmouth on 6 December 1798, the register recording that he died '. . . of a decline which had been upon him for six months.' He was just 50 years old.

Stephen had married Cornelia Barclay (1753–1817) by whom he had five children. There were four daughters, the eldest, Susan (1780–1832), marrying twice, her first husband being Colonel William Johnstone, by whom she had two daughters, Charlotte and Susannah. Johnstone died in 1813 and Susan's second husband was Lieutenant-General Sir Hudson Lowe, whom she married on 30 December 1815 and then accompanied to

St Helena, where he was Governor during the former Emperor Napoleon's exile there. Stephen and Cornelia had three other daughters: Anna Maria married William Lawson: Charlotte married a soldier, Lieutenant-Colonel Child, while Phila, as far as can be discovered, did not marry.

Stephen and Cornelia had only one son, who was born in 1778 in New York City and was named after the commander of the British troops in North America at the time, Major-General Sir William Howe (1729–1814). During the war against the French in Canada Howe had led the first assault up the steep path to the Plains of Abraham in the Battle of Quebec (1759) and then took part in the war against the American colonists, being in command at the Battle of Bunker Hill (June 1775) and becoming overall commander of British troops in October 1775. Howe defeated George Washington at the Battle of Long Island (August 1776) and then occupied New York City. He was replaced by Sir Henry Clinton in May 1778 and returned to England, where he was knighted and made a lieutenant-general for his victory in the Battle of Long Island.

Between the arrival of the first Stephen in New York in 1686 and the general departure of the De Lanceys with the other Loyalists at the end of the American Revolution, the family had done extremely well for themselves. On the other hand, they had also played a full part in New York's political, social and legal life. Both the men and women of the family had married well, and many of the men had also fought in the army against the French, the native Americans and, latterly, against the Revolutionaries. From being one of the richest families in the world, however, their loyalty to the Crown cost them most of their fortunes and it was now up to the next generation to start again. One of those to achieve fame was the younger Stephen's son, William Howe De Lancey.

NOTES

1. *Gentleman's Magazine,* April 1800.
2. Correspondence of General Haldiman, B Lib Add 21.825.
3. Stephen was certainly in England in 1786, since he proved his father's Will on 17 January of that year.
4. Beverley Record Office, Book BO p 139, Lease document dated 15 October 1789. Information kindly supplied by Mrs Berna Moody of Beverley.
5. PRO CO 285/4. p 259.
6. Carmichael, G, *The History of the West Indian Islands of Trinidad and Tobago,* p 308.
7. PRO CO 285/5. The certificate was signed by George Cummings MD, and counter-signed by the Clerk of the Council.

CHAPTER II
Military Beginnings

As soon as he was old enough, William Howe De Lancey went to Beverley Grammar School, but he was forced to change schools when his father moved the family yet again, this time to London, before leaving to take up his new post as Chief Justice of Bermuda. Once there, William transferred to Harrow School, arriving on 12 December 1789 and leaving in December 1791.[1] The young man elected to join the army and on 7 July 1792 he was gazetted a cornet in the 16th Light Dragoons at the tender age of 15.

Meanwhile, developments across the English Channel were leading inexorably towards war with France. The British had remained aloof from the early events surrounding the French Revolution and declined to join the alliance set up in early 1792 by Austria, Brunswick, Hesse, Piedmont and Prussia, and which led to the invasion of France in August of that year. The beheading of King Louis XVI on 21 January 1793 was, however, the final straw for the British government and resulted in the immediate expulsion of the French ambassador in London. This spurred the French into declaring war on England, starting a conflict which was to dominate Europe for twenty-two years and in which William Howe De Lancey was involved from its start until he became one of its last casualties.

Following the outbreak of war, the British Army expanded rapidly with many new regiments being raised, one of them being the 80th Regiment of Foot (The Staffordshire Volunteers),[2] which was heavily supported by the Earl of Uxbridge, even to the extent of giving commissions to sons of his friends, rather than selling them. He also appointed his son, Lieutenant-Colonel Lord Henry Paget, as its first commanding officer on 12 September 1793. The 80th Foot assembled at Chatham and only ten weeks later was sent to the island of Guernsey, where it remained for less than a year, before moving yet again, this time for active service, arriving in Flushing in the Netherlands in late September 1794[3] where it was part of the British contribution, commanded by the Duke of York, to a combined Austrian-British-Dutch force.

The Netherlands (1794–1795)
De Lancey, now 16 years old, was promoted to lieutenant on 26 February 1793, and in 1794 he took advantage of the Earl of Uxbridge's generosity to transfer to the 80th Foot in search of active service. He joined the

regiment in early October direct from England, which was fortunate for him, since the transports which took the battalion from Guernsey to Flushing had not been fumigated following their recent return from the West Indies. As a result, the 80th lost a third of its strength from yellow fever within weeks of disembarking.

As if the outbreak of yellow fever was not bad enough, the campaign which followed was one of the most disastrous ever undertaken by the British Army, with the 80th Foot suffering particularly badly. Poor command, shocking commissariat and medical support, and shortage of ammunition for artillery and muskets were exacerbated by an almost complete lack of cooperation between the three allies. Then, as if all those problems were not enough, the winter proved to be the worst in living memory.

Once ashore, the 80th moved to join the other seven British battalions, which were commanded by General Sir David Dundas (1735–1820), whose wife was De Lancey's Aunt Charlotte. In a fierce local engagement on 31 December 1794, the 80th was involved in its first major action when it drove the French out of the town of Tael and pushed them back across the frozen River Waal. The 80th repelled a French counter-attack and spent the night in the open in a snowstorm.[4]

After some confused fighting in which the 80th – and De Lancey – was heavily involved, the British force made a twenty-five mile (40 km) night withdrawal in a blizzard so severe that anyone who sat down was frozen to death within minutes. The British then marched some 170 miles (270 km) along the southern edge of the Zuyder Zee, with the severe wintry conditions causing further heavy losses. Despite this, the 80th held together better than most other battalions and was frequently selected for rearguard duties, which involved holding the pursuing French at bay until the main body had got away. This dismal British retreat continued throughout March and the sadly depleted force finally reached the safety of the Hanseatic city of Bremen on 5 April 1795, from where the 80th Foot sailed on 24 April, arriving at Portsmouth on 9 May. In this brief campaign the 80th Foot lost 228 dead, with a further 210 so badly affected they were declared unfit for any further service, some fifty percent of the battalion.

For the young De Lancey it was as thorough a baptism of fire as could be imagined, and he echoed the view of many participants in the campaign, that 'all that they had learnt was what one ought not to do.' One of them, whom De Lancey was to meet frequently throughout his life, was Lieutenant-Colonel Arthur Wellesley, who had taken command of the 33rd Foot in 1793, at the very tender age of 24.

The French Coast (1795–1796)

On disembarking, the 80th marched to the New Forest area where it retrained and found recruits to fill the many gaps in its ranks. It was, however, given a remarkably short time to recover from its experiences, since in July it was ordered to undertake a totally different operation, embarking at Southampton for a projected amphibious raid on Brittany in support of French Royalists. The intention was to land troops on the island of Quiberon, which would then be used as a base from which to invade the mainland. Some British troops did indeed get ashore, but not the 80th, and when, after three weeks at sea, it was learnt that the force ashore had been defeated, the battalion returned to Southampton.

Just twelve days later the 80th sailed on yet another amphibious operation, this time as part of a much larger force, which was intended to support French Royalists in La Vendée. Again, the intention was to seize an island, in this case the Île Noirmoutier on the southern end of the mouth of the River Loire, and to use it as a base for an attack on the mainland. When the British arrived, however, they discovered that the island could be reached from the mainland at low tide, so the plan was changed and 1st British Brigade, of which the 80th was a part, was put ashore on the Île d'Yeu, where they remained from late September until early December. Possession of this island, some twelve miles (20 km) offshore, proved to be of very limited strategic value and the single attempt to invade the mainland was a fiasco, in which the British troops failed to get ashore at all, while the few French Royalists who did succeed proved to be no match for the more energetic Revolutionary troops and were quickly defeated. By this time the Île d'Yeu was seriously over-crowded and both the British garrison and the local inhabitants quickly ran desperately short of food for the men and forage for the horses. As a result, the British were forced to withdraw, although it took two weeks to embark the troops, another two weeks to sail to Southampton and yet a further week to disembark, the whole enterprise coming to a dismal conclusion on 6 January 1796.

The Far East (1796–1798)

Once again, the 80th was allowed only a brief respite and on 12 April it sailed to join the British garrison at the Cape of Good Hope, which had recently been captured from the Dutch, who were now on the enemy side in the war. The 80th disembarked at Simon's Town on 26 July and although its stay was relatively brief, it took part in one major – and very unusual – operation in which land forces combined with naval forces to capture an entire Dutch naval squadron.

Seven Dutch men-of-war were on their way to the East Indies and put into Saldanha Bay, some sixty-two miles (100 km) north-west of Cape Town, for water. News of their presence rapidly reached the British commander-in-chief, Major-General Francis Dundas,[5] who devised a neat operation in which British warships blockaded the mouth of the bay, while a military force, which had marched across sandy, waterless and

11

deserted country in four days, arrived in time to prevent the Dutch sailors from landing. The 80th Foot, which had only been in the colony a few weeks, was one of the army units involved and watched from the shore as the Dutch admiral bowed to the inevitable and surrendered on 17 August. The 80th then returned to Cape Town and sailed for India on 6 December. The 33rd Foot, which had served alongside the 80th in Flanders and was still commanded by Lieutenant-Colonel Wellesley, arrived at the Cape at the same time as the 80th and also departed at the same time; the two battalions arrived in India in February 1797; the 33rd in Calcutta and the 80th in Madras.

The 80th remained in Madras for only two weeks before sailing again, this time for Ceylon. Once there, the battalion was split between various stations, but De Lancey was soon on the move again. He had been promoted captain on 20 October 1796 and transferred to the 17th Light Dragoons, a fashionable cavalry regiment of which his uncle, General Oliver De Lancey, was colonel. But, while he was awaiting a ship to take him back to England to join his new regiment, Major-General John St Leger passed through Ceylon on his way from England to Calcutta and invited De Lancey to join his staff as aide-de-camp (ADC). Since St Leger was on his way to take command of the Honourable East India Company's cavalry, this was a prospect that De Lancey, now himself a cavalryman, would have been foolish to refuse.

The arrival of St Leger and his staff in Calcutta was noted with great interest by a British businessman, who was also an inveterate observer, gossip and diarist, William Hickey, who recorded that St Leger arrived in Calcutta on 20 March 1797 accompanied by three staff officers, one of whom was '. . . Captain De Lancey, as his aide-de-camp, a high spirited, fine, dashing youth, who, though no more than eighteen years old, had a troop of dragoons . . .'[6] St Leger had been a close friend of the Prince Regent in England, his health and pocket having suffered accordingly, and the trip to India was intended to repair both. The European inhabitants of Bengal were enormously flattered by the presence of such an important personage with such intimate contact with the throne and threw a succession of parties and entertainments, which De Lancey as ADC had no choice but to attend.

One such event was a bacchanalia at the Dutch settlement of Chinsurah, some thirty miles (48 km) up-river from Calcutta, where Hickey and a number of friends owned country villas. Hickey invited St Leger and his staff to Chinsurah for a week at the beginning of June, which started off with three days of horse-racing, a sport of which General St Leger was inordinately fond.[7]

As 4 June was the King's Birthday, Hickey hosted a dinner for sixteen guests, including General St Leger, De Lancey, another regular attender at such parties, Lieutenant-Colonel Arthur Wellesley, still commanding officer of the 33rd Foot, and the Dutch governor. This particular party lasted from 3pm to 3am the following morning and passed with 'the utmost hilarity and good humour', including a spirited and greatly admired rendering of 'The British Grenadiers' by the general. The company then met again for breakfast at 10am: '. . . when all complained more or less of headache or slight sickness, except the gay young Captain De Lancey, who protested he never was better in his life, and had slept uninterruptedly, from which "he was sure the wines were sterling"'. The party carried on throughout the 5th, following which the Dutch governor, overwhelmed by this hospitality, threw a party of his own, which started on the afternoon of the 6th and only ended when all were exhausted at dawn on the 7th.

One of the reasons that General St Leger was able to spend so much time carousing was that the governor-general, Sir John Shore, had shown his opinion of the Board of Directors of the Honourable East India Company in distant London by refusing to accept St Leger's appointment as commander of the Company's cavalry. This led to a furious row within the British community in Bengal, with Shore standing firm, while St Leger broadcast his views of the governor's behaviour to anyone who would listen. St Leger found many ready listeners since Shore was highly unpopular, William Hickey recounting how, when threatened by invasion '. . . our sagacious Governor-General, Sir John Shore, also conceived that his presence [with the troops] might prove of much benefit, possibly by frightening any of the enemy who should come within view of him, as there certainly never existed a more hideous ugly fellow'.[8]

In mid–1797, however, St Leger was designated the commander of a British expedition, which was initially intended to attack either Manila, the capital of the Spanish Philippines, or the French-owned island of Mauritius. The former was selected and contingents from each of the three British presidencies – Bengal, Bombay and Madras – were ordered to meet each other in the anchorage off the Company's trading station at Prince of Wales's Island (modern-day Penang) on the Malay Peninsula.

The Bengal contingent, comprising St Leger and his staff, the 33rd Regiment and a Bengal Native Infantry battalion, assembled at Calcutta, but there were many hesitations. Wellesley reported laconically that on 20 May they were ready to sail, on 23 June they were still ready, and on 12 July that they would sail in early August. This last was actually achieved and on 10 September Wellesley was writing from Prince of Wales's Island that they would shortly be departing for Manila.[9]

St Leger's other two contingents duly arrived, and he was about to set sail for Manila when a warship arrived with an urgent message calling the whole thing off. Disappointed, St Leger and his staff duly returned to Calcutta, arriving in mid-November, where the general and his brigade-major were struck down with a fever so serious that the former's life was despaired of. This illness did not, however, affect De Lancey, who seems to have been an extraordinarily healthy man, never recording any absence from the army due to sickness.

St Leger recovered to be appointed to command at Dinapore, near Patna, but it was now time for De Lancey to return to England and he sailed in early 1798, arriving later that same year.[10] On his return, De Lancey was granted a period of leave before joining the 17th Light Dragoons at Canterbury in September 1799. He stayed with this regiment barely a year, living the normal life of a home-based cavalry officer, before being promoted to major and returning to the infantry, but this time to the 45th Regiment of Foot. Since this battalion was in the West Indies, however, and was not due to return to Great Britain in the near future, he sought and was granted permission to remain in England until its return.

Thus, by the age of 21 De Lancey had four years of arduous campaigning behind him, with experiences ranging from the Flanders campaign, fought in virtually Arctic conditions, to the tropical heat of the Cape of Good Hope, India, Ceylon and Penang. The campaigns in Flanders and off the French coast had all been disastrous, being typical examples of the inept strategy, tactics, leadership and logistics which have characterised so many British campaigns in the early years of a war. He had, however, obtained a thorough grounding in regimental soldiering, while his brief spell as an aide-de-camp gave him a taste for working at headquarters. In addition, he had gained considerable experience of working with the Royal Navy and of amphibious landings and withdrawals, and had also made friends with the young Lieutenant-Colonel Arthur Wellesley, all of which were to stand him in good stead in the years to come.

NOTES

1. Information kindly supplied by the Archivist, Harrow School.
2. Later 2nd Battalion, The South Staffordshire Regiment.
3. Vale, *History of the South Staffordshire Regiment*, pp 40–43.
4. In 1809, when situated outside Badajoz, De Lancey had to complete a 'record of service' which was required by the bureaucrats in the distant Horse Guards; 'the action at Thuyle [Tiel]' was proudly placed at the head of the list of battles in which he had been engaged.
5. Major-General Francis Dundas was not related to the General David Dundas, mentioned earlier.
6. Hickey, W, *Memoirs,* p 154.
7. He was the founder of the 'St Leger', now the oldest classic horse-race in the world.
8. Hickey, *op cit;* p 147.
9. These letters are in University of Southampton, WP 1/6, all, as a matter of interest, clearly signed 'Wesley'. The file also includes a long and most perspicacious memorandum by Wellesley, describing 'Pulo Penang' (the

island's correct Malay name) and assessing its strategic and commercial importance to Britain.

10. Like so many of his contemporaries, Major-General St Leger did not survive the rigours of the Indian climate, dying in May 1799 from an apparent over-exposure to the sun. [Hickey, *op cit*, p 219]

CHAPTER III

Learning His Trade

When Captain William Howe De Lancey joined the 17th Light Dragoons at Canterbury in late 1798, one of his fellow officers was his cousin, Major John De Lancey. This officer left the regiment in May of the following year to become the ninth student in the First Department of the newly founded Royal Military College (RMC) at High Wycombe and returned in January 1800, when he may well have been one of the people who encouraged William to follow the same course. Another could have been his Aunt Charlotte's husband, General Sir David Dundas, the commander-in-chief at the time, who was a stalwart supporter of this new system of staff training and visited the college regularly. In any event, whilst awaiting the return of the 45th Foot from the West Indies, De Lancey took an important decision which was to alter the course of his military career for ever and applied to attend the RMC. He was duly accepted and reported for duty on 23 May 1801, where his name appears as the fifty-third in the college records.[1]

Staff Training

The need for proper and realistic training for officers of the British Army had been recognised for many years, but it was principally due to the efforts of a cavalry officer from the Channel Islands, Lieutenant-Colonel John Gaspard Le Marchant, that such training became formalised. After considerable lobbying by him and his supporters, the RMC was established at High Wycombe on 4 May 1799, consisting of two elements: a 'First Department' to train aspiring staff officers; and a cadet college to train officer cadets.[2]

The novelty of training and employing professional staff officers should not be underestimated. Until that time there had been no formal body of staff officers, and generals' staffs consisted of a military secretary, a few aides-de-camp and a small number of officers, who were 'borrowed' for short periods from regiments under the general's command. Thus, when Major De Lancey of the 45th Foot volunteered for the brand-new RMC, he was taking a daring step into the unknown.

The college comprised a governor, lieutenant-governor (Le Marchant) and the chief instructor, an elderly, retired French general named Jarry, whose distinguished military career had included seven years as aide-de-camp to Frederick the Great of Prussia. Jarry gave many lectures himself, although since he only spoke French, this caused some confusion among the students, very few of whom could understand the language. There were four other lecturers: two professors of mathematics, one of French, and one of fortifications. There was no set course length, the students arriving and departing throughout the year and completing each of five stages at their own pace, the only requirement being that they pass each stage before proceeding to the next (suggesting that the late twentieth century fashion for 'modular' courses may not be the daring innovation its proponents believe it to be).

Entry to the RMC was not easy. First, the potential student had to obtain his commanding officer's recommendation for staff training, which might not always be forthcoming when the commander knew that the young officer concerned would be held against his battalion's strength during his absence. Second, the candidate had to undergo a stiff oral examination, conducted by Le Marchant and Jarry in person. On top of this, the official view was that not only was the college very expensive to run, but it was also, in effect, robbing the army of officers who would otherwise be on duty with their regiments. To compensate itself, the government charged all students thirty guineas (£31.50 = £1,100) for each year they were under instruction, laid down that there would be a six-day working week and that the only leave would be a short official vacation from 29 November to 30 January annually, which had to be spent in approved military activities.

The work-level was high, the officers having to study or attend lectures from nine until four in winter and eight until three in summer, the subjects covered being mathematics, drawing, fortification, French, German, and 'General Jarry's instructions'. Jarry was adamant that subjects should not be learnt parrot fashion and he constantly reiterated his requirement that a staff officer had to think for himself, stating that: 'An officer who proposes to serve on the Staff should be acquainted with infantry and cavalry manoeuvres. It is not these manoeuvres that are taught at Wycombe, but the use and reason of them.'

An essential element of Jarry's teaching was the importance of 'the ground' and the fact that modern operations were on such a scale that it was no longer possible for the commander himself to see all the terrain over which his force would move and fight. As a result, Jarry stressed the importance to staff officers of personal reconnaissance, tactical sketching ('drawing') and simple map-making, so that the commander could better understand the nature of the ground. This was of particular importance in an era in which maps were not only in extremely short supply, but were also notoriously inaccurate. Other subjects included cavalry and infantry manoeuvring, field fortifications, the siting of artillery, the choice of routes, the conduct and control of marches, and the choice and selection of camp-sites (a subject known at the time as 'castramentation').

The reputation of the infant establishment was considerably enhanced by General Sir Ralph Abercrombie's expedition against the French in Egypt in 1801. This started on 8 March with a brilliantly conducted and totally successful amphibious 'opposed landing' against a French force in a position dominating the beach, and culminated in the defeat of the French on 31 August. The significance for the RMC was that three of the students most advanced in their studies had been taken off their course and sent as part of Abercrombie's headquarters' staff, where they proved a brilliant success and drew high praise. This played a major part in securing official endorsement for the establishment, which became the First (or Senior) Department of the Royal Military College on 24 June 1801.

De Lancey was as busy as the other students during his time at the First Department, one of the highlights being in the summer of 1802 when he was a member of a team of students who took part in a 'survey' of the south coast from Rye to Sandwich. This resulted in some excellent maps and sketches, which proved invaluable in the subsequent invasion 'scare' when Napoleon's armies were poised on the French coast. De Lancey also used the 1801/1802 vacation to soldier, however briefly, with the 45th Foot, the only time he ever served with them.

De Lancey graduated from High Wycombe on 14 September 1802 but was held on its books for a time thereafter, his record of service stating that he used the 1802/1803 vacation to take advantage of the period following the Treaty of Amiens (later known as 'the short peace' [27 March 1802 to 16 May 1803]) to visit France, after which he returned briefly to High Wycombe.

Having taken the daring step of attending the course at the RMC, De Lancey now faced two alternatives for his future in the Army. One was to continue to serve as a line officer in a cavalry or infantry regiment, with occasional tours of duty on a headquarters staff, which would lead him, first, to command of a regiment and, then, provided he was reasonably successful, to general's rank, commanding a division or corps.

The second choice was to transfer to the newly established permanent staff of the Quartermaster-General's (QMG) department, which would involve a continuous succession of staff appointments, thus ensuring him jobs at the centre of affairs, but, on the other hand, exposing him continuously to the whims and vagaries of senior officers and depriving him of the opportunity to command a regiment, the goal of every ambitious British Army officer. An added hazard was that, since the permanent staff of the QMG's department had only just been created, the future for any officer who joined it was not at all clear, but, despite this, De Lancey chose to transfer, stating in his record of service '. . . shortly after my return in 1803 to High Wycombe [I was] appointed extra permanent Adjutant in the Quarter Master General's Department.' This meant that he was struck off the roll of the 45th Foot and remained with the QMG's

Department until his death in 1815, making him one of the earliest professional staff officers (nicknamed 'Wycombites') in the British Army.[3]

De Lancey's first two postings in this new sphere were to headquarters in the British Isles: Yorkshire District (1803 March 1806), then Ireland (March 1806–March 1808). During that time he was promoted, although since all officers held two ranks, one in the army as a whole, the other in his regiment or department, his promotion to lieutenant-colonel came in two stages: in the army on 1 January 1805 and in the QMG's Department in 1807. Whilst in Ireland his immediate superior as Deputy Quartermaster-General was Colonel George Murray (1772–1846) of the 3rd Foot Guards, starting a working relationship that was to endure for the next eight years.

The Swedish Expedition
De Lancey's years of relative obscurity ended in 1808. In the constant realignments that characterised the Napoleonic wars, that was the year in which the Emperor Napoleon and Tsar Alexander of Russia signed the Treaty of Tilsit, which included a demand on Sweden to abrogate its coalition with Britain. This the Swedish king, Gustav IV Adolfus (r. 1792–1809) refused to do, and with his territories in Finland and Zealand under threat from Russia and France, respectively, he sent a plea for support to London. The British, always keen to bolster resistance to the French, despatched a force in April 1808 of some 11,000 men under the command of Sir John Moore, with Lieutenant-General Sir John Hope (1765–1823) as his second-in-command and Colonel George Murray as his Quartermaster-General. It would seem no coincidence that Murray took his subordinate from Ireland, Lieutenant-Colonel De Lancey, as his principal assistant.

Moore's instructions from the British government left him a large degree of personal discretion, but did include specific orders not to place himself under the command of a king whose sanity was in some doubt. Moore also received the traditional instruction given by every British government to commanders venturing onto the Continent, that he was not to engage in any enterprise so far inland that he would not be able to re-embark in an emergency. The British force arrived off the Swedish port of Gothenburg in April 1808 and matters got off to a bad start when the king refused permission for the British troops to disembark. The transports were very crowded and after tense discussions some officers were allowed to live ashore, while the troops were permitted to disembark in small groups onto an island in the bay for recreation and exercise. Moore went to the royal capital, Stockholm, where he remonstrated with the king and, after disagreeing with the monarch's impracticable military plans, he found that the only way to escape from this 'friendly' capital was to disguise himself as a peasant and leave at night. On his return to

Gothenburg, he immediately ordered his transports to sail for England, which they reached in July.[4]

With Moore to the Peninsula

Apart from Great Britain and Sweden, the only continental country not under French dominance and thus outside the 'Continental System' was Portugal, and having nominally sought and received permission from Spain, Marshal Junot took an army through Spain to invade Portugal, occupying Lisbon on 1 December 1807. In a series of high-handed actions, the French then seized control of Spain and forced King Carlos IV and his son Ferdinand to renounce the throne in favour of Napoleon's brother Joseph. These actions provoked a national uprising, guerrilla warfare broke out on a massive, if uncoordinated, scale and the French garrisons were soon isolated in their citadels. The Spanish regained control of a number of cities, including Madrid and Saragossa, and then in the Battle of Baylen a French force of 20,000 was forced to capitulate (22 July 1808), following which the men were either butchered on the spot or despatched to prison hulks where they were left to rot. This was the first defeat of one of Napoleon's vaunted armies, and, apart from being a blow to French prestige and morale, it also left Marshal Junot and his army isolated in Portugal.

In order to encourage this resistance to Napoleon the British sent an army to Portugal under the command of Wellington (then Major-General Sir Arthur Wellesley), who started operations as soon as he was ashore. Then, in a somewhat farcical development, he was superseded in command by two officers who, although senior to him, were far less competent. Wellington defeated the French at their first engagement, the Battle of Vimiero (21 August 1808), following which Junot found himself in an untenable position but managed to extricate himself by the Convention of Cintra (30 August 1808), under the terms of which his troops surrendered and were then taken by British transports back to metropolitan France.

Meanwhile, reinforcements had been despatched under Sir John Moore. As in the recently concluded Swedish expedition, Lieutenant-Colonel George Murray was the Quartermaster-General at the headquarters, with Lieutenant-Colonel De Lancey in his department, but 'attached to General Hope's division'. There was some confusion about where Moore's troops would land, but eventually they went ashore at Merceira, the heavy surf making the operation so difficult that it took five days for it to be completed.

Following the Convention of Cintra most British troops were withdrawn from the Peninsula, together with the three most senior officers, including Wellington, leaving Moore in command. He found himself in a most unhappy situation, principally because the Spanish authorities and people were somewhat antagonistic to their British allies and did very little to help them in terms of cooperation, providing intelligence and the sale of supplies. In addition, the Spanish army, with which Moore was under orders to cooperate, was poorly led, trained and organised.

Moore's British forces were split into three wings under Baird, Hope and himself, respectively. De Lancey was with Hope's division, which was sent via Badajoz, Talavera and Madrid to Valladolid. When Moore received intelligence on 28 November that the Spanish armies had been defeated and that Buonaparte was in Spain, he considered, rightly, that he had little option but to order a general withdrawal into Portugal. This was opposed by the Spanish authorities, who were supported by the British minister in Madrid, but as one Spanish army after another was defeated Moore had no choice but to begin the long withdrawal. Hope's division was compelled to make a forced march to rejoin Moore and De Lancey found himself taking part in yet another wintry retreat and the division managed to rejoin Moore on 7 December, having narrowly avoided being cut off by the French.

Moore's fighting withdrawal continued, with some elements of the British troops, discouraged by the continuous retreat, appalling weather, harassment from the pursuing French and the hostile population, becoming disorderly, although they always managed to rally when actually under attack. Moore's columns reached Corunna on 11 January and fortunately he had already sent word to the Royal Navy to meet him there, rather than at Vigo, as originally planned. Once outside Corunna discipline was restored and, if little else worked properly, at least the staff work for the embarkation was extremely well organised, as described by an eyewitness, Lieutenant Basil Hall, RN of HMS *Endymion*, who will appear more than once in these pages:

> Each soldier took his place in the boats and was rowed on board the particular ship destined to receive him. It may not be uninteresting to mention, that, on visiting the field before the battle, we found the officers of each regiment in possession of tickets, specifying the name and number of the transport in which their corps was to be embarked. Accordingly, when the troops marched into Corunna in the middle of the night, they proceeded, without any halt, straight to the shore, where they found the men-of-war's barges and launches, and the flat-bottomed boats of the transports, all ranged in order ready to receive them. As soon as it was known what regiment was approaching, a certain number of the boats were brought to the edge of the beach – no noise or confusion took place – the soldiers stepped in – the word was given to shove off, and in half an hour the empty boats were on their way back again to the point of embarkation, having deposited

these freights in their respective vessels – and happy enough, we may well believe, they must have been to find rest for their feet at last. [5]

The final battle took place on 16 January when the French attacked in force, but in a bitter fight they were held by the rear-guard. It was during this fighting, however, that Sir John Moore received his fatal wound and he was hurried back into the citadel. His staff tried to help but there was nothing that any of them could do and Moore died during the evening. The military situation was so desperate that his personal staff had no choice but to carry the body to a bastion, where they dug a shallow grave and buried their much-loved general, an action that was immortalised in the lines:

> . . . Not a drum was heard, not a funeral note,
> As his corpse to the rampart we hurried;
> Not a soldier discharged his farewell shot
> O'er the grave where our Hero we buried.[6]

The Final Hours at Corunna
Moore's second-in-command, General Baird, was also wounded that night, leaving Sir John Hope to command the final evacuation, assisted by De Lancey and others of his staff. They ensured that every man had been embarked, with Hope even touring the streets to ensure that nobody remained, and then, their job done, they made their way to the shore, where they split up and, the last to leave, they commandeered a few small local boats to take them to the ships. One of these boats contained three of the staff officers and their progress was once again reported by Lieutenant Basil Hall, RN:

> . . . before breakfast-time the next morning, the fleet of men-of-war and transports were standing out to sea. As we in *Endymion* had the exclusive charge of the transports, we remained to the very last, to assist the ships with provisions, and otherwise to regulate the movements of the stragglers. Whilst we were thus engaged, and lying to, with our main-topsail to the mast, a small Spanish boat came alongside, with two or three British officers in her. On these gentlemen being invited to step up, and say what they wanted, one of them begged we would inform him where the transport No. 139 was to be found?
>
> "How can we possibly tell you that?" said the officer of the watch. "Don't you see the ships are scattered as far as the horizon in every direction? You had much better come on board this ship in the mean time."
>
> "No, sir, no," cried the officers, "we have received direction to go

on board the transport 139, and her we must find." "What is all this about?" inquired the captain of the *Endymion*, and on being told of the scruples of the strangers, insisted upon their coming up. He very soon explained to them the utter impossibility, at such a moment, of finding any particular transport amongst between three and four hundred ships, every one of which was following her own way. We found out afterwards that they only were apprehensive of having it imagined that they had designedly come to the frigate for better quarters. Nothing, of course, was further from our thoughts; indeed, it was evidently the result of accident. So we sent away their little boat and just at that moment the gun-room steward announced breakfast. We invited our new friends down, and gave them a hearty meal in peace and comfort – a luxury they had not enjoyed for many a long and rugged day.

Our next care was to afford our tired warriors the much-required comforts of a razor and clean linen. We divided the party amongst us; and I was so much taken with one of these officers (William Howe De Lancey), that I urged him to accept such accommodation as my cabin and wardrobe afforded. He had come to us without one stitch of clothes beyond what he then wore, and these, to say the truth, were not in the best condition, at the elbows and other angular points of his frame. Let that pass, – he was as fine a fellow as ever stepped; and I had much pride and pleasure in taking care of him during the passage. We soon became great friends; but on reaching England we parted, and I never saw him more. [7]

Coming from a Royal Navy officer this was praise indeed and clearly shows that whatever else may have deteriorated in the long retreat, the staff work at Moore's and Hope's headquarters remained extremely efficient. De Lancey, at the hub of Hope's headquarters and with his considerable previous experience of amphibious operations, would have been deeply involved in it all. Once back in England, De Lancey spent only the briefest time ashore, as had happened when he was with the 80th Foot, and he sailed again in March 1809, this time as Assistant Quartermaster-General to a new expeditionary force. The commander was Wellington, whom De Lancey had known at the Cape of Good Hope and in Calcutta, while his immediate superior, the Quartermaster-General, was Colonel George Murray, who had been his chief in Ireland and the senior QMG staff officer on Moore's expeditions to both Sweden and the Peninsula.

NOTES

1. The details of William Howe De Lancey's attendance are taken from 'Royal Military College – Register of the Officers of the First Department' pages 1–2,

which is held in the archives of the former Army Staff College, Camberley. Details are at Appendix C.

2. The first class of twenty-six students assembled at High Wycombe on 4 May 1799, but the formal 'opening' did not take place until 24 June 1801, which was the official birthday of the now-defunct Army Staff College.
3. The term 'Wycombites' was a play on the name 'Wykamists', given to those who had attended Winchester College, a well-known boarding school, which produced many officers for the British Army.
4. The Swedish king was deposed the following year.
5. Hall, Basil, *Fragments of Voyages and Travels,* Vol I, pp 354–355.
6. *The Burial of Sir John Moore at Corunna* by Charles Wolfe (1791–1823).
7. Hall, Basil, *ibid*, pp 367–369.

CHAPTER IV
The Peninsular War: 1809–1814

The major part of William De Lancey's military career was spent in the Peninsula as an officer of the Quartermaster-General's Department, and it is thus important to place these two factors in their proper perspective. A cursory glance at the map of Europe might suggest that the British campaign in Spain and Portugal, which lasted from 1807 to 1814, was a peripheral matter – a 'sideshow'. But for the French it was an ever-increasing problem – the 'Spanish Ulcer,' as Napoleon termed it – tying down many troops and resulting in the loss of some 800,000 men. It also became the graveyard of the reputations of many of France's leading generals.

One reason for the British choice of the Peninsula was that, unlike the Continental powers, the government and people steadfastly refused to consider conscription, making it out of the question for a British army to take an equal part alongside the mass armies of countries like Russia, Prussia and Austria in the campaigns in central and eastern Europe. Instead, the British government provided subsidies and huge quantities of weapons and ammunition for virtually any country prepared to fight Napoleon, maintained the mastery of the seas, took part in a number of minor campaigns – and fought in the Peninsula. There they could challenge Napoleon, but, since the Royal Navy's control of the seas was virtually unchallenged, they had a guaranteed escape route for the army, should it ever be required.

Another important factor was that this was an Allied campaign, with three armies – British, Portuguese and Spanish – each playing a major role. Wellington was the Commander of the Forces of the British Army throughout the campaign and for most of the time was also the commander-in-chief of the Spanish Army, although this responsibility was exercised through an otherwise exclusively Spanish chain of command. His authority over the Portuguese Army was, however, more direct, since it was commanded by a British officer on loan to the Portuguese government – Lieutenant-General William Carr Beresford (1764–1854) – who was given the Portuguese rank of Marshal-General, while numerous British officers were seconded to the Portuguese service at all levels down to battalion commander.

Despite the evacuation from Corunna, the British government

determined that the Iberian peninsula remained the most promising theatre in which to oppose Napoleon and selected Wellington to lead a second expedition. Accordingly, Wellington returned to Lisbon – which had never been abandoned by its British garrison – on 22 April 1809, his strategic concept being to establish a strong base, to hold Portugal until his forces were ready, and then undertake a systematic campaign, in which the combined British/Portuguese army would act in cooperation with the Spanish Army and guerrillas. This would, he hoped, create an insoluble problem for the French, who would need to disperse their men to guard their lines of communication and to combat the guerrillas, but would need to concentrate to deal with Wellington's regular forces. It was a dilemma the French never solved.

Wellington also perceived another problem the French created for themselves. Their 'revolutionary' armies were capable of marching very rapidly – and considerably faster than the British – but did so by abandoning the well-established system of supply depots for a practice of living off the land. This meant that the arrival of a French army had much the same effect as a swarm of locusts, with the sheer volume of supplies required (food for men, fodder for horses, wood for fires) stripping the area bare within days, while the brutality of their foragers and the fact that they did not pay made matters even worse. This not only antagonised the population, but also meant that a French army had to move on within a relatively short period in order to find a new area to occupy.

By May 1809 Wellington had some 26,000 British and Hanoverian troops, plus a further 16,000 Portuguese, under command. Before commencing major operations, however, he carried out a significant reorganisation of his British forces, which was to pay great dividends as the campaign wore on, by integrating brigades, hitherto independent, into a divisional structure, and giving the divisional commander a permanent allocation of cavalry and artillery, together with a small command and administrative staff. As the campaign progressed he also created even larger formations consisting of several divisions, which were usually known as *corps d'armée* (corps, for short).

Once he considered his force ready, Wellington placed part of it to cover the French under Marshal Victor (1764–1841) and then attacked Marshal Soult (1769–1851), who was occupying Oporto with a force of some 24,000 troops. Wellington used four wine barges to get troops across the River Douro, taking Soult completely by surprise and routing his army (12 May 1809). The British then marched into Spain, where, at least in theory, they could depend upon the support of the Spanish Junta (government), its army and the large bands of guerrillas.

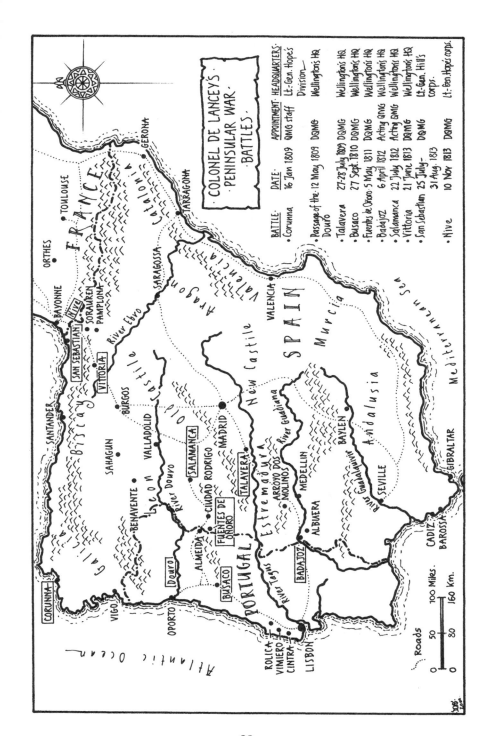

Battle of Talavera (27–28 July 1809)
The first major test came at Talavera, where Wellington (21,000 troops) and the Spanish General Gregorio de la Cuesta (33,000 troops) held off an attack by the combined forces of Marshal Victor and King Joseph Buonaparte (47,000 troops). It was a defensive action in which the Allied infantry was sited on the 'reverse slope', a tactic which became a Wellington favourite thereafter, and one which repeatedly misled the French, right up to Waterloo. The hard-fought battle was tactically a draw, but strategically an Allied victory, not least because Major-General 'Black Bob' Craufurd arrived the following morning with his Light Brigade (it did not become the Light Division until the following year) after a harrowing march, in the final stretch of which they covered sixty-three miles (100 km) in twenty-six hours, in blazing heat and with standard loads on their backs. With the British reinforced, the French retired to Madrid, having lost some 7,400 against the Allied 6,500.

Busaco (27 September 1810)
After a year's hard campaigning, Wellington undertook a strategic retreat to spend the winter behind the lines of Torres Vedras, in the course of which he fought a major battle at Busaco, matching his Anglo-Portuguese army against the French under Marshal Massena. Once again the British were in a defensive position on the reverse slope and the ever-impulsive Ney rushed his men to the crest of what he took to be an unoccupied hill. The French infantry laboured up the slope only to find the ridge lined with fresh British infantrymen, who rose, as if from the ground, fired several volleys and then charged. The French were pushed, pell-mell, down the hill and Massena was compelled to withdraw, enabling Wellington to continue his withdrawal.

The Lines of Torres Vedras (1810–1811)
The initial part of the campaign had made Wellington realise that the Spanish were not ready to support an offensive undertaking, but he was also repeatedly reminded from home that he commanded Britain's only field army and that his country could not afford its loss. There were other British armies in the field, to be sure, but none on the same scale, and, as Wellington well knew, Parliament and the country remained adamantly opposed to conscription. These factors led him to decide in late 1809 to fortify a position overlooking Lisbon from the north.

Known as 'the Lines of Torres Vedras', this position was intended to be impregnable and to afford both a secure base for future operations in the Peninsula, or, should matters deteriorate, protect the port of Lisbon while the British expeditionary force re-embarked, either to return to England or to redeploy elsewhere within the Peninsula. There were three lines of fortifications which, after a vast amount of work, were ready for occupation when Wellington's army reached them on 10 October 1810. Massena followed up, but when he reached the line of forts his probes concluded that they were totally secure. The French army remained facing the fortifications until both men and horses were starving; then, with only 40,000 remaining out of the 65,000 he had started with, Massena had no choice but to pull back.

Battle of Fuentes de Oñoro (3–5 May 1811)

Massena was determined to restore his tattered reputation and assembled the best of his surviving troops to relieve the besieged French garrison at Almeida. When Massena found Wellington blocking his advance at Fuentes de Oñoro, he tried, but failed, to outflank him in a battle which was marked by the resistance of British infantry squares to French cavalry charges. The Allies lost 1,800 out of 35,000 engaged, while Massena's casualties were 2,800 out of 45,000 and then, having done nothing to restore his reputation, he was replaced by a new commander, Marmont.

By the middle of 1811 the French had some 355,000 men in the Peninsula, organised into six armies, although this force was not as formidable as it sounds, since few of the 'armies' were any larger than a British division and there was a vast amount of territory to be covered. In addition, the Spanish guerrillas made travel very hazardous, with, for example, a single messenger requiring an escort of at least a squadron of cavalry. To cap it all, the personal relationships between the French commanders were such that cooperation was poor, intermittent and bad-tempered.

Battle of Albuera (16 May 1811)

Meanwhile, Marshal Beresford (32,000 men) was besieging Badajoz, but when threatened by Soult (18,000) he was forced to raise the siege and to face this new threat, taking a position near the town of Albuera, with the Portuguese on the left, the British in the centre and the Spanish on the right. The Spanish were heavily attacked, but held, although when Lieutenant-Colonel John Colborne took his British brigade to their aid, he was forced by his divisional commander to expose an open flank. French cavalry appeared out of a snowstorm and caught the British at their weakest spot, causing heavy losses, although a counter-attack by the 4th (British) Division saved the day. Some reckoned this to be the bloodiest battle of the Peninsular campaign and to give just two examples: the 1st Battalion, 3rd Foot lost 643 out of 755, while the 2nd Battalion, 7th Foot lost 483 men out of 568.

Ciudad Rodrigo (7–20 January 1812)

The French retained and held the main passes, but in early 1812 Wellington resumed the offensive, directing some diversionary attacks in the province of Estremadura and then falling upon the fortress of Ciudad Rodrigo in order to open the way into Spain. The weak French garrison fell after twelve days, much sooner than Marmont had anticipated and as a result he failed to reach the fortress with a relieving force.

Badajoz (6 April 1812)

Wellington now controlled one of the passes into Spain and turned to the other, which was dominated by the strong fortress at Badajoz, which was well-built, well-sited, and had a capable commander, Governor Armand Philippon (1761–1836), who had already successfully resisted one siege in 1811. Nevertheless, Wellington decided that it must be taken and operations began on 16 March 1812. The outer works were quickly taken, the French being driven back into the citadel where Philippon conducted an imaginative defence, but by 6 April three breaches had been opened and, having received news that Soult's army was approaching, Wellington ordered the assault for that night.

The main attack was pressed home against fierce opposition into two breaches and one British 'forlorn hope' after another struggled to penetrate the skilfully sited defences. Some forty attempts were made in the space of two hours and Wellington recalled the dazed survivors at midnight, when, on the verge of failure, he was given the surprising news that the two diversionary attacks had succeeded. The French defenders holding the main breaches were overwhelmed from their flanks and rear and the fortress fell. After these appalling experiences, there followed two days of anarchy as the British soldiers rampaged through the city and were so far out of control that the officers had no option but to withdraw and let the madness work itself out.

Moyle Shearer, an officer in the 34th Foot, served in the Peninsula from 1809 to 1814 and subsequently wrote one of the most perceptive and balanced accounts of the campaign. In discussing the question of what he termed 'marauding' he says:

> But when troops are neither fed, clothed or paid with regularity, they are tempted beyond their strength; and the military man, who has served, learns how and when to make allowances for those disorders, which the world is ever too forward to characterise as barbarous and licentious. My opinions of the moral excellence of soldiers is very superior to that generally entertained; and I think that we should find as much virtue, and as many amiable qualities, among ten thousand soldiers, as a similar number of individuals taken, without selection, from the bosom of civil society.[1]

Battle of Salamanca (22 July 1812)

The way now clear, Wellington advanced into Spain in June 1812 and three weeks later both he and the French Marshal Marmont found themselves marching towards the town of Salamanca on the River Tamus. Between 15 and 21 July 1812 the two commanders tried to outmanoeuvre each other, the French proving once again that they could march faster than the British, until Wellington, hearing of the approach of another army commanded by King Joseph, was forced to consider retreat and, as a necessary preliminary, ordered the baggage train to move first.

The long column of carts and carriages raised such a large dust-cloud that Marmont – who, like most French leaders had a low opinion of Wellington's abilities, believing him to be over-cautious and defensive-minded – thought that the British were already in full-scale retreat and moved to attack. This disdain for his opponent led Marmont into marching his troops in a thin line across the front of the Allied position and, seeing this, Wellington seized the opportunity with enthusiasm. The Allied attack rolled back the French advance guard onto the main body, achieving a brilliant victory in which Marmont was wounded and his army totally defeated, losing some 13,000 men, of which about half were captured. Wellington lost 5,200, of which the most notable was Major-General Gaspard Le Marchant, the founder of the Royal Military College, who died charging at the head of his cavalry brigade.

Advancing rapidly, Wellington took temporary possession of Madrid on 12 August 1812, but on receiving intelligence that the French were concentrating to deal with him, he evacuated the capital on 1 September. Eventually the British went into cantonments near Ciudad Rodrigo, and although the French followed up, by November they had stripped the countryside of supplies and were compelled to retreat.

Battle of Vittoria (21 June 1813)

By 1813 the French forces in the Peninsula were in dire straits, with Wellington pushing them ever back towards France, while not only had Soult been recalled (at King Joseph's behest), but numerous troops had also been withdrawn to reinforce Napoleon's hard-pressed armies in Germany. Wellington resumed the offensive and in a series of brilliant manoeuvres put the French on the defensive everywhere, so that King Joseph, who had reoccupied Madrid, was forced to abandon it again and withdraw towards the border with France. When he reached the River Ebro, however, he halted to enable other isolated French garrisons to join him and thus avoid being mopped up by the increasingly successful Allies. And Joseph was still there, near the town of Vittoria, when Wellington caught up with him on 21 June 1813.

There were three French armies present, comprising some 63,000 troops, but with a huge baggage train (which included the booty from the years of occupation) and a great horde of camp-followers. Wellington divided his army into four columns and went straight into the attack, which was helped when one column found a bridge over the River Zadorra, which the French had neglected to destroy or guard. The Allies scored an overwhelming victory, capturing some 150 guns, 2,000 baggage carts, King Joseph's silver and three million dollars in specie, but it would have been an even greater triumph had many British soldiers (and not a few officers!) not been diverted by the capture of the French baggage-train and the opportunities for plunder that offered. Following this disastrous defeat, Napoleon removed his brother Joseph from command, replacing him with Marshal Soult, the officer Joseph had so recently sacked, who arrived with the title of 'Lieutenant of the Emperor'.

Battle of Sorauren (26 July–1 August 1813)
Soult, wishing to demonstrate to Napoleon that he was a better general than his predecessors, attempted to re-enter Spain with a force of some 30,000 men in order to raise the British siege of Pamplona. The French achieved some initial success, pushing back the garrisons holding two passes but, even though greatly outnumbered, Wellington's 16,000 men stood and held the attack, once again deployed in line to defy and disperse the French columns. Both sides called up reinforcements and both were on the verge of running out of ammunition on the night of 29 July, but it was the British who received the crucial resupply. The following morning Wellington discerned that the French were about to retire and ordered an immediate advance which caused confusion in the French ranks. The fighting lasted for six days, but by the end the French had been pushed back across the Pyrenees. Soult had lost 13,000 (against Wellington's 7,000) and left the two besieged garrisons in Spain unsupported. As a result, San Sebastian fell to the British on 31 August and Pamplona to the Spanish on 31 October.

Invasion of France (October 1813–April 1814)
Wellington crossed the River Bidassoa (7–9 October 1813) and advanced into France, while Soult's army, which had lost yet more men in drafts to Napoleon's other armies, could only fight delaying actions. At the Nive (10 November) Soult tried to overwhelm a British detachment but was forced back after some stiff fighting in which the French lost 4,500 out of 18,000, and the Allies 5,300 out of 45,000. More stiff fights took place at the Nive (9–13 December 1813) and Orthes (27 February 1814). The final battle took place at Toulouse (10 April 1814) with an assault on the city, which was well laid out and had good defences. The Allies had 6,700 casualties, but it turned out to have been unnecessary, as two days later they received news that Napoleon had abdicated.

Wellington's Headquarters

As Commander of the Forces, Wellington had a complicated and demanding task. His principal aim was to defeat the French, but to achieve this he had to maintain his army in a foreign country, and ensure that it was properly organised, trained, administered and supplied. He also had to cooperate with the governments and military authorities of Portugal and Spain, with the Spanish guerrillas, and last, but certainly not the least demanding, he had to deal with the British government at home. Wellington could not exercise these many responsibilities on his own and he assembled a body of trained and experienced staff officers to help and advise him, and to carry out whatever functions he was prepared to delegate to them.

Personal Staff

Wellington was served directly by a Military Secretary – Lieutenant-Colonel Lord Fitzroy Somerset – whose task was to organise and run Wellington's private office, to deal with much, but by no means all, of the incoming and outgoing correspondence, and to control personal access to the commander. Wellington and his corps and divisional commanders were also served by aides-de-camp (ADCs), whose task in war was to convey their commander's oral and written orders to subordinates, and, albeit to a lesser extent, to ensure that he was provided with accommodation and food. A general officer entitled to ADCs was issued with a fixed monetary allowance, scaled according to his rank, from which to pay them, although some, including Wellington, employed more, meeting the extra costs from their own pockets. Selection of ADCs was, however, entirely the general's own business, Wellington remarking on one occasion that he would as soon select a wife for a general as his ADC.

This staff was organised on practical lines although, as was usual with the British Army, these were not always totally logical or comprehensible to outside observers and even, on occasions, to insiders either. In essence, Wellington's military staff was split into two, which, as a contemporary officer explained, consisted of:

> . . . the Adjutant- and Quartermaster-General's departments, the chief of the former being charged with all that relates to the discipline, arms, ammunition and clothing of the troops, while the duties of the latter extend over the movements, quartering, encamping, taking up positions and control of camp equipment. To every division of the army is attached an officer of each branch.[2]

The Quartermaster-General

During the seventeenth and most of the eighteenth centuries British field armies included an officer known as the 'harbinger', who was responsible for travelling ahead of the army in order to select future sites and to plan the routes to reach them. This euphonious title was changed to that of 'quartermaster-general' during the 1686 Irish campaign, and by the time of the Peninsular War the responsibilities had expanded to include routes, the equipment required for cantoning and encamping the troops, all matters relating to quarters, marches, camps, plans and dispositions for defence, embarkation, disembarkation, and general conveyance of the troops.

Routes

The term 'route' had a very particular meaning and applied to a document, always brief and simple, which was the authority to be on the move, laying down the roads to be followed, towns to be passed through, where overnight halts were to be made, where supplies and forage could be found, and how long to take. The Peninsular army was used to frequent and rapid moves, and whether it was a division of 10,000 men, a squad of six, or even an individual, the QMG staff issued the 'route', one copy to the party concerned in the move and others to depot commanders, town majors and commandants along the way; troops deviated from it or moved without it at their peril.

One example will serve to illustrate the principle and is the 'route' issued to the commandant of the headquarters, Colonel Colin Campbell, for a move of the civil department of the headquarters:

Frenada, May 20th, 1813 – Route for the headquarters of the army.
    The military department will move on the 22nd instant to Ciudad Rodrigo.
The Civil Department

May 22nd. Almeida. Depot of provisions.
May 23rd. Pinhel.
May 24th. Cotimos.
May 25th. Villa Nova de Foscoa
May 26th. Terro de Moncorvo. Depot of provisions.
May 27th. Halt.
May 28th. Tornas and Lagouca.
May 29th. Villa Dalla.
May 30th. Sendim.
May 31st. Miranda de Duero. Depot of provisions.
(signed) G.MURRAY, Q.M.G.

To the Commandant of headquarters[3]

Judge-Advocate Larpent, a civilian staff officer, described in a letter home how his group followed this 'route' to the letter, arriving in Miranda de Duero right on schedule on 31 May (although they then found that Wellington had moved again, so they had to obtain another 'route' in order to catch up with him). Larpent also tells a story which illustrates the all-embracing effectiveness of the QMG's department where routes were concerned:

> Colonel F – who commanded the artillery at the battle of Salamanca, and who is very well spoken of by every one, but at times, I believe, is slow, was once with Lord Wellington at an audience when things went wrong, and Lord Wellington got irate, who told him pretty nearly that his friend concerning whom he was inquiring "might go to h—." Colonel F— came muttering out, "I'll go, Sir, to the Quarter-Master-general for a route," which Lord Wellington heard, and laughed at well.[4]

Quartering

Wellington's Peninsular army became a well-drilled and smooth-running organisation, not least where the provision of accommodation was concerned. When a force was due to move into a town there was a well-practised drill, in which a QMG staff officer played the key role, being the first to arrive, following which he made a quick reconnaissance and then discussed his requirements with the local magistrates or mayor. Having decided on the allocation of general areas of the town to units, he then selected the sites for specific installations, such as guard rooms, alarm posts, gun parks for the artillery, stabling for animals, and depot areas for the Commissariat. Once this was done he met the quartermasters, who had come forward from every unit, and gave them their areas; the unit quartermaster then made a detailed allocation, his orderlies marking each doorway in chalk with the company identification letter and the number of men to be accommodated. The QMG staff officer also took a building for the headquarters, which included an office for himself, where he could be consulted to resolve disputes and to provide additional accom-modation for new arrivals.

Operational Moves

If the division or brigade moved into a field position, the drill was somewhat simpler, with the commander and the QMG staff officer usually arriving in the proposed area together. The general selected the best ground for the encampment according to the tactical situation, the positions of the enemy, the need for advance picquets, and com-munications with divisions or brigades on either flank. The QMG staff officer then divided the area chosen by his commander into unit areas and briefed the quartermasters of the advance parties accordingly. Not only did the QMG staff plan such operational moves, but they also provided the 'conducting officers' who led the columns along the routes and delivered them to their destination.

QMG Corps
In addition to staff officers, the QMG Department also had direct control of several organisations, the largest being the Royal Staff Corps, which had been raised in 1798, mainly to provide the army with a body of engineers which was independent of the Master-General of the Ordnance, who controlled the Royal Engineers. By the time of the Peninsular War, the Royal Staff Corps fulfilled three functions. First, the soldiers were engineers trained to act as supervisors for fatigue parties provided by the infantry; for example, in clearing roads and building bridges. Secondly, as Wellington's army grew in size and the operations covered an ever wider area, good communications became increasingly important, and the Royal Staff Corps became involved in providing despatch offices to control mail and couriers, and eventually a semaphore service, as well. Finally, since the officers of the Royal Staff Corps were under the direct control of the QMG's department and thus readily available, a number were frequently employed as additional staff officers.

The second of the QMG's corps was the Royal Waggon Train, raised in 1800 to provide an ambulance service for the wounded, and the use of its waggons for other purposes, such as to convey baggage, stores or unwounded soldiers, was strictly forbidden. Detachments of the Royal Waggon Train were allocated to divisions, where they came under the orders of a QMG staff officer, although those that were detached to regiments were actually tasked by medical officers.

Next came the Corps of Staff Guides, which was raised in the Peninsula in 1809 to assist the QMG staff in police duties, as well as reconnoitring roads and acting as conducting officers for columns during a march. The corps originally consisted of officers and men seconded from cavalry regiments, but since many of its duties involved interpreting between the local population and the army, a number of Spaniards were also recruited. The corps was some one hundred strong by 1814 and was commanded by Major Scovell of the QMG staff, but it was disbanded at the end of the Peninsular War.

Finally, the collection of intelligence about the enemy was not well coordinated during the early years of the Peninsular War, but an officer of the QMG's department, Lieutenant-Colonel Colquhoun Grant, was made responsible for the intelligence service from about 1812 onwards.

Control of Equipment
The QMG's department controlled the storage and issue of certain items of equipment, including blankets, greatcoats, camp-kettles, canteens and their straps, and tents for the troops; horse-shoes and portable forges for the horses; and felling axes, bill-hooks and general tools for defensive works. Such items may seem trifling by twentieth century standards, but were of great importance in the Peninsular and Waterloo campaigns.

NOTES

1. Shearer, Moyle, *Recollections of the Peninsula*, pp 131–132.
2. A Staff Officer, 'Recollections of Waterloo' in *Colburn's United Services Magazine*, 1847, Pt III, pp 2–3.
3. Larpent, FS, *'Private Journal'*, Volume 1, p 152.
4. Larpent, FS, *ibid*, Volume 1, pp 121–122.

CHAPTER V

De Lancey in the Peninsula

The Quartermaster-General's department to which De Lancey belonged was an example of the British Army's method of applying ranks and titles to staff appointments, which has never been noted for its logic, consistency or the ease with which outsiders could comprehend its workings. The head of the department at Wellington's headquarters was the 'QMG to the Forces', and there was an equivalent at both corps and division HQ, designated Assistant Quartermaster-General (AQMG), a lieutenant-colonel, who had an unusual relationship with his commander. The AQMG was under the command of the commander, but, on the other hand, the QMG at army headquarters clearly considered these departmental officers to be 'his' and the term 'QMG's Department' embraced all QMG officers in the Peninsula, wherever they were. They were, in essence, on loan to the commander, and while the main operational orders and directions were passed down the command chain, from Wellington to corps commander to divisional commander, there was a parallel chain in which orders were passed down and information passed up between QMG staffs, with the commander being informed where the matter was considered to be one of importance. This meant that QMG officers were serving two masters, but, although there may occasionally have been friction, particularly during the brief period when Gordon was QMG, the system worked effectively and smoothly. There were also subordinate QMG staff officers at all levels – majors, captains and a few lieutenants – whose title was Deputy Assistant Quartermaster-General (DAQMG).

Most of these were regimental officers, that is to say, they were infantry or cavalry officers who were detached from their regiments and worked with the QMG's Department for a period of time, at the end of which they would return to their regiments. A few, however, elected to become full-time staff officers, thus severing their connection with their regiment, De Lancey being one of these.

George Murray

De Lancey's first chief in the Peninsula was Colonel George Murray (1772–1846), both men being appointed to Wellington's staff on 1 April 1809. A Scotsman, Murray was commissioned into the 71st Foot in 1789, but transferred to the 34th Foot shortly afterwards and to the 3rd Foot

Guards in 1790, with whom he remained for the rest of his career. As a regimental officer he served, like De Lancey and Wellington, in the Dutch campaign (1793–95) and then took part in the raid on Quiberon (1795), but this was followed by a short spell in the West Indies. After this he had a succession of appointments on the QMG staff, first in the Egypt expedition (1801), followed by the Horse Guards (1803–4)[1] and then Ireland. After taking part in several operations, he headed the QMG staff in General Sir John Moore's Swedish expedition, and on his return he went, still with Moore, to the Peninsula. Murray got on very well with Wellington and was promoted to brigadier-general in July 1811 and to major-general in December 1811. This last promotion, however, made him too senior for the QMG post in the Peninsular Army and despite strenuous objections from Wellington, he was posted to Ireland. Murray's replacement in the Peninsular did not arrive until August 1812, and De Lancey, still a lieutenant-colonel, filled the vacancy.

James Willoughby Gordon

De Lancey's second chief, who arrived to take over from Murray, was a totally different character. Colonel James Willoughby Gordon (1773–1851) was the archetype of a particular breed of staff officer who combine high efficiency, good intelligence, hard work and painstaking attention to detail, with extreme ambition, ruthlessness (particularly where their own interests are concerned), deviousness and, on occasions, outright deceit. Gordon had risen by a mixture of personal ambition, royal influence (he had been taken up, first, by the Duke of Kent and later by the Duke of York) and 'interest', the latter involving a large network of people with similar concerns (it would be too much to describe such self-centred people as friends). He reinforced his position yet further by marrying an aristocratic heiress, whose circle of relatives spread wide through the English and Welsh nobility.

Gordon survived no fewer than three major setbacks, any one of which might well have sunk a lesser man. The first occurred shortly after he had been appointed Deputy Barrackmaster-General in 1804 when his chief, General Oliver De Lancey (1749–1822), William Howe De Lancey's uncle, was accused of misappropriating government funds. General De Lancey was forced to resign, but Gordon emerged unscathed. The second occurred in 1809 when he was serving as Military Secretary to the Commander-in-Chief at the Horse Guards, the Duke of York, and the latter was accused of allowing his mistress to manipulate the 'purchase' system. Gordon had to give evidence to the Parliamentary committee investigating the affair – which he did with great flair, proving a master of the minutiae of the conduct of his office – but although the charges could not be substantiated, the Duke felt obliged to resign, as did Gordon on 1 October 1809. Within days Gordon was appointed Commissary-in-Chief, which he held until the Duke of York returned as Commander-in-Chief in 1811, when Gordon moved on to the even more prestigious post of Quartermaster-General of the Army, still at the Horse Guards.

Gordon's third debacle was on an even greater scale. It came as a surprise to all (except, perhaps, to Gordon himself), when the Duke of York selected him to relieve Murray in the Peninsula, while retaining his post at the Horse Guards. This enabled Gordon to draw the salaries for both posts, but it may have been that there was a more important consideration where he was concerned in that, while he had occupied every top staff post in the Horse Guards, he had not done so in an operational headquarters; in modern parlance, he lacked field experience. Indeed, although there is no proof, it does not seem beyond the bounds of possibility that Gordon used his undoubted influence with the Duke of York to engineer Murray's promotion and posting in order to create a vacancy that he could then fill. Whatever the background, Gordon arrived at Wellington's headquarters in August 1812, which forced De Lancey to revert to the deputy position, and Gordon, as he had done in all his previous posts, immediately set out to enhance both the efficiency of his department and his own role and status in the headquarters.

During his time at headquarters, Murray had gradually and informally assumed the role of Wellington's chief-of-staff. When Gordon arrived in August 1812, however, he brought with him a letter from the Commander-in-Chief proposing to Wellington that Gordon was to combine the roles of QMG and chief-of-staff. Gordon expanded upon this during his initial interview, explaining to a bemused Wellington that he had been studying the French Army's staff system prior to his arrival. Wellington appears to have contained himself during the interview, but let off steam by writing to Colonel Torrens, the Military Secretary[2] to explain that, while he was not opposed to a rearrangement of the staff, even, indeed, to combining the Adjutant-General's and Quartermaster-General's departments into one, even on first acquaintance, '. . . I don't think that the present Quarter-Master General [Gordon] ought to be the superintendent, if such an alteration were to be made.'[3]

As so often in his military career, Gordon's theory was sound, but his abrasive personality prevented the system from working properly and he proceeded to infuriate his subordinates (who had to suffer in silence) and to upset his colleagues, not least the Spanish liaison officer (and good friend of Wellington's), General Miguel D'Alava, whose comments on the arrogant Englishman were scarcely repeatable. Nor was that all, since Gordon was a supporter of the parliamentary opposition and, with stunning impropriety, started to send extracts from Wellington's official papers home to his friends to be used in Parliament and the press to embarrass the government. Wellington caught him out in this and thereafter refused to show 'secret' reports to his QMG, a most extraordinary state of affairs. On top of that, the performance of the QMG's department – previously so efficient – was found seriously wanting in various tactical respects.

It would have been highly embarrassing for all concerned if an officer who had been personally nominated for his post by the Commander-in-Chief had been publicly dismissed for incompetence, but fortunately Gordon himself provided the answer, when he was found to be suffering from haemorrhoids (piles). This required urgent treatment in England, an item of news which raised some wry smiles around the headquarters, where he had won few friends. Seizing the opportunity this offered, Wellington wrote a highly adverse report to the Commander-in-Chief in which he said that:

> Colonel Gordon does not turn his mind to the duties to be performed by the Quartermaster-General of an Army such as this, actively employed in the field: notwithstanding his zeal and acknowledged talent, he has never performed them, and I do not believe that he ever will or can perform them. I give this opinion with regret, and I hope His Royal Highness will believe that I have not formed it hastily of an officer respecting whose talents I, equally with His Royal Highness, had entertained a favourable opinion.[4]

Somewhat surprisingly, Wellington added that, if it was felt in London that such a step would be too hurtful to Gordon, then he would be allowed to return to the Peninsula, but:

> . . . if he is wise he will not return, as he must feel what is notorious to the whole army. Besides which his health and the habits of his life render him in some degree incapable of performing the active and laborious duties of his office in the field . . .[5]

Thus, Gordon departed, unmourned, after barely four months in the job, but totally unaware of the chaos that he had created, and with no knowledge of the letter Wellington had sent to Torrens. Indeed, he was full of promises to return as soon as his condition was cured and he chose not to depart quietly, since he took the opportunity (without being requested to do so) to visit a regiment of the Life Guards on his way back to England and to submit a highly critical report on them to Wellington.

In London, Torrens, the Military Secretary, received two letters on 7 January 1813, the first being Wellington's letter of 20 December 1812 describing Gordon's failure in the Peninsula, and the second a letter from Gordon to announce that he had just arrived in Plymouth and would be in London within hours. Torrens rose to the occasion with a letter to Gordon of which Machiavelli would have been proud, congratulating

Gordon on his safe arrival and wishing him a swift recovery in 'the repose you will find in your Domestic circle.' However, as Torrens went on to explain, Wellington intended to take the field very shortly and out of the kindest consideration for Gordon's complaint, and in ignorance of Gordon's strong desire to return to the Peninsula the moment the complaint had been cured, the Commander-in-Chief had directed Murray to return to the Peninsula at once. According to Torrens, 'it never occurred to His Royal Highness that he was acting in contradiction to your wishes and intentions.' Even Gordon realised that to demand a return to the Peninsula would make the Commander-in-Chief look foolish and precipitate, something which the cunning Torrens knew he would never do.

Gordon duly obtained an opinion from two eminent London surgeons, in which they described the severity of his condition and the urgent need for an operation, following which, they declared, Gordon would be unfit to ride a horse for a minimum of twelve months. Gordon wrote to Wellington on 13 January, explaining all this and, game to the last (or, perhaps, just giving the appearance of it), he told the Commander of the Forces just how desolated he was to be unable to keep his promise to return to the Peninsula.[6]

Wellington requested that Murray be returned to the Peninsula as quickly as possible and De Lancey once again held the fort from Gordon's departure in early December to Murray's return on 17 March 1813, one of his main tasks being to calm the ill-feeling caused by Gordon during his brief stay.

De Lancey

Of all the staff officers who passed through the QMG's department in the Peninsular Army, De Lancey was the only one to serve from the very first day (1 April 1809) to the very last (25 June 1814), without a single known break for leave, wounds or illness.[7] Throughout this time De Lancey was graded as the Deputy Quartermaster-General, but, as described above, he spent two periods as Acting Quartermaster-General, first to cover the gap between Murray's departure and Gordon's arrival (December 1811 to August 1812), which included the major battles of Badajoz (19 April 1812) and Salamanca (22 July 1812), and, secondly, between Gordon's abrupt departure and Murray's return (December 1812 to March 1813).

De Lancey's service in the Peninsula can be traced through his Army Gold Cross, with four battles recorded on the arms of the cross and five on the clasps.[8] This shows him to have been present at Corunna, Talavera, Busaco, Fuentes de Oñoro, Badajoz, Salamanca, Vittoria, San Sebastian, and the Nive. Indeed, there were only seven officers in the entire Peninsular Army who also had five clasps and only six with more.[9]

Wellington was careful to ensure that De Lancey received frequent 'mentions in despatches', one noteworthy occasion being the Salamanca Despatch (22 July 1812), where he recorded that:

> ... I am particularly indebted to Lieut. Colonel De Lancey, the Deputy Quarter Master General, the head of the department present, in the absence of the Quarter Master General, and to the officers of that department and of the Staff corps, for the assistance I received from them.[10]

By this stage, however, De Lancey was beginning to feel hard done by. The incident which brought matters to the surface was the appointment of an officer he considered to have contributed less than he had to the campaign, Colonel Arentschildt, as a Royal aide-de-camp, a much sought-after reward for distinguished service. Accordingly, he discussed the situation with Wellington, who wrote to the Horse Guards on his behalf:

> I enclose a paper of memorandums which De Lancey has put into my hands, which shows that he has not been much favored; and I have to say of him, that he was at the head of the Quarter Master General's department during nearly the whole of last campaign, and in the battle of Salamanca; and that he always rendered me the greatest assistance, and gave me every satisfaction.[11]

This elicited a rapid but singularly unsatisfactory reply from the Military Secretary (Colonel Torrens):

> ... By the Memorial you enclosed respectively, Colonel De Lancey's service, it certainly appears that favors have not been dealt out to him according to his deserts, as they may have been to others. But at the same time you will observe that the turn his professional fortune has taken appears to be attributable to his having left the line for the permanent staff service. There can be few men who in retracing their military career have not reason to say "If I had not done that, or accepted this or that, I should have been in such & such a situation" and there are still fewer who have not to say that they were passed over in the rank of Major. The Army is altogether a lottery and Colonel De Lancey has not drawn the prize which many have, who probably deserve it less. The only thing the Duke can do in the present case is to recommend De Lancey for the first vacant Aide de Campship & this His Royal Highness desires me to inform you he will not neglect.[12]

British Army officers will immediately recognise from this that the patronising 'keep up the good work and it will all come right in the end' approach and the despairing ' if only you hadn't done so-and-so in your youth' used in letters from today's Military Secretary have changed but little in the past two hundred years.

By 'leaving the line' Torrens is referring to De Lancey's transfer to the Permanent Staff of the QMG's Department and is implying that had he not done so, then preferment for honours and promotion might have come more readily. The implication that this was a long-term mistake must have been particularly galling to an officer who had spent over four years constantly at Wellington's side.

Above all, Torrens' suggestion that the whole system was 'altogether a lottery' can have done little to inspire De Lancey's confidence in the Horse Guards, one of whose responsibilities was to ensure fairness in promotion and reward. To this day Torrens' letter is marked with Wellington's pencilled comment, 'Inform Col De Lancey', although it is to be doubted that sight of it gave the latter the slightest satisfaction. Indeed, the unfairness of that 'lottery' was demonstrated even more convincingly with the news that Gordon, whose failure had been so great and so public (at least in the Peninsula), was rewarded with promotion to major-general and a knighthood within twelve months of returning to England.

Throughout Murray's first tour and Gordon's brief appearance, De Lancey spent all his time at Wellington's headquarters, but following Murray's return he was detached to a corps headquarters, where he was the senior QMG staff officer, which was probably intended by Wellington and Murray to give him a greater feeling of independence and responsibility. He was certainly with Lieutenant-General Sir Thomas Graham's corps in 1813, when he personally conducted the arrangement of terms for the capitulation of the fortress at San Sebastian[13] and was mentioned in Graham's despatch as a result.[14] He impressed Graham so much that when the latter was sent to take command of the British forces in the Netherlands later in 1813, he wrote to Wellington asking specifically for De Lancey to join him as his Quartermaster-General, but when Wellington asked De Lancey whether he would like to go, he declined politely.[15]

Lieutenant-General Sir John Hope took over the corps on Graham's departure, but De Lancey remained, which doubtless suited them both, because they had served together in both the Swedish expedition and the first Peninsular campaign. Wellington may, however, have had a hidden motive in leaving De Lancey there, since he may have hoped that the cool, calm De Lancey might keep the hot-headed and impulsive Hope out of trouble – the general regularly placing himself in the position of greatest danger. If this was the case, then De Lancey failed, since at the Battle of the Nive Hope personally led a counter-attack which prevented the French from retaking Bayonne, being wounded in the instep as he did so, leading Wellington to complain gently to Torrens that:

I have long entertained the highest opinion of Sir John Hope, in common, I believe, with the whole world, but every day's experience convinces me of his worth. We shall lose him, however, if he continues to expose himself in fire as he did in the last three days; indeed, his escape was then wonderful. His hat and coat were shot through in many places, beside the wound in his leg. He places himself among the sharpshooters, without, as they do, sheltering himself from the enemy's fire. This will not answer; and I hope that his friends will give him a hint on the subject.[16]

While obviously well-intentioned, Wellington was the last man entitled to give lectures about general officers unnecessarily endangering themselves in battle, since he himself regularly took the most astonishing risks. Indeed, there were many occasions, both in the Peninsula and at Waterloo, when Wellington's British soldiers shouted at him to get out of the firing line, partly out of affection but mainly because they did not want to lose such a respected and trusted commander.

Death deprived De Lancey of the opportunity to write his own memoirs, so there are only occasional personal glimpses of him during the Peninsular War. Wellington was a hard task-master and, as Gordon's experiences showed, did not hesitate to dismiss those who failed to live up to his exacting standards, so De Lancey's six years at his side clearly show that he met the standards set. On operations his task was to run the department (or to assist in running it when Murray or Gordon was present) and to assist Wellington in his command tasks.

That De Lancey was frequently in the thick of the fighting cannot be doubted. One account states how in the 1809 campaign, 'Colonel De Lancey had gained and continued in the rear of the enemy all night, and joined us at daybreak with an officer he had taken.'[17] On another occasion an officer describes how, at the siege of Badajoz, he found himself close to Wellington in the final stages of the battle, when:

> Suddenly turning to me and putting his hand on my arm, he [Wellington] said: 'Go over immediately to Picton and tell him he must try if he cannot succeed on the Castle.'
>
> I replied: 'My lord, I have not my horse, but I will walk as fast as I can, and I think I can find the way. I know part of the road is swampy.'
>
> 'No, no!' he replied. 'I beg your pardon. I thought it was De Lancey.' [18]

Similarly, at the Battle of Vittoria, a brigade commander (Major-General Sir FP Robinson) clearly appreciated De Lancey's closeness to the commander when he recorded that:

. . . William De Lancey was upon the hill, and I understand he exclaimed that, By G— it was the most brilliant attack he ever saw, and that he would not sleep till he had made a proper report to Lord W—.[19]

When not actually engaged in operations, the pace was slightly different, although the standards were still the same, as Judge-Advocate General Larpent describes:

Lord Wellington, whom I saw every day for the last three or four days before he went, I like much in business affairs. He is very ready, and decisive, and civil, though some complain a little of him at times, and are much afraid of him. Going up with my charges and papers for instructions, I feel something like a schoolboy going to school. [20]

Another staff officer , Captain Thomas Browne, describes how:

. . . At nine in the morning the heads of all departments waited upon him with their respective reports. These comprised returns of various descriptions, & the correspondence of their several departments during the preceding day, on which they had to take his instructions. Before ten o'clock all this business was dispatched, & the details of his directions were committed to the Junior branches of the General Staff.[21]

De Lancey was one of those responsible for transmitting Wellington's directions, and his signature appears on numerous documents issued by the headquarters, ranging from 'routes' and instructions to Wellington's more general correspondence. Of many examples, one stinging rebuke (possibly slightly 'tongue-in-cheek') concerning a cavalry officer is worthy of note and shows that De Lancey had learnt his master's style:

Sir,
I am directed by the Commander of the Forces to acquaint you, that he cannot direct a reply to be made to Captain Campbell's letter of the 12th Instant (with inclosures) until a copy can be made of the letter in question, as Captain Campbell's writing is perfectly illegible to him and his Lordship requests that you will recommend to Captain Campbell to pay a little more attention to his writing as it is impossible in many cases to allot the necessary time to trace the Characters in his letters without neglecting other public business.
(Signed) W De Lancey.
DQMG[22]

NOTES

1. The headquarters of the British Army was located in the building on Whitehall known as the Horse Guards.
2. The Military Secretary was responsible for advising the Commander-in-Chief (the Duke of York) on appointments for senior officers and for implementing the Duke's sometimes arbitrary and erratic decisions.
3. Wellington to Torrens, 29 September 1812, *Supplementary Dispatches*, Volume VIII, pp 433–434.
4. Wellington to Torrens, 20 December 1812, *op cit*, Volume VIII, pp 499–500.
5. Wellington to Torrens, *op cit*, p 500.
6. Although not part of the De Lancey story, it should be added that Gordon retained the post of Quartermaster-General at the Horse Guards until his death, although he was never fully employed as such.
7. He was still in France on 20 June 1814. Wellington memo, dated Paris, 20 June 1814. *Supplementary Despatches*, Volume IX, p 145.
8. This Gold Cross, complete with ribbon and clasps, was sold by the Harvey family at some time in the late nineteenth century and in 1906 was in the possession of a Major JA Hay, although how he came to acquire it is not known. Since then it is known to have been in a collection in South Africa whence it was bought in 1988 by a collector in California. It was then purchased in 1995 by the National Army Museum, London, where it is now on permanent display. Information supplied by Gale Hawkes, Esq. of Washington, USA.
9. Information supplied by P Haythornthwaite, Esq.
10. Wellington's despatch following the Battle of Salamanca: General the Earl of Wellington, KB, to the Earl Bathurst, Secretary of State, dated Flores de Avila, 24 July 1812.
11. Wellington to Torrens, 24 March 1813. *Dispatches*, Volume X, p 232.
12. Torrens to Wellington, 14 April 1813; Southampton WP/1/368 folder 4. As far as is known, De Lancey never received the appointment of ADC.
13. *Dispatches*, Volume XII, pp 101–102.
14. *Dispatches*, *op cit*, p 65.
15. *Dispatches*, Volume XI, pp 460–461, 472.
16. Wellington to Torrens, 15 December 1813. *Dispatches*, Volume XII, pp 371–2.
17. Anon, An Account of the British Campaign of 1809, *Colburn's United Services Journal*, Number 7, July 1829.
18. Fraser, E, *Soldiers Whom Wellington Led*, page 236.
19. *Journal of Army Historical Research*, Volume XXXIV (1956), p 161.
20. Larpent, Volume I, p 44.
21. Browne, TH, *The Napoleonic Journal of Captain Thomas Henry Browne*, p 156.
22. De Lancey to Sir Stapleton Cotton, 16 February 1812. National Library of Scotland NLS 46.3.16 f 71.

CHAPTER VI
By Special Request

The Peninsular War having been brought to a successful conclusion, the British Army was dispersed in accordance with the government's directions, which Wellington's staff achieved with their now customary efficiency. A large force, predominantly infantry, was sent direct to America, where Britain and the United States were at war, while the remainder of the infantry returned to Ireland or England by sea. The cavalry and the horse artillery simply marched across France using a 'route' provided by the QMG department, in which a two-page document was sufficient for the move of eighteen cavalry regiments, three troops of horse artillery and 11,300 horses along two roads, one from Bordeaux to Boulogne (38 days) and the other from Toulouse to Calais (44 days). That such a large and complex operation could be accomplished without a hitch and on schedule with so little paperwork speaks very highly of the standards of staff work, discipline and mutual understanding achieved by the Peninsular Army.[1]

De Lancey was deeply involved in all this, but when his turn came to go home in late 1814 he returned to a country he had not seen for six years. His mother had moved to Colchester and other members of his family were in London and Beverley, but his posting was as Deputy Quartermaster-General in the army headquarters at Edinburgh in North Britain (Scotland), where he took over from Major-General TB Reynardson, neither the first nor the last time that he was to relieve a more senior officer without himself being given the same rank.[2] It can be imagined that the arrival of this Peninsula veteran caused something of a stir in the Scottish capital: he was still relatively young, just 38 years old; he had been in the war from start to finish; and he had been one of the closest confidants of the great national hero, the Duke of Wellington. Then, to add to his glamorous image, he was knighted in the victory honours list, being created a Knight Commander of the Order of the Bath in the *London Gazette* of 3 January 1815.[3]

None of the many reminiscences of life at Wellington's headquarters in the Peninsula makes any mention of De Lancey indulging in dalliances with Portuguese or Spanish ladies during the recently concluded campaign, but when he arrived in Scotland events moved fast. Quite when and how De Lancey and Miss Magdalene Hall met each other cannot now be established, although Captain Hay says that he met them both when he visited the Hall family residence at Dunglass in December 1814.[4] De Lancey's earlier meeting with Basil Hall had nothing to do with it, but, whatever the background, the records show that the banns were read in March and the wedding took place in Greyfriars Church in Edinburgh on 4 April 1815, following which the newly-weds went to Dunglass.

They had been there but ten days when fate in the shape of Napoleon Buonaparte cruelly intervened. When the victorious powers made peace with France in 1814, they recognised the restored Bourbon government of King Louis XVIII and then set about restoring order to the rest of Europe. The Congress of Vienna opened in September 1814 with all states sending prestigious political or military representatives; the head of the British delegation, for example, was Viscount Castlereagh, until he was replaced by Wellington in February 1815. While this was going on, the deposed Emperor Napoleon had been exiled to the Mediterranean island of Elba, where he was allowed to live in some style, including a guard of some 800 soldiers, but this proved to be too small a territory for a man who had once ruled virtually the whole of continental Europe.

The diplomats were still conferring in Vienna when, on 7 March 1815, news reached them that Napoleon had escaped, only to be followed by even more disturbing tidings on 10 March, when they learned that he had landed at Cannes on 1 March and commenced a triumphal march on Paris. The plenipotentiaries at Vienna took very quick action: they resurrected the treaty signed at Chaumont in 1814 (25 March) and appointed the most prestigious Allied general, the Duke of Wellington, to be the commander-in-chief of the Allied armies. Wellington spent a few days tidying up his affairs at Vienna and then rode to Brussels, arriving on the night of 4/5 April 1815.

Wellington was profoundly disturbed by what he found, especially his army, which was made up of a motley collection of contingents from a variety of national armies, some of them of dubious reliability, but he was particularly concerned by the poor quality of his staff officers. As a result, he quickly told the Military Secretary at the Horse Guards in London – still the redoubtable Torrens, but now Major-General Sir Henry – that he must have men who had served under him in the Peninsula. This was not, however, a matter of cronyism, but rather of practicality, since, with an attack by a well-trained, homogenous French army led by Napoleon imminent, it was vital to get an effective and efficient staff system in operation as soon as possible. It needed to be a system which would respond quickly and predictably to Wellington's wishes and method of command, in which he understood the individuals and they understood him, and the Peninsular model was the obvious, indeed the only, choice.

His Prussian liaison officer, Major-General Baron von Müffling, was a fascinated observer of Wellington's method of command which he described as follows:

> The Duke was accustomed to direct *alone* all the strategical operations of his army; and in defensive battles to indicate from his central point of observation the moment for assuming the offensive . . . The Duke, more than any one in Europe, had reason to know the value of a command which, proceeding from one master-mind, directs great operations and battles . . .[5]

But, not even Wellington could operate entirely on his own and a second man was also essential: an efficient and effective chief-of-staff, upon whom the commander-in-chief knew he could rely. That post had been filled in the Peninsula by Murray, who was Wellington's first choice for this post in Brussels, but meanwhile it was being filled by someone quite unsuitable.

Major-General Sir Hudson Lowe

At the time of Wellington's arrival in Brussels the Anglo-Dutch Army was commanded by General the Hereditary Prince of Orange, who two years previously had been one of Wellington's ADCs in the Peninsula and who was now served by a number of senior British staff officers. One of these was the Quartermaster-General, Major-General Sir Hudson Lowe, and, since he reappears several times in this story, he needs to be properly introduced, not least because his career had been quite unlike that of the majority of British officers of the time. Lowe had seen plenty of active service, but this had been split between the Mediterranean (1787–1812) and north-eastern Europe (1813–15), and he had never served in the Peninsula; thus, he knew (and was known by) only a few of his contemporaries.

Commissioned into the 50th Foot in 1787, Lowe served with them in Gibraltar, Corsica and Portugal, but was then selected to raise and command an *émigré* unit, designated the Corsican Rangers, which he took on General Abercrombie's 1801 expedition to Egypt. His unit was disbanded as a result of the Peace of Amiens in 1802 and he returned briefly to England, but was then despatched on a secret mission to Portugal. In 1803 he was promoted to lieutenant-colonel and instructed to raise a new unit, this time designated the Royal Corsican Rangers, which he commanded at numerous actions in the Mediterranean. The most notable was the siege of Capri in October 1807, after which he had been forced to capitulate, although his resistance had been so effective that he and his men were given full honours of war and allowed to rejoin the British forces in Sicily.

In December 1811 Lowe returned to England on leave and was

promoted colonel in the following month, but his next employment did not come until January 1813 when he was sent to north-east Europe to report on foreign units in British pay. This involved visiting the Swedish, Russian and Prussian armies, and he achieved a good rapport with all three, but particularly the latter, becoming particularly friendly with Prince Blücher and Lieutenant-General von Gneisenau. He accompanied the Prussians into France in 1814 and was the man who brought the news of Napoleon's first abdication to London, where he was knighted and promoted to major-general. In June 1814 he was sent as QMG of the Anglo-Dutch army in the Netherlands, where he worked hard to develop some order into the newly established headquarters.

During his career Lowe made many friends and was well thought of by people as disparate as the British General Sir John Moore, Tsar Alexander of Russia and the Prussian Prince Blücher. He was also admired by many of his subordinates. Colonel Basil Jackson recorded that he had worked closely with Lowe in the Netherlands in 1815 and that he could not:

> . . . recollect any single instance of his breaking out into any unseemly bursts of anger, or showing any real uncourteousness. He was very much liked by all who served under him, being at all times kind, considerate, generous and hospitable . . .[6]

Not all considered him quite so highly, however. Lieutenant-Colonel Sir John Colborne of the 52nd Foot was Military Secretary to the Prince of Orange at the time when Lowe was his QMG. Lowe retained that post when Wellington arrived, but Colborne, a discerning and rarely cruel man, described Lowe as 'a great fidget' and recounted how:

> . . . Sir Hudson Lowe always hesitated in his replies, a thing the Duke of Wellington could not endure. On one occasion the Duke said, 'Where does that road lead to, Sir Hudson?' Sir Hudson began drawing his plans from his pocket before answering. The Duke, putting his hand to his mouth, turned round to an officer with him, saying, 'D—d old fool!'[7]

Other staff officers, more mentally agile and aware of Wellington's nature, knew that it was infinitely preferable to give a firm and immediate answer without reference to any papers and then to check the accuracy of their statements. If necessary, they then went to the commander and made a correction, a tactic employed by many staff officers to this day.

In a discussion after the war with Thomas Creevey, Wellington again described Lowe as 'a damned fool' and explained how the latter had tried to educate the British commander on the excellence of Prussian equipment and tactics, which can only be described as exhibiting a tactlessness bordering on folly. Lowe was the target of several of Wellington's celebrated put-downs, which would have silenced a more perceptive officer, but Lowe blundered on, and since it would have been impossible for a commander to work with a subordinate he had so little respect for, Lowe had to go. Wellington and Torrens did, however, show a great deal of consideration for Lowe and the latter found him an appointment in the Mediterranean, an area which Lowe both understood and loved, and he was tactfully eased out of his appointment in the Netherlands.

De Lancey's Return

Wellington's first choice to replace Lowe was Murray, but he had been sent as governor of Canada in late 1814, with the acting rank of lieutenant-general. Although an urgent summons was despatched for his return, it was realised that there would be several months' delay (in the event, Murray did not join the army until it was in Paris). Wellington, therefore, asked for Murray's old number two, and his friend of many years standing, Colonel Sir William De Lancey, and Torrens was able to inform Wellington on 16 April that 'De Lancey is going out to you immediately.'[8]

While these great events were unfolding on the Continent, the newly married De Lanceys were enjoying the tranquillity of Spring at Dunglass and the news that Napoleon had escaped from Elba and that Wellington had been appointed to command an Anglo-Dutch army in the Netherlands probably caused them little immediate concern. This was closely followed by a second message from headquarters in Edinburgh telling De Lancey that he was required by Wellington and that he was to travel at once to take up his old post as Deputy Quartermaster-General. De Lancey had no choice in the matter, although his bride was appalled at the prospect of being left alone after such a brief, but blissfully happy, period of marriage, so she persuaded her husband that she should accompany him to the south.

They arrived in London on 21 April and De Lancey hurried to the Army headquarters at the Horse Guards to see Torrens. While clearly knowing where his duty lay, De Lancey had some serious reservations about the position in which he was being placed, as Torrens explained in a letter to Wellington:

> De Lancey is in town on his way to go out. He has his scruples as to the indignity of returning to service in the field in the same position only which he so long held; and he has requested of me to withhold the notification of his actual appointment until he communicates with you personally, lest you should imagine that he looks upon the arrangement as one favourable to him. I told him the very handsome and complimentary manner in which you asked for his services, and assured him that nothing could be so gratifying, in my view of the

case, to his military and professional feelings, as the desire you expressed to me of having him again with you; and that the expectation of Murray's arrival, and the existing appointment of Lowe, precluded the possibility of your offering him more in the department than the situation of Deputy Quartermaster-General. It would be desirable to place him on the Staff as a Colonel, in order that his situation may not be less advantageous than when he held the same in the Peninsula . . .[9]

Several thoughts may have been running through De Lancey's mind. First, he was, not unnaturally, ambitious and wished to make progress in his military career, and the job in the Netherlands, while not a step backwards, was certainly no step forwards, either. Secondly, this would be the third time he would act as a locum tenens for this most important appointment, and he knew that as soon as Lieutenant-General Murray arrived he would be reduced to the deputy's position yet again.

Torrens seems to have been as eloquent in speech as he was with the pen, since De Lancey, still a colonel, duly set out for the Netherlands, leaving Magdalene to follow as soon as he sent for her. Of course, at that point nobody had any means of knowing how long the new war would last and perhaps either Torrens or Wellington gave De Lancey some promise of early promotion or other reward, once things had settled down.

Brussels

De Lancey was in Brussels by 25 May 1815[10] where he was forced to undergo a careful briefing from the pedantic and long-winded Lowe, prior to the latter's departure on 2 June.[11] De Lancey then moved quickly to re-establish the 'Peninsular system' and thanks to Wellington's machinations he was soon surrounded by old colleagues from Spain. Indeed, on the day of the Battle of Waterloo, of the sixteen AQMGs, all had served in the Peninsula; these were, as in Spain, a mixture of permanent QMG staff (four) and regimental officers seconded to the department (twelve), with seven of them graduates of the Staff College at High Wycombe. These were assisted by twelve DAQMGs, who were captains and lieutenants in rank.

De Lancey was immediately immersed in the preparations for the forthcoming campaign, but he also found time to make arrangements for Magdalene, so that when she arrived on Thursday 8 June she was able to move straight into an apartment. For a few days they lived an almost normal life and Magdalene reported afterwards that her husband spent only about an hour a day in the office and the remainder with her, something which has caused some adverse comment in later years.[12]

The most likely explanation for this is, however, not difficult to find.

First, De Lancey had a staff of tried and tested officers, well acquainted with each other, and who were performing tasks which they had learnt thoroughly in the Peninsula. Secondly, De Lancey's officers knew that their chief, a much-liked and highly respected man, had been married for just one week before he was summoned to Brussels and, of course, at that stage nobody knew what the forthcoming campaign would involve or how long it would last. Thirdly, they were invited in turn to have dinner at the De Lanceys' house, where they met the charming and lovely Magdalene, and would have quickly realised that she was desperately in love with their chief and that, while by no means unsophisticated, she had no experience of either the army or of life outside Britain. It would, therefore, have been the most natural thing in the world, at least in the British Army, for the staff officers to make it tactfully but firmly clear to their chief that, for a few days at least, his main priority lay with his wife, that they would manage very well without his constant supervision, and that, in any case, they would let him know as soon as his presence was essential.

That moment was not long in coming, the first alarm being given on the night of 12/13 June when, following a stream of intelligence reports about French movements, De Lancey had to go to the office to write new orders for Wellington's signature. Lieutenant-Colonel Sir George Scovell called in at the office at 6 a.m. on 13 June where, to his surprise, he found De Lancey hard at work. His chief explained that 'he had been employed all the night preparing the Duke's orders for all the Divisions to move to a certain point, but that these orders would not be sent off before Napoleon had committed himself to a certain line of operations'.[13]

On Thursday 15 June the De Lanceys had an invitation to the Duchess of Richmond's Ball[14] but apparently decided not to attend, since Magdalene made no preparations. Nevertheless, her husband felt compelled to accept a dinner invitation from an old comrade, General Miguel D'Alava, the popular and respected Spanish ambassador to the King of the Netherlands, who had been the Spanish liaison officer with Wellington in the Peninsular campaign.

D'Alava's dinner had been under way for about an hour when a mounted officer arrived to hand De Lancey a message. This proved to be so urgent that De Lancey purloined the officer's horse and went at once to Wellington's house to deliver the message personally to the Commander of the Forces.[15] Having been given his instructions by Wellington, De Lancey hurried back to his house, which was only a few doors away, to set the army in motion to meet the French threat, but despite the urgency of the task, he still found time to reassure Magdalene and to tell her to be ready to leave for Antwerp at six o'clock the following morning.

A young officer on the QMG's staff, Lieutenant Basil Jackson, was walking in the park when:

... a soldier of the Guards, attached to the Quartermaster-General's office, summoned me to attend Sir William De Lancey. He had received orders to concentrate the Army towards the frontier, which had until then remained quiet in cantonments. I was employed, along with others, for about two hours in writing out "routes" for the several divisions, foreign as well as British, which were despatched by orderly Hussars of 3rd Regt. of the German Legion, steady fellows who could be depended on for so important a service. To each was explained the rate at which he was to proceed, and the time when he was to arrive at his destination; he was directed also to bring back the cover of the letter which he carried, having the time of its arrival noted upon it by the officer to whom it was addressed.[16]

As soon as the first set of 'routes' had been issued, however, Jackson became involved in one of the many staff drills evolved by the QMG's Department in Spain, under which all important messages were prepared in duplicate, the first copy being sent, as described, by orderlies provided by one of the cavalry regiments under command. Experience had taught, however, that something could go wrong – the orderly could lose his way or misunderstand his instructions, the horse could be lamed, or they could be waylaid by the enemy or guerrillas. So, it was a standing procedure for a second copy to be sent by hand of officer, and so:

> ... This business over, which occupied us till after nine, De Lancey put a packet into my hand directed to Colonel Cathcart – the present Earl – a thorough soldier and highly esteemed by the Duke, who then filled, as he had previously done in Spain, the arduous post of Assistant Quartermaster-General to the whole of the Cavalry.[17]

De Lancey worked steadily, meeting Wellington's requirements as they arose, one of them being that, after the initial 'routes' had been distributed, new information required an amendment to be issued, which resulted in another set of cavalry orderlies and officers being despatched. De Lancey split his time between the QMG's office and his own house, where Magdalene kept quiet, interrupting only occasionally to supply her husband with cups of 'green tea' but he also went twice to Wellington's house, on the first occasion finding the commander in discussion with Major-General von Müffling, the Prussian liaison officer.

De Lancey finished his work at about 2 a.m. when he delivered the final document and then returned to his own house where he and Magdalene spent their remaining few hours together discussing their plans and leaning over their balcony, watching Picton's 5th British Division assemble below and then march off into the morning mist.

At six o'clock in the morning Magdalene left for Antwerp with her groom, West, and her maid, Emma. De Lancey knew that she would be in good hands, as he had already given full instructions to Captain Mitchell of the 25th Foot, the Deputy Assistant Quartermaster-General in the city, who could be relied upon to ensure that his chief's wife was safely looked after.

The Battle of Quatre Bras

Having seen his wife safely on her way De Lancey finished off some work in Brussels before following Wellington, von Müffling and Lord Fitzroy Somerset (Wellington's Military Secretary) to Quatre Bras. The time of departure from Brussels and of arrival in Quatre Bras of these two parties vary slightly in the different accounts[18] but they were definitely there by 10.30 a.m., since that was the time that Wellington wrote a letter to Blücher[19] which was apparently based on information he had received from his chief-of-staff in a document known as the 'De Lancey Memorandum' (this is discussed in detail in Appendix D). De Lancey was at his usual place at Wellington's side for most of the day at the Battle of Quatre Bras where the Allied army held Napoleon's advance. Afterwards De Lancey accompanied his chief to the inn which was to be their overnight headquarters, where his first task was to issue orders:

> Genappe June 16 1815.
> The troops to continue on the same ground as they occupied at the close of the action this day, placing picquets in their front and communicating to their right and left. The 1st Brigade and 2nd Brigade of Guards to bivouac in rear of Quatre Bras, having their light companies to their front. The Brunswick Battalions and Nassau troops to occupy the wood on the right of the position, placing picquets round the wood and communicating with the cavalry on their right. (Signed) W DE LANCEY DQMG
> General HRH the Prince of Orange is requested to communicate this order to his Corps, to the Brunswick and Nassau troops. (Signed) W DE L.[20]

Having issued these and other orders, De Lancey's mind turned to Magdalene and he snatched the opportunity to write a letter to his wife, which, to her great delight, reached her at Antwerp at midnight the following day.

On the morning of the 17th Wellington received news of Blücher's defeat the previous day at Ligny and the subsequent Prussian withdrawal, and realised that he would have to pull back alongside his ally. When Wellington had been in the Netherlands in 1814 he carried out a personal reconnaissance of the routes approaching Brussels from the south, accompanied by Lieutenant-Colonel James Carmichael Smyth, a

Royal Engineers officer,[21] as a result of which Smyth tasked a team of surveyors with preparing a map of the area. In 1815 one completed copy of this map was presented to the Prince of Orange,[22] but another, almost complete, remained in the surveyors' office at Brussels and on arriving at Quatre Bras on 16 June, Smyth realised that this map would be needed.

The map was, therefore, despatched from Brussels by hand of a Lieutenant Waters, a Royal Engineer officer blessed with the somewhat improbable first names of Marcus Antonius, who stowed the document in a small bag attached to the horse's saddle. Waters arrived at Quatre Bras during the battle and became embroiled in a small cavalry action in which he was unhorsed and ridden over. On recovering, the hapless officer realised that his horse – and, of course, the precious map – were nowhere to be seen and with so much fighting going on and so many riderless horses wandering about, his chances of recovering the vital document seemed slim. By the greatest of good fortune, however, he chanced upon his horse unconcernedly attacking a peasant's vegetable patch, and to his immense relief the map was where he had left it. Waters then immediately delivered the map to the Royal Engineers' Brigade-Major Oldfield, who was able to produce it the instant it was requested by Wellington.[23]

The following morning Wellington used that map to brief De Lancey, watched by some interested spectators, including the Prince of Orange's chief-of-staff, Major-General de Constant Rebecque, who recorded that:

> The Duke seated in a hut of foliage behind the farm of Quatre Bras dictates his marching orders to Colonel De Lancey. According to these orders the army must begin moving at 10 a.m. in order to take up the position in front of Waterloo, where the Duke's headquarters will be.[24]

Wellington's Military Secretary, Lieutenant-Colonel Fitzroy Somerset, was also on the spot:

> . . . and he despatched De Lancey, the Q^r M. General, to make out a position in front of the Forest of Soignes, which the Duke proposed to take up with his Army. The troops began to move from Quatre Bras about 9 o'clock.[25]

De Lancey duly went back, selected a position for the army, marked it out and briefed the staff officers who were to act as guides for the regiments as they arrived following their withdrawal from Quatre Bras. De Constant Rebeque also went to Mont St Jean where he found De Lancey:

> . . . seated on the ground with a large sketch map of the position before him. He does not foresee that he will be killed the next day at

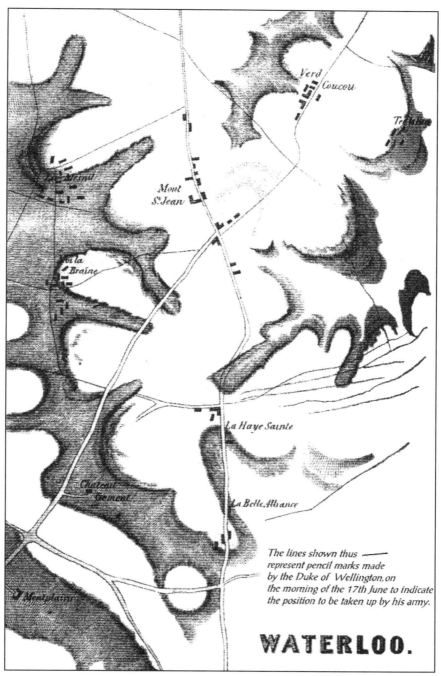

The lines shown thus ——
represent pencil marks made
by the Duke of Wellington, on
the morning of the 17th June to indicate
the position to be taken up by his army.

WATERLOO.

A small portion of the Waterloo Map which was being carried by De Lancey when he was hit by a cannon-ball. (From CD Yonge, The Life of Field Marshal Arthur, Duke of Wellington, *Chapman & Hall, London, 1860, Volume I).*

61

this same place. He tells me the order of battle intended by the Duke on the position; he requests me to place the troops of the Low Countries.[26]

Fitzroy Somerset, however, makes it clear that De Lancey did not follow his commander's directions precisely:

The Duke left Quatre Bras between 2 and 3 o'clock & proceeded leisurely towards Waterloo; on arriving near to La Belle Alliance he thought it was the position the Q^r M Genl would have taken up, being the most commanding ground but he had found it too extended to be occupied by our troops, & so had proceeded further on & had marked out a position on the right next Braine le Comte & extending thence to the left across the high Road which joined on the rear and near Mont St Jean. About four o'clock the Duke found the Troops on it & looking at the position finding the ground between Braine le Comte & Hougoumont broken, He ordered the right to be thrown back, the angle or elbow in the rear of Hougoumont and the extreme right on Merbe Braine, intending that Braine le Comte should be occupied by a battery. The Infantry had been conducted to their respective positions by the Staff Officers . . .[27]

Fitzroy Somerset's record is supported by Lieutenant-General Sir Hussey Vivian:

3rd. That the position of Waterloo is by no means a strong one cannot for a moment be disputed. How far the statement that the Duke had the year before selected it is correct I will not pretend to say, but I will mention an anecdote told me by poor Sir Fredk. Ponsonby after the Battle, and what I heard him often repeat. He said 'he knew it to be a fact that the Duke had himself halted some Regiments in position on the Bruxelles side of Genappe, meaning to have halted his Army there, having that town and the small river that runs through it to his front, but that De Lancey, his Quartermaster-General, who had been sent to the rear, came to him and described to him the position of Waterloo, and that the Duke determined to retire from that on which he was then halted to take up that on which the Battle was fought.'[28]

These two accounts differ slightly in the detail, but the over-riding conclusion is the same: that it was De Lancey who selected the position. It is also an indication of De Lancey's abilities that he not only made such a brilliant selection of the ground, but that he felt sufficiently secure in his relationship with Wellington that he could make such a major decision with such confidence.

The veracity of Somerset's account is not open to serious challenge, as explained by Elizabeth Longford:

> So much has been written about Wellington's inspired and highly individual choice of the cross-roads on the Mont-Saint-Jean ridge for his Waterloo battle-ground, that it is hard to believe his first preference was for something different. Yet Somerset was close to Wellington and had long been renowned for his truthfulness, exact execution of his master's orders and accurate echo of his master's voice.[29]

At some during that morning Lieutenant Basil Jackson, the young QMG staff officer, was instructed to make his way from Quatre Bras to the new position at Mont St Jean where he was to report to De Lancey to act as a guide. By this time the withdrawal from Quatre Bras was in full swing and, although three separate routes were in use, the *chaussées* were overcrowded with men, horses, guns, waggons, tumbrels and wounded, all jostling for position, a situation exacerbated by the different nationalities and languages of those involved. Jackson took a short cut across the fields, which took him into the centre of the village of Genappe, where he beheld such chaos that he decided that personal intervention was required. He was soon sorting things out, helped by the fact that:

> . . . Happily I was acquainted with some pithy expressions in two or three languages, which were familiar to the ears of those I had to deal with; and these, together with the flat of my sword, proved very efficacious in the end. While in the thick of this scene of tumult and confusion, I felt some one clap me on the shoulder, and looking round saw Sir W De Lancey. 'You are very well employed here,' said he; 'remain, and keep the way clear for the troops; I shall not want you at Waterloo.' Encouraged by my chief's commendation I redoubled my efforts, and had the satisfaction of seeing the defile free.[30]

Having seen the rearguard safely covering the withdrawal, Wellington joined De Lancey in the afternoon, and as the French were making no move against his right, he closed his British troops inwards from Braine L'Alleud to the Nivelles road, leaving Chassé's Dutch-Belgian division to hold the village. It seems likely that it was at this point that he made the pencilled marks on the map which Oldfield has recorded were made by the Duke himself. The marks have the slightly irregular appearance of having been done without anything firm beneath the paper, and probably when it was held in one hand on horseback; they mark the left of the position, showing roughly how he intended to hold it, one possible

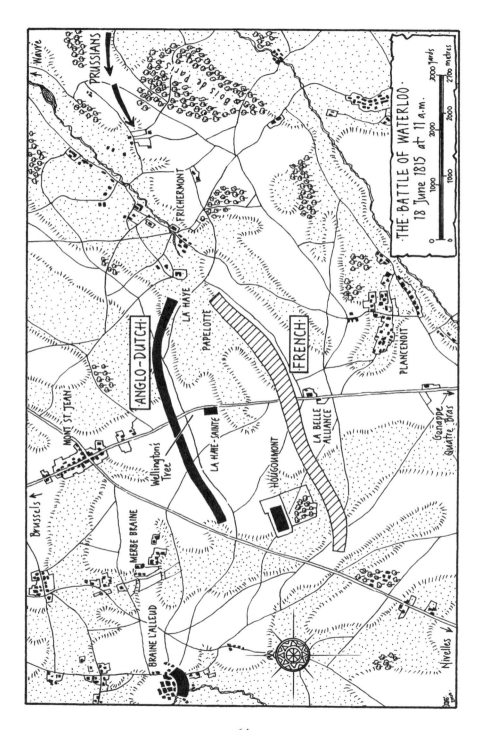

THE·BATTLE·OF·WATERLOO
18 June 1815 at 11 a.m.

PRUSSIANS

Wavre

FRICHERMONT

LA·HAYE

PAPELOTTE

ANGLO–DUTCH·

MONT ST·JEAN

Wellington's
Tree

LA·HAYE·SAINTE

FRENCH·

PLANCENOIT

LA·BELLE
ALLIANCE

Genappe
Quatre Bras

Brussels

HOUGOUMONT

MERBE BRAINE

BRAINE L'ALLEUD

Nivelles

64

explanation being that Wellington made them when pointing out to von Müffling the line on which he wanted the Prussians to join him.

The men of the headquarters spent the night of 17 June in the village of Waterloo, where Wellington, the Prince of Orange and Lord Uxbridge, by privilege of rank, occupied the better houses. The staff, however, stayed in the small thatched cottages that lined the *chaussée*, and on Saturday 15 July 1815 – barely a month after the battle – an English lady passing through the village on her way to the battlefield noted that De Lancey's name was still to be seen chalked on the door of one such cottage.[31] It was to be his last night of comfort and ease.

After taking over from Sir Hudson Lowe, De Lancey proved that if he still had reservations over the manner in which he had been appointed – and despite knowing that Murray was on the way from Canada to replace him – he gave of his best, which was very good, indeed. He got the army on the move on the night of 15 June and, although there was undoubtedly some confusion, this is not surprising, bearing in mind the size of the army, the disparate nature of its elements, the inexperience of many of the units and the changes necessitated by the rapidly developing situation. His written orders were clear and concise, leaving the recipients in no doubt as to what was required of them. He was cool and collected, concentrating on the great responsibilities that rested on his shoulders, but still able to find the time to pause and encourage a junior officer like Jackson. Whether it was receiving orders from Wellington at Quatre Bras or seeing to their implementation at Mont St Jean, De Lancey was the master of his profession.

NOTES

1. Ward, SGP, 'The QMG's Department in the Peninsula', *Journal of the Society of Army Research,* Volume XXIII, pp 133–154.
2. His posting order was dated 1 July 1814 and appointed him Deputy Quartermaster-General in Headquarters North Britain in Edinburgh from 25 June 1814. Commander-in-Chief's Out Letters PRO WO 3/573 p 2.
3. This list created no fewer than 181 KCBs and, while no doubt delighting the recipients, it caused great umbrage in higher ranks of both the Navy and the Army. In the Army's case, the entire list was decided in London without any reference to Wellington, who was most annoyed. One problem arose because the second class of the Order of the Bath (i.e. KCB) was extended to the rank of lieutenant-colonel and an arbitrary threshold for qualification was set at five clasps on the Peninsula Medal. This resulted in major-generals commanding divisions being ignored, while some of their subordinates received knighthoods. The normally phlegmatic Torrens confessed in a letter to Wellington that this one issue had caused him 'more anxiety & labour & worry! than I ever endured!' Letter Torrens to Wellington, 16 January 1815. PRO WO 3/63.
4. Hay, Captain William, *Reminiscences 1808–1815 Under Wellington*, p 204.
5. von Müffling, Major-General Baron, *Passages From My Life; Together with*

Memoirs of the Campaign of 1813 and 1814, pp 215–16.

6. Jackson, B, *Events of a Military Life,* Volume ii, p 59.
7. Moore Smith, GC, *The Life of John Colborne, Field Marshal Lord Seaton,* pp 213, 246
8. *Supplementary Despatches,* Volume X, p 84.
9. Letter Torrens to Wellington, 21 April 1815, *Supplementary Dispatches,* Volume X, p130
10. Gurwood, *Dispatches,* Volume XII, p 426.
11. According to the Monthly Returns in University of Southampton WP 9/7/1, Lowe was QMG on 25 April, and was again shown as QMG on 25 May but with pencil note 'Removed from staff 2 June.' De Lancey was shown as DQMG on 25 May and as QMG on 25 June. In the same book the 'Staff Appointments' section shows De Lancey's official posting-in date as 9 May 1815.
12. See, for example, SGP Ward, 'The Quartermaster-General's Department in the Peninsula,' *The Journal of the Society of Army Historical Research,* Volume XXIII, pp 149–150.
13. *Copy of Memorandum of Service at the Battle of Waterloo* by General Sir George Scovell, *GCB,* PRO WO 37/12.
14. Their names are on the list given in *A Sketch of the life of Georgiana, Lady De Ros, with some reminiscences of her family and friends, including the Duke of Wellington,* by the Honourable Mrs JR Swinton, John Murray, London, 1893.
15. This was almost certainly the message sent by Lieutenant-Colonel Sir George Berkeley, Wellington's representative at the Prince of Orange's headquarters at Braine-le-Comte. That headquarters had received information at 12 a.m. (midday) that the French had crossed the frontier from Major-General Dörnberg, but, due to the prince's absence, it was not passed on to Brussels until 2 p.m.
16. A Staff Officer (Basil Jackson), 'Recollections of Waterloo,' *Colburn's United Service Magazine;* 1847, Part III, p 3.
17. Jackson, Basil, ibid
18. Various times are given for Wellington's movements on the morning of 16 June. '. . . about five we were on horseback . . . and reached Quatre Bras about eleven A.M' (von Müffling, p 230). 'The Duke left Bruxelles about 8 in the Morning and proceeded as quickly as possible to Quatre Bras where he got about 10 o'clock.' (Fitzroy Somerset. *Account*).
19. Hofschröer, P, *1815: The Waterloo Campaign,* p 232, quoting Ollech, General von, '*Geschichte des Feldzuges von 1815',* Berlin, 1876.
20. De Bas, Colonel F, *Prins Frederik der Nederlanden en zijn Tijd,* Vol 3 Part 2, p 600. It should be noted that although De Bas' book is written in French, this order is given in the original English. I am obliged to J Hussey Esq. for drawing my attention to this and the two following extracts from De Bas' book.
21. Memorandum dated 22 September 1814, *Dispatches* (1838), Vol XII, pp 125–129.
22. An officer named Robinson claimed to be the author of the map: 'Superintended under the orders of Major Genl. J Carmichael Smyth RE the making of the Plans of the Fortresses in the Netherlands. He provided also under his direction a Plan of the Ground about Waterloo previous to the battle, which was consulted continually in the course of that eventful day and found in the breast coat pocket of the DQMG after he was killed.' Letter from Robinson to Lt Gen Sir Hussey Vivian, Bart, Master-General of the Ordnance dated 4 April 1838. PRO WO/44/692 File 389.

23. Raglan Papers, Gwent County Record Office, Cwmbran, Wales. Box: 'Wellington C Nos 130–155 Miscellaneous Letters and Papers.' This box contains a copy of the 'De Lancey map' fully annotated and certified by 'J Oldfield, Colonel, late Captain and Brigade-Major, Royal Engineers; 31st January 1845.'
24. De Bas, Colonel F, *Prins Frederik der Nederlanden en zijn Tijd*, Vol 3 Part 2, p 621.
25. Raglan Papers, Gwent County Record Office, Cwmbran, Wales. Box D 3134. Manuscript volume *Lord Fitzroy Somerset's account of the Battle of Waterloo*.
26. De Bas, Colonel F, *op cit*, p 634.
27. This is taken verbatim from the original, which is in Lord Fitzroy Somerset's own hand, in the Gwent Record Office. Raglan Papers, Fitzroy Somerset, *op cit*.
28. Siborne, Major-General HT, *Waterloo Letters*, Letter #71, p 152.
29. Longford, Elizabeth, *Wellington: The Years of the Sword,'* p 441.
30. A Staff Officer, *Recollections of a Staff Officer*, Part 1 p 11.
31. An Englishwoman (Mrs Eaton), *Narrative of a Residence in Belgium*, etc,' p 260. The marking of staff officers' quarters by chalking their name on the lintel was one of Wellington's instructions from the Peninsula, laid down in a General Order issued on 4 July 1809.

CHAPTER VII
Waterloo

The Battle of Waterloo is one of the few true turning points in history, where the day before there was one dispensation and the day after quite another. Napoleon had dominated Europe for a generation and to the forces under Wellington and Blücher, all of whom had been fighting for virtually all their adult lives, it must have seemed, as they awaited the French attack, that they were faced by many more years of war. But by evening it was all over, in a bloody battle in which most of the fighting took place in an area some three miles long by two miles wide; a tiny cockpit in which to decide the fate of Europe for the next fifty years.

Immediately to the south of the large farm buildings of Mont St Jean lie two parallel ridges, running approximately east-west and separated by a valley approximately three miles long. The southern ridge is generally identified by the inn 'La Belle Alliance' which lies at its centre and it was this feature which, according to Fitzroy Somerset, Wellington had mentally selected. De Lancey, however, decided that the southern ridge would not be suitable for an army as small as Wellington's and decided on the northern ridge, instead. Not only was this more suited to the size of force available, but it would also enable Wellington to employ the tactic he had developed in the Peninsula, where the troops on the reverse slope could lie down, giving them shelter from enemy artillery, while also enabling them, when they rose as a body on a signal, to create surprise and dismay among the advancing enemy ranks.

The main Charleroi road, a wide, paved trunk road (known locally as a *chaussée*) ran north-south down the centre of the battlefield and was the main axis of Napoleon's advance; the last, short stretch of his direct route from Paris to Brussels. There was a second significant road, which headed south-west from the junction at Mont St Jean to the town of Nivelles. The area was covered with a number of smaller roads, many of them little better than farm tracks, most of which crossed the battlefield in a roughly west-east direction. Some of these were 'sunken' for at least part of their length, with the surface some 6–10 feet (2–3m) below the level of the surrounding fields. This particularly applied to the track running across the front of the Allied right (i.e., from the crossroads above La Haye Sainte westwards to the Mont St Jean-Nivelles road) where the sunken road, with its steep banks, formed a major tactical obstacle to troop movement, especially for cavalry.[1]

To the north of the battlefield was the village which gave its name to the battle Waterloo and between that and the battlefield was the hamlet of Mont St Jean. In front of the main Anglo-Dutch position were three groups of buildings which served as outposts: on the left, the Ferme Papelotte; in the centre, Ferme La Haye Sainte; and on the right, in the hollow between the two ridges and surrounded by a small wood, Château Hougoumont.* On the French side the only building of any significance was the inn, La Belle Alliance,[2] which was on the eastern side of the Charleroi road, overlooking the valley.

The area in which the battle took place was mostly cultivated and under wheat, which, immediately prior to the deployment of the Allied troops, was taller than most of the soldiers. Underfoot, the ground was very wet following a violent thunderstorm on the afternoon of 17 June which had led into a night of heavy rain. The horses, troops, guns and supply carts then churned it into a sea of dense mud, and by the morning of 18 June the 'going' was especially difficult for heavily loaded infantrymen, cavalry horses and artillery alike.

The situation is well described by a participant in the battle, Captain Hay:

> ... I may as well give the best idea I can of the nature of the ground on which so great a contest was about to take place. The length from one end to the other, i.e. from left to right, I do not think exceeded three miles if so much, the breadth not two miles. From about the right centre of the British position was a gentle slope in the ground, at some points a little more abrupt than others, which slope ended on a flat bottom of about three hundred yards broad at the widest place. Rather to the right-hand side of the flat ran a deep lane, and, on the British side, close to that lane were some low hedges and small enclosures occupied by an infantry brigade.
>
> On the French side of the flat, the ground just opposite was rather more bold, the land lying in a considerable degree more on a slope; on the French's left of this was a flat valley, again a gentle rise in the lay of the land towards the extreme left of the enemy's position ...
>
> ... The country around was covered with growing crops of wheat and rye in full ear, and, from the rain that had fallen and the height of the corn, it was like riding through a pond ... As to lying down to

---

* Throughout this chapter the terms 'left', 'centre', and 'right' are used in accordance with the military convention that they are expressed as seen when the side concerned was facing the enemy. Thus, Château Hougoumont was on the British right and the French left.

septicaemia (the result of a gas attack) in February 1916. By kind permission of The Royal Artillery Institution and Cuneo Fine Arts.

15. Dunglass House was totally rebuilt under the personal supervision of Sir James Hall, a long and very expensive project. It was completed in 1813 and resulted in one of the finest houses in Britain. By kind permission of F Usher, Esq.

16. Lieutenant Peter Reynolds, 2nd Battalion, Irish Guards, Magdalene Harvey's great-great-grandson. Born in 1916, he was captain of the Cricket XI and President of Pop at Eton, but was killed commanding his platoon at Boulogne in 1940. A sketch by Antony Devas. By kind permission of his sister, Mrs Mary Birch Reynardson.

rest, it was out of the question, as the road was knee deep in water; consequently the night was spent uncomfortable. We heard, the whole night long, the moving of the French troops into position. Fires we had none, from lack of fuel, so the camps looked more dull than usual.[3]

Hay was woken at 6 o'clock on the morning of the battle to find that:

> . . . the rain which had continued in a more or less degree throughout the night, had now ceased, and the morning was very cool and very dull.

In the early morning a dense mist lay in the valley between the two positions, which, once fighting started, was replaced by a heavy pall of smoke from the guns and muskets. In addition, conflict between so many men in such a small area generated a vast amount of noise – a mixture of muskets, guns, bugles, drums, men shouting and screaming, and horses neighing – many reports describing how difficult it was to pass orders.

The Cavalry Charges

Before battle commenced, Wellington rode along the Allied line, both to check the positions and to encourage his troops. He was wearing a plain blue coat, low cocked hat and a short cloak, and was accompanied by his staff, the British officers, including De Lancey, being dressed similarly to Wellington, except for the Adjutant-General, Major-General Barnes, who wore his full-dress embroidered coat, which 'rendered him very conspicuous'. One of those staff officers describes the entourage as being:

> . . . composed of at least forty. There was his personal Staff, consisting of a Military Secretary and six or eight Aides-de-Camp; the Adjutant and Quartermaster Generals, each with his suite of half-a-dozen officers; the Commanding officers of Artillery and Engineers, with their followers. Besides our own people, we had Generals Alava, Müffling and Vincent, all attended by Aides-de-Camp; so that we formed an imposing cavalcade.[4]

As was his custom, Wellington stopped here and there for a chat or a cheery word and accepted an invitation for a cup of tea with the Rifles. The British troops, most of whom knew him as 'Old Douro' (from the first title he had earned in the Peninsula), respected him as being firm but fair and ever mindful of their welfare, doing his best to ensure that they were properly fed and clothed, and, in particular, that they were not exposed to unnecessary danger. Above all, perhaps, they respected him for his personal courage as he rode about the battlefield apparently oblivious to the shot and shell. He, in his turn, had a great affection and respect for them. History remembers his remark '. . . they are the scum of the earth' but overlooks that this was a reference to the many recruits who were jailbirds, debtors and the like (a consequence of the government's opposition to conscription), and forgets the all-important second part of his sentence: '. . . but see what fine fellows we have made of them.' On the other side of the valley Napoleon also reconnoitred his position and was roundly cheered by his troops as he galloped along the line, accompanied by his suite. He remained, however, a distant figure and did not stop to talk.

Reports of the time at which the battle commenced vary between 10.30 a.m. and midday, such differences probably being no more than an indication of the imprecise nature of timekeeping in the early nineteenth century. All agree, however, that the action started with a barrage from the massed French artillery, located forward of La Belle Alliance. This barrage did comparatively little damage to the British who were mostly on the reverse slope and out of sight of the French guns. But Bijlandt's Dutch brigade, which, having fought under Napoleon in previous campaigns, was on the forward slope and suffered accordingly.

With that, the battle for Hougoumont started on the right of the British position, and then at about 2 p.m. the first major French attack was mounted by some 16,000 men of D'Erlon's corps, with its left resting on the Charleroi-Brussels road and its right angled towards the village of Smohain. The assault reached the main Allied position where there was fierce fighting and the issue was in the balance when the British cavalry intervened, the Union Brigade charging into the French right and the Household Brigade, led by Lord Uxbridge in person, into its left. In many cases Highlanders of the 92nd Foot grabbed horses' stirrups as they galloped by to rush them into the fray and a fierce fight followed, with no quarter given on either side.

Unfortunately for the British, the cavalry charge got out of hand, their momentum carrying the troopers into the French artillery positions, where they were counter-attacked by French *cuirassiers* and forced to withdraw, with considerable slaughter on both sides. D'Erlon's attack was repulsed with great loss of life and many taken prisoner, but the Household and Union cavalry brigades virtually ceased to exist.

Both Napoleon and Wellington knew that Blücher was on his way, but the question was whether he and his gallant Prussians could arrive before the French broke through the Anglo-Dutch position and continued their advance on Brussels. Wellington ordered his infantry to withdraw a short distance and to lie down, once again giving them cover and enabling them to catch their breath. The apparent disappearance of much of the Allied infantry led Ney to conclude that Wellington had begun to retreat and, acting quickly, he ordered General Farine to lead his cavalry brigade towards Mont St Jean to discover what the Anglo-Dutch army was doing. Unfortunately, the divisional commander objected vociferously to Marshal Ney issuing orders direct to one of his brigade commanders, instead of through the proper chain of command, whereupon Ney, renowned for his quick temper, impetuously ordered the entire cavalry corps to charge against the unseen British positions. There was no gainsaying Ney, who shouted that the future of France depended upon success.

The eighteen squadrons of cavalry started from their position on the right of the Charleroi-Brussels road, crossed that road at an angle and then trotted up the slope with Hougoumont to their left and La Haye Sainte on their right. The Anglo-Dutch artillery waited until the French were only some sixty yards distant and then opened a withering fire, but despite suffering heavy casualties, the French pressed forward by sheer weight of numbers. Meanwhile, the British infantry stood up and formed squares, each of four more or less equal-sized walls, all with fixed bayonets. Each wall was composed of either three or four ranks, depending on the numbers available, with the front and second rank kneeling, the butts of their muskets resting on the ground and their fixed bayonets forming a formidable barrier, while the third and (if available) fourth rank stood, firing volleys whenever the attacking cavalry were within range. In the centre were officers, musicians, drummers, the colours, wounded and staff officers, while the gunners continued to fire their guns until, at the very last second, they, too, fled into the centre of the squares.

Seeing that Milhoud's corps was in trouble, Napoleon ordered Kellermann's cavalry corps and the Guards heavy cavalry – thirty-seven squadrons in all – to their aid. These followed across the valley, preceded in this case by *voltigeurs* (skirmishers), their progress impeded by fallen men, loose horses and the ever-present mud. Again the British guns poured fire into them, their cannonballs cutting swathes through the French cavalry columns. Once they had weathered this storm the French cavalry found themselves faced by the British squares and again, despite the utmost bravery, the attack petered out. Indeed, there was a short period when an eerie and almost total silence fell on the battlefield as the French cavalry rode around and behind the British squares, occasionally approaching a particular square and halting, whereupon a few individuals – usually officers – would press forward, waving their helmets on the point of their swords, shouting to their men to attack; but the sight of the grimly determined British infantry with their fixed bayonets was sufficient to prevent such a rash undertaking. This stalemate was broken when what remained of the British heavy cavalry charged and the survivors of the French cavalry withdrew across the valley.

Ney now carried out a smaller-scale attack, using one infantry division and part of another belonging to Reille's corps (which was still concentrating its efforts on the stubborn British in Hougoumont) supported by surviving cavalry from Milhaud's corps. The attackers struggled across the valley and up towards the British, but were soon repulsed, although by now the soldiers of the Anglo-Dutch army were drawing on their last reserves of courage. Many officers and senior non-commissioned officers had been killed or wounded, and large areas of ground were covered with dead, dying and wounded men and horses.

The Attack on La Haye Sainte

Napoleon now ordered Ney to take La Haye Sainte where, despite its exposed position and an increasingly serious shortage of ammunition, a battalion of the King's German Legion (KGL), a German-manned unit but an integral part of the British Army, had held out all day under its commanding officer, Major Baring. In a bitterly fought engagement the French gradually prevailed. The Prince of Orange ordered another KGL battalion to go to the aid of the beleaguered garrison, but insisted, despite advice, that it did so in line, as a result of which it suffered very heavy casualties from a French cavalry charge. The Prince then repeated the error with the 8th KGL.

Having taken La Haye Sainte, Ney rushed both infantry and artillery reinforcements forward across the valley and up the slope past the farm, but although his men reached the ridge line they could get no farther. Nevertheless, the Allied position was in grave danger, with the French threatening to break through its centre, although, fortunately for Wellington, at this time Napoleon's attention was diverted to the French right where the advance troops of Blücher's army took the village of Plancenoit, although they were subsequently pushed out again by two battalions of Napoleon's Old Guard.

De Lancey is Wounded

One of the major features of the battle was that, throughout the day, Wellington was constantly in the thick of the fighting, and was repeatedly warned by his soldiers – sometimes in the strongest, but still respectful, terms – to take cover, all to no effect. The peril of his exposure and the good fortune which enabled him to survive totally unscathed can be gauged by the deaths and wounds inflicted upon his personal staff and his staff officers.

The Duke's Military Secretary, Lord Fitzroy Somerset, lost his right arm from a shot fired from La Haye Sainte at about 7 p.m., while Lord Uxbridge, commanding the cavalry, was riding beside Wellington just before the end when a cannonball virtually severed his leg and he had to be carried off the field. Wellington had eight aides-de-camp, of whom two, Lieutenant-Colonels Charles Canning and Sir Alexander Gordon, both of the 3rd Foot Guards, were killed. The losses among the General Staff, some of them at subordinate (i.e., corps and divisional) headquarters were also heavy. Of twenty-four on the adjutant-general's staff, two were killed and six wounded, the latter including the Adjutant-General himself, Major-General Sir Edward Barnes, in his scarlet jacket. There were more QMG staff present – thirty altogether – but their losses were greater also, with nine wounded.

One of that nine was De Lancey, who at about 3 p.m. was with the Commander of the Forces near 'Wellington's Tree', on the main ridge immediately above La Haye Sainte. There are two slightly different versions of what happened next, although both stem from Wellington. According to Fraser's account:

> In the afternoon of the 18th, I have this on good authority, he [the Duke] took off his cloak, and Sir William De Lancey, who was his most intimate friend, in order not to put the Duke to any inconvenience, dismounted; and was fastening the Duke's cloak to the front of his own saddle when he was struck down; he most unfortunately gave orders to those who were carrying him from the field, to leave him there; and to go back, and fight. He was found alive the next morning; and his life might have been saved under other circumstances . . .[5]

Wellington himself, when describing the incident to another author,[6] said that:

> De Lancey was with me, and speaking to me when he was struck. We were on a point of land that overlooked the plain. I had just been warned off by some soldiers (but as I saw well from it, and two divisions were engaged below, I said 'Never mind') when a ball came bounding along *en ricochet*, as it is called, and, striking him on the back, sent him many yards over the head of his horse. He fell on his face, and bounded upwards and fell again. All the staff dismounted and ran to him, and when I came up he said, 'Pray tell them to leave me and let me die in peace.' I had him conveyed to the rear . . .[7]

Whether mounted or dismounted at the time he was hit, De Lancey was lying in a very exposed spot, with the battle raging around him, and his friends could only devote a limited time to tending him. It would seem that someone removed his blue coat to examine the wound, as the Waterloo Map was removed from his pocket.[8]

His cousin, Lieutenant-Colonel De Lancey Barclay of the 1st Foot Guards, an assistant adjutant-general, saw what had happened and instructed four soldiers to carry him off the field in a blanket. With the battle raging fiercely they could do little other than leave the wounded man in a barn and hurry back to their posts, and, in any case, De Lancey was certain that he was about to die and was most insistent that he be left alone to do so in peace.

Indeed, there was a general assumption that De Lancey had died, Wellington recording in his despatch written that night that Colonel De Lancey:

> . . . was killed by a cannon shot in the middle of the action. This officer is a serious loss to His Majesty's service, and to me at this moment.[9]

Wellington was, however, wrong, because De Lancey survived the night and at some time the following morning a staff officer chanced upon him and immediately summoned Lieutenant-Colonel Sir George Scovell, one of De Lancey's AQMGs and an old friend from the Peninsula. Scovell hastened to his chief, moved him to a nearby peasant's cottage and then sent a message to Wellington, who was in Brussels writing his despatch. Scovell penned a note to Lady Magdalene, which he sent via General McKenzie, the British commander at Antwerp, requesting that she be told of the situation. He also summoned expert medical help and De Lancey was bled twice.

On the morning of Tuesday 20 June Wellington passed through Mont St Jean on his way from Brussels to rejoin his army, and called in to visit the wounded De Lancey, where:

> . . . I saw him in a barn, and he spoke with such strength that I said (for I had reported him killed), 'Why! De Lancey, you will have the advantage of Sir Condy in "Castle Rackrent" – you will know what your friends said of you after you were dead'.[10] 'I hope I shall,' he replied. Poor fellow! We had known each other since we were boys.[11] But I had no time to be sorry. I went on with the army, and never saw him again.[12]

In describing the incident many years later, Wellington, not a man to give idle praise, said that De Lancey: '. . . was an excellent officer, and would have risen to great distinction had he lived.'[13] Again, Fraser reported that:

> THE DEPUTY QUARTER-MASTER GENERAL, who was in attendance on the Duke's person at Waterloo was one of his favourite officers; and I believe that the Duke felt his death more than that of anyone else . . .[14]

This statement by Fraser is borne out by Wellington's words in his Despatch, quoted above: the phrase 'a serious loss to His Majesty's service' was one he used on several other occasions, but no other instance can be found of the more personal note of '. . . and to me . . .'.

Another officer, Lieutenant-Colonel Sir Augustus Frazer, commander Royal Horse Artillery at Waterloo, and who had known De Lancey in the Peninsula, was with Wellington throughout the battle and wrote: 'Poor De Lancey! He is our greatest loss; a noble fellow and an admirable officer.'[15]

Later that day Scovell was still with his wounded chief when a former cavalry officer, Captain Hay, suddenly appeared to announce that he had just arrived with Lady Magdalene De Lancey, who was waiting some distance away while he came forward to ascertain how her husband was. Scovell told Hay to bring her forward and when she arrived he went out to greet her and to warn her about her husband's condition, before escorting her into the cottage.

With this reunion, it is time to turn to Lady Magdalene and to trace the path which had brought this gentle and refined woman, who hailed from a wealthy, comfortable and intellectual background, to desperation, suffering, squalor and death on the bloody battlefield of Waterloo.

NOTES

1. This road is no longer 'sunken' since the earth was removed by the Belgians in the years following the battle in order to construct the Butte de Lion as a tribute to the Hereditary Prince of Orange, who was wounded during the battle.

2. The name, La Belle Alliance, was particularly apt for the place where Blücher and Wellington met after the battle, but the name actually came from an earlier event, when the inn-keeper's daughter married a local farmer.

3. Hay, Captain William, *Reminiscences 1808–1815 Under Wellington*, London, 1901, pp 175–7.

4. A Staff Officer, 'Recollections of Waterloo', *Colburn's United Service Magazine*, 1848, Part I, p 183.

5. Fraser, Sir WA, *Words on Wellington: The Duke – Waterloo – The Ball*, JC Nimmo, p 262.

6. Samuel Rogers Recollection, quoted in *Dictionary of National Biography*, pp 754–755

7. A story has prevailed for many years that De Lancey was not struck by the cannonball, but was wounded by the shock wave. This is contradicted by the two quotes from Wellington, which both agree that he was actually hit. Further, Wellington's personal surgeon, Dr Hume, told Sir Augustus Frazer that after De Lancey's death: '. . . he had opened the body; eight ribs were forced from the spine, one totally broken to pieces, and part of it in his lungs'. (Frazer, *Letters*, p 582) It is not credible that such wounds could be caused by the ball's slipstream.

8. The question of what happened to De Lancey's military papers is discussed at Appendix D.

9. Gurwood, *Dispatches* (1838), Volume XII, p 483.

10. Wellington was referring to *Castle Rackrent*, a novel by his friend Maria Edgeworth, published in 1800. It concerns a number of people involved in a

debt-ridden Irish estate, where the leading character, Sir Condy Rackrent, expresses 'a great fancy to see my own funeral afore I die', whereupon his servant Thady announces his 'death'. At the wake Sir Condy's supposed corpse lies under a pile of greatcoats listening to the mourners' opinions of him, although he is disappointed at 'not finding there had been such a great talk about himself after his death as he had always expected to hear'. Eventually, thirst gets the better of him and 'his honour got up to drink with them, and sent for more spirits from a shebean-house, where they very civilly let him have it upon credit'. [This author cannot forbear to recommend *Castle Rackrent*, not because it is Irish, written by a woman, or has some particular literary merit – although it is all of those – but because it is a cracking good story and every bit as fresh and funny today as when it was written 200 years ago.]

11. Wellington went to Eton and De Lancey to Harrow, so it is presumed that Wellington was referring to their regular meetings in Calcutta and at Hickey's country villa in the 1790s.

12. Conversation between Earl Stanhope and the Duke of Wellington while out hunting, 12 October 1839. From *Notes of Conversations with the Duke of Wellington 1831–1851* by Philip Henry, 5th Earl Stanhope, John Murray, London (2nd edition), 1886, pp 182–183.

13. Stanhope, *op cit*.

14. Fraser, *op cit*, pp 98–99.

15. Frazer; *op cit*; p 582.

The Hall coat of arms is a blue shield with a silver chevron and three storks' heads, surmounted by a crest of a stork holding a piece of rock. The family motto is Dat Cura Quietam *(Care Gives Peace of Mind). (Michael Heywood)*

PART TWO

Magdalene Hall

CHAPTER VIII
The Halls of Dunglass

Magdalene Hall's background could scarcely have been more different from her husband's. He came from a Huguenot, American Loyalist family which had produced administrators, jurists, businessmen and many soldiers; indeed, he was himself a professional soldier to his fingertips. She, on the other hand, was the child of a Lowland Scottish family, which moved almost exclusively in intellectual circles at the centre of the Scottish Enlightenment and which had no virtually no connection with the army at all.[1]

Magdalene was born at the family country home on 20 March 1793, the fourth child and second daughter of a most remarkable couple, Sir James Hall of Dunglass (1761–1832), the fourth baronet, and his wife, Lady Helen, née Douglas (1762–1837). Sir James came of a distinguished family (see Table II), whose ancestors had become wealthy in commerce and law, and then, like others in that position, sought land, which they found on the North Sea coast at Dunglass, a few miles south of Dunbar, straddling the border between the counties of Berwickshire and Haddingtonshire (present-day East Lothian).

Originally the property of the Scottish Crown, by the thirteenth century the Dunglass estate had passed to the Pepdie family and thence, through marriage, to Sir Thomas Home of Home, during the reign of King Robert III of Scotland (1390–1406). Apart from the periods 1516–22 and 1528–50 when it reverted to the Crown, the Homes held the property until 1644, when they sold it to Major-General Sir John Ruthven, whose son, Sir William, inherited in 1649. By 1685 the property had passed into the hands of one Edward Callender, a London merchant, and it was from him that John Hall, a wealthy Edinburgh businessman, purchased it in 1687.

The other necessity for success was a title and that came on 8 October 1687: a baronetcy 'with remainder to male heirs whatsoever'. The Scottish baronetage originated as a money-raising device to finance the settlement and expansion of the North American colony of Nova Scotia, which had been annexed to Scotland in 1621. For several decades thereafter a Nova Scotia baronetcy could be obtained for the sum of £3,000 (£300,000), which included the title, a coat of arms, a badge and a grant of land in the colony. Payment and the grant of land were abolished over the course of the seventeenth century, but the grant of titles to deserving Scotsmen continued. Now Sir John Hall of Dunglass, he served as Lord Provost of Edinburgh from 1689 to 1691 and again from 1692 to 1694, and represented the city in the Scottish Parliament from 1689 until his death in 1695.

Initially the Hall estate consisted only of the castle and a small area around it, but excluded the lands and castle of Cockburnspath, which was owned by the Nicolson family, but when they became encumbered by debt in 1694 it was sold at a public auction. The purchaser was Sir John Hall, who joined it with his newly purchased Dunglass estate, creating a property covering 8,835 acres (3,575 hectares), which extended some eight miles (13 km) along the North Sea coast from just below Dunbar in the north to Fast Castle Head in the south, and inland deep into the Lammermoor Hills.

Sir James Hall, 4th Baronet

Magdalene's father, James, was born in 1761 and started his education in Edinburgh but then, like many children of wealthy Scottish families, went south to London, where he attended Elim's Military Academy in Kensington. The early death of his father, Sir John Hall, 3rd baronet, in 1776 meant that James succeeded to the baronetcy when just 15 years old and he returned to Edinburgh to discover that his father's sister, Miss Isabella Hall of Coveyheugh (near Reston in Berwickshire) had been appointed his guardian, until he attained his majority. Known to the family as 'Aunt Tibby', Isabella Hall became responsible for the new baronet's education, business and domestic affairs, and, as maiden aunts tended to do, she espied a likely, striking and energetic girl of good family, Lady Helen Douglas, second daughter of Dunbar, 4th Earl of Selkirk. Aunt Tibby invited the girl, first to the Edinburgh house and, subsequently, to Dunglass, and then withdrew into the background, content to let nature take its course.

James went up to Cambridge (Christ's College) on 17 November 1777, where, although he left in March 1779 without obtaining a degree (a by no means unusual event in those days), he made his mark as an intelligent and diligent young man, his main areas of interest being architecture, chemistry, geology and physics. He then made the first of many trips abroad, before returning to Edinburgh to spend some time at the university, again making his mark, not only as a keen student, but also as a devoted socialiser and party-goer, with a particular enthusiasm for dancing.

Then came that essential part of any young man's education – The Grand Tour – which in James's case lasted from 1783 to 1785. During the early part of this extensive journey he stayed with his cousin, William Hamilton, the son of the 3rd baronet's sister, Kitty, whose husband, William Hamilton of Bangour, had been forced to flee Scotland after supporting the Pretender in the rebellion of 1745. Hamilton's château was close to the famous Brienne military academy, where James took lessons in mathematics and French, and where, as we shall see later, he caught the eye of a Corsican cadet, some ten years his junior, who had arrived in 1778. It is also clear that Aunt Tibby's romantic machinations were bearing fruit, since the one stipulation James made before going abroad was that if any other young man appeared to be taking an undue interest in Lady Helen, his aunt was to inform him at once and he would return post-haste to claim what he clearly had come to regard as his own.

James's Grand Tour covered Austria, Bavaria, France, Italy, Prussia and Switzerland, as well as numerous minor German kingdoms and principalities, his peregrination taking him as far east as Berlin and south to Sicily. He showed a detailed interest in every place he visited, making copious notes covering the geology, flora and fauna, as well as social customs and art. As always throughout his life, his wealth, title and intellect combined to give him *entrée* to the highest scientific circles and meeting the leading men of the day.

He returned home briefly in 1785 and then went back to Paris, where he became friendly with a famous chemist, Lavoisier. Despite the exciting events in France, James returned to Scotland in 1786, where, on 9 November, he finally married his Lady Helen at what he described in a letter to his uncle, William Hall, as a 'fine, merry wedding'.

Sir James went abroad again in 1789 to visit France, but this time he was accompanied by three of his wife's brothers, including the eldest, Basil William Douglas-Hamilton, Lord Daer (1764–94), who had already established a reputation as something of a radical. They were in Paris when the French Revolution broke out and ignored a warning to leave, watching the events in the streets, listening to the debates in the National Assembly, and joining in the impassioned arguments in the salons. They met many of the important figures of the Revolution, including Robespierre, but eventually life became too dangerous and James and two others left, although Lord Daer remained, and was a fascinated spectator of the assault on the Bastille. Lord Daer expressed considerable support for the ideals of the Revolution, alienating himself from many of his family, and, following his death shortly afterwards in Florence, his name was rarely mentioned by his relations, except by the forthright Lady Helen.

When in Scotland, James's and Helen's second home was 132 George Street, Edinburgh, a wide and fashionable thoroughfare, running parallel to and above Princes Street in the New Town. James became a noted savant, carrying out many scientific experiments and writing learned theses on a wide variety of subjects, but with particular interests in geology, in which he carried out many experiments, and architecture.

The Scottish Enlightenment

One of the strongest influences on Magdalene's parents, which, in its turn, had a major effect on her upbringing, was that period of intellectual and scientific ferment known as the 'Scottish Enlightenment'. Like most historic 'periods' this has an ill-defined beginning and end, but is generally acknowledged to have burned at its brightest from about 1760 to the end of the century. It was a time of remarkable developments in philosophy, the sciences, such as chemistry, physics, geology and medicine, and the arts, especially painting (particularly of portraits), literature and poetry. Nor were more practical matters neglected, with architecture, bridge-building, industrial mechanisation and canal construction all receiving attention, while the more progressive landowners sought to introduce new and more efficient agricultural methods on their estates.

One of the leading lights of this period was Adam Smith (1723–90), philosopher, economist and author of *An Enquiry into the Nature and Causes of the Wealth of Nations*, the influence of which survives to this day. There were also Smith's close friend David Hume (1711–76), historian, philosopher and author of *A Treatise of Human Nature* (1739), and Joseph Black (1728–99) the chemist whose discoveries included carbon dioxide and latent heat. Another was Robert Adam (1728–92), who integrated architecture and interior decoration to produce buildings with a coherent theme. His early style was the 'neo-classical', which included such buildings as Harewood House, Syon House and Osterley Park in England, although he later turned to a more eclectic and 'picturesque' style, one of the foremost examples of which is Culzean Castle in Ayrshire, Scotland. On the literary scene, Robert Burns' career as a poet was both brilliant and short, his principal works being written in the 1780s, while Sir Walter Scott brought the novel to a new peak of sophistication and influence, although this was towards the end of the period, his main works being published between 1814 and 1826.

Sir James Hall moved with ease in these circles, although the most powerful influence on him appears to have been that of James Hutton (1726–97) the 'father of scientific geology'. Hutton's book *Theory of the Earth* incensed both the supporters of the biblical time-scale (who had established to their satisfaction that the earth had been created in 4004 BC) and the followers of other theories, such as Professor Robert Jameson of Edinburgh University.[2] In his search to prove his theories, Hutton made many journeys to examine rock formations, on several of which he was accompanied by the young Sir James Hall; indeed, one such expedition was mounted from Dunglass Castle.

The premier scientific body in Scotland was the Philosophical Society, which was founded in 1737 and renamed the Royal Society of Edinburgh in 1783. Sir James was elected a member of this august body in 1784 at the early age of 23 and was its president from 1806 to 1820, the building being, most conveniently, just 400 yards from his house in George Street. James moved with equal ease in learned circles in London, being elected a Fellow of the Royal Society (FRS) in 1804 and was one of the founder members of the Athenæum Club in 1824.

Hall had laboratories in his houses at Dunglass and Edinburgh, and carried out notable experiments, many of them designed to support the theories of James Hutton. After much trial and error he managed to create marble and sandstone artificially. The latter event earned him some notoriety when he emulated a famous scientific predecessor by rushing down George Street (fortunately, fully clothed) to a neighbour's house, brandishing the cup of sandstone he had just created and loudly proclaiming his success.

James travelled widely in England, taking advantage of the great improvement in the stagecoach service, and he and his wife regularly stayed in London, Harrogate and Bath. Apart from the social side, James took advantage of such journeys to visit cathedral cities in pursuit of his architectural interests, rock formations in pursuit of his geological interests, and farms to view the latest advances in agriculture.

James was a very sociable man, entertaining guests regularly in Dunglass, Edinburgh, London and Bath, an activity in which he was enthusiastically supported by his wife in the intervals between bearing at least ten children. He was a noted dancer, and among his social interests was an Edinburgh gentleman's chess club, which met in different houses each week in the winter months, and of which Sir Walter Scott was also a member.

In May 1806 James was nominated by the 5th Earl of Selkirk, his brother-in-law, to be a representative Scottish peer and while this was under consideration, another peer who knew him well described Hall as 'a declared democrat and an avowed atheist, but clever'. The proposed peerage fell into abeyance with the dissolution of that particular Parliament, but Hall was then nominated by Lord Falmouth to become Member of Parliament for Mitchell, a small Cornish constituency mid-way between Truro and Newquay, a seat which was in that peer's gift. Although the constituency was almost as far from his home in Edinburgh as it was possible to be, Hall was elected in the 1807 General Election. He made his maiden speech on 15 March 1808 thereafter joining in many debates, establishing a reputation as an entertaining speaker, who always took an independent and well thought-out line. His son Basil was impressed by the hours of research his father devoted to studying and discussing a topic prior to rising to talk about it in a debate, a degree of preparation by a Member of Parliament which was as remarkable then as it would be today. Politics does not appear to have interested him for long, however, as he was granted leave of absence due to illness in

December 1810 and did not stand for re-election in the 1812 General Election.

Despite his many other interests, James was passionately interested in his estate, its farms and people. He brought many new agricultural methods to Dunglass and undertook many improvement tasks, building several major bridges and developing the roads. He had inherited the family fortune and property, but, in addition, his father's brother William and sister Isabella (Aunt Tibby) both died unmarried and left him all they had. Unfortunately, the illness which caused him to leave Parliament in 1812 seems to have had an increasing effect on him in later years. He was still travelling regularly within Great Britain as late as 1820, but thereafter he seems to have remained in Scotland and died in Edinburgh in June 1832.

Dunglass

The Halls' great love was the family seat at Dunglass, overlooking a spectacular gorge, known as the 'Dene', which was some three miles (5 km) long and carried the Dunglass Burn below the family house and past Dunglass Mill to the sea. The first recorded castle at Dunglass was built during the Middle Ages, sited to dominate the Dunbar-Berwick road, but this was burnt down in 1547 and was replaced by a large residence, whose main claim to fame was as the last Scottish house to accommodate a Scottish king, when, in 1603, James VI spent the night there on his way south to claim the English throne as James I.

By the end of the eighteenth century, this house had become so weakened as to be positively dangerous, and Sir James decided that he had no alternative but to demolish it and start again. The new house was built according to James's interpretation of the best of contemporary architectural practice and he employed an Edinburgh architect, Richard Crichton, to design it and an Edinburgh painter, Alexander Naysmith, to prepare sketches and models as the design progressed. One of Sir James's many interests was architecture, particularly the Gothic, on which he published an *Essay on the Origin and Principles of Gothic Architecture* in Edinburgh in 1797 (27 pages with 6 plates) but a greatly expanded version, *Essay on the Origin, History and Principles of Gothic Architecture"* (150 pages with 60 plates) was published by John Murray in 1813, the year of the completion of James's new house.

Curiously, despite his fascination with the Gothic, Sir James's own house was built according to the principles of the 'Picturesque' school, of which the leading lights were Robert Adam, Vanbrugh and Sir Uvedal Price.[3] This required houses to be dramatic in overall appearance, to combine light and shade with irregularity of plan, and to combine with the surrounding landscape to produce a generally 'picturesque' effect.

The design and construction of this large mansion took place between

1807 and 1813, with Sir James exercising detailed supervision. The end result was one of the most important and imposing houses in Scotland, but this very expensive project was undertaken at a time of considerable inflation due to the Napoleonic War and, despite his considerable wealth, Sir James began to experience some financial embarrassment. During this lengthy period, Sir James, Lady Helen and their older daughters, including Magdalene, lived in the new steward's house, which had been completed first for just such a purpose, while the younger children lived near Berwick with a governess.[4]

Lying hard by Dunglass House was the Collegiate Church of Dunglass which was built in the fifteenth century. By Sir James's time, although in good repair, it was no longer in use as a church, and during the years in which the mansion was being rebuilt, the north transept was used as a potato store, the sacristy housed the carpenter's shop, and the main aisle was used for the carriages. These were moved out at some time in the nineteenth century and, while the building remains in good repair to this day, it is only occasionally used for worship.

Lady Helen Hall

Lady Helen was a small woman, but extremely dynamic and greatly respected by all who knew her. Much of her childhood was spent on her father's estate at St Mary's Isle, where, with her numerous brothers and sisters, she was allowed a considerable degree of freedom, and wild games were the order of the day. She was reputed to have had a teenage tendresse for a dashing naval officer known as 'Pygmy' Douglas, so-called not on account of his lack of stature, but because he was in command of HMS *Pygmy*, a cutter sent to try to apprehend a pirate then operating off the Galloway coast. This cannot, however, have been serious, since Aunt Tibby did not consider it necessary to summon Sir James. Once married, Helen's devotion to Sir James, his interests and her growing family was absolute. She bore her husband a large number of children and then ensured that those who survived infancy – there may have been some who died very young – were properly educated, the girls as well as the boys.

Helen had a number of idiosyncrasies, one of which was rising very early, following which she usually filled in her time by spinning, then much in vogue in society circles in Scotland. Such early rising took its toll, however, and she always went to bed early, except when company was present. She also suffered badly from travel sickness after dark, which meant that journeys to or from London by stagecoach could take up to two weeks, instead of the more usual seven days.

She was a firm advocate of the then unheard-of practice of keeping windows open throughout the day and night, which bred a certain toughness in her family, especially when they were at Dunglass, which was on an exposed position overlooking the North Sea. She entertained frequently, supported all of her husband's many interests, and managed the tenanted houses and shops which were not part of the farms. She also oversaw the construction of the estate-owned and tenanted houses, Cockburnspath Inn, the extension of the church tower and a new passage between the main tunnel and the cellars at Cove Harbour.[5]

Having played such an important role in their courtship, Aunt Tibby lived with the Halls as a more than welcome guest from the time of their marriage until her death in 1804. She played a major role in bringing up the children and was on particularly good terms with Lady Helen. After her death her memory was perpetuated by her favourite walk in the grounds at Dunglass, which was known as 'Miss Hall's Walk'. She was also a noted seamstress, although one of her most ambitious projects, a large carpet, remained unfinished at her death. However, Lady Helen ensured that it was completed as a tribute to her good friend, with all lady visitors being encouraged to undertake some work on the project; in view of Lady Helen's forceful personality, this must have been an invitation that was difficult to refuse.

Lady Helen was a great letter-writer, an activity mostly undertaken before breakfast. She never, so far as is known, attempted any literary work, which is to be regretted as her letters are models of clarity, while two surviving documents are minor masterpieces. One of them opens with characteristic abruptness: 'My Will written with my own hand, Helen Hall', which was clearly (and almost certainly deliberately) written without any assistance from lawyers and had no witnesses, but left absolutely no doubt as to what was to be done with her possessions, which, she wrote, '. . . I bequeath as follows, among my family, in remembrance of me.' It also contains a charm and a personality entirely lacking in the dry legalese of Wills drawn up with professional assistance, one example being:

> To my daughter Katherine Lady Russel & my beloved son-in-law Sir James Russel [I bequeath] the Buhl Table, with rich embossed Tea set on it (of which there is an inventory). Also a large specimen of Dunglass Pebble. We thought it a pity to lose the large size of it by cutting it into any article, & so I had it merely sawed up through and polished. It was found by Magdalene when a girl riding on the shore of Dunglass. When she married Mr Harvey she took the other half with her – which I suppose he now has.[6]

The second document is prefaced 'I like to keep this memorandum of how I happened to have my property independent of my husband.' As she explained, her father, Dunbar, 4th Earl Selkirk, told his daughters that he knew of several cases where families had been brought to financial ruin by the bad or unwise behaviour of the husband. As a result, Selkirk considered it '. . . a very great advantage in married life' that the wife should have money in her own name, which could not be touched by her husband's creditors, enabling her to support herself and her children and even, perhaps, to save her unworthy partner from absolute want. When her father died in 1799, the main legacy was left in the form of land (the Baldoon estate in Galloway) and proved a troublesome legal and financial problem for some years, the problems being exacerbated by the deaths over a period of ten years of her father and four brothers, the land eventually ending up in the hands of the youngest, Thomas. There was a series of protracted and ill-tempered arguments. The sale had been agreed but the contract not yet signed when Sir James Hall, who had no direct concern with the business but who did have some knowledge of land prices, insisted that the property was being grossly undervalued. Sir James was proved correct and the eventual outcome was that the purchasers paid a much greater sum, with Lady Helen receiving £20,000 (£820,000), instead of the maximum of £10,000 (£410,000) she had originally expected.

Lady Helen felt some regret that her husband, who had contributed greatly to the increase obtained, was given no share by Thomas, Earl of Selkirk. Thus, in 1808, when Sir James was 'pinched for money' due to the enormous expense of re-building Dunglass, Lady Helen split her inheritance down the middle and gave her husband £10,000, 'it being agreed by all of us, that we should like best to have it so'.[7]

Lady Helen died in 1837 at the age of 75, having outlived her husband and all but four of her many children. Her memorial plaque in the family vault in the Dunglass Collegiate church is unusually effusive and indicates the strength of her character and the force of her impact on others:

> . . . her powerful mental qualifications and accomplishments rendered her a conspicuous member of the social circle of her time; she was eminently characterised by the warmth and constancy of her friendship, and by her sympathy and active charity towards the poor.[8]

The Halls and Robert Burns

Robert Burns, the poet, came to national prominence in the early 1780s and moved to Edinburgh in November 1786, where he was lionised by society and welcomed in many aristocratic drawing-rooms. It would appear that he must have met the Halls in the capital, since he was invited to visit Dunglass when on his 'Border tour'. This peregrination began on Saturday 5 May 1787 when Burns mounted his mare, Jenny Geddes, and accompanied by Robert Ainslie, a law student, headed southwards. Burns was on his own during the return journey when he spent several days with the Sheriff family at Chapelhill Farm, near Cockburnspath, where he was sought out by Sir James:

> . . . Sir James Hall of Dunglass having heard of my being in the neighbourhood comes to Mr Sheriff's to breakfast – takes me to see his fine scenery on the stream of Dunglass – Dunglass the most romantic sweet place I ever saw – Sir James & his lady a pleasant happy couple – Sir James shows me a favourite spot beneath an oak where Lady Helen used to ponder on her lover Sir James then being abroad – he points out likewise a walk for which he has an uncommon respect as it was made by an Aunt of his to whom he owed much . . .[9]

Burns also described the visit in another document:

> . . . Mr Sheriff tired me to death; but as my good star directed, Sir James Hall detained him on some business as he is Sir James's tenant, till near eleven at night, which time I spent with Miss — till I was, in the language of the royal Voluptuary, Solomon, 'Sick of Love!'. Next morning, Sir James who had been informed by the Sheriffs of my Bardship's arrival, came to breakfast with us and carried me with him, and his charming Lady & he did me the honor to accompany me the whole forenoon through the glorious, romantic deane of Dunglass. – I would not stay dinner . . .[10]

Burns was always particularly critical of aristocrats who lionised him in what he took to be a condescending manner, so his very friendly description of the Halls indicates that they got on unusually well together. Later that year Burns dined with Lady Helen's radical brother, Lord Daer, in Edinburgh, and the two seem to have got on famously:

> This wot ye all whom it concerns,
> I, Rhymer Rab, alias Burns,
> > October twenty-third,
> A ne'er-to-be-forgotten day,
> Sae far I sprachl'd up the brae,
> > I dinner'd with a Lord.
>
> . . .
>
> Then from his Lordship I shall learn,
> Henceforth to meet with unconcern
> > One rank as well's another;
> Nae honest, worthy man need care
> To meet with noble youthfu' Daer,
> > For he but meets a brother.[11]

The Halls and Sir Walter Scott

Sir Walter Scott and Sir James knew each other well, meeting frequently in Edinburgh, including at a private chess club, whose meetings rotated between the members' Edinburgh residences, but the famous author also knew many of the Hall children. He had a particularly close friendship with Basil, which lasted over many years, and it is clear from various letters that he knew both James and Magdalene. Indeed, according to Hall family tradition, 'Ravenswood,' the main setting of the novel, *The Bride of Lammermoor*, is based on the Dunglass estate, while Fast Castle, whose ruins lie at the eastern end of the family estate, was, so the Halls believe, the original 'Wolf's Crag.'[12]

Nor was that the only link between the Halls and *The Bride of Lammermoor*. Scott's story was loosely based on a real-life tragedy involving David Dunbar of Baldoon (the estate whose sale brought Lady Helen so much money), who was attacked by his demented bride on their wedding night. Dunbar's wife died some two weeks later and he subsequently married a daughter of the 7th Earl of Eglinton, only to die following a fall from his horse in 1682. His daughter, the heiress to Baldoon, married Lord Basil Hamilton, and was Lady Helen's great-grandmother.

A Gifted Family

It is clear that Sir James and Lady Hall were an exceptional couple. James came into his fortune and property by accident of birth but had the rare ability to use both wisely; he also had the intellect necessary to devote his time to the pursuit of scientific and artistic goals. His frequent scientific papers, numerous experiments and ability to hold his own in discussions with the leading men of the age earned him the respect of his peers and a long presidency of the Royal Society of Edinburgh, being described by Cockburn in his *Memorials* as '. . . the most scientific of our country gentlemen.' He also – due to the good offices of Aunt Tibby – found an exceptionally suitable wife and, in an era not renowned for marital fidelity, they remained devoted to each other throughout their lives, with not even a whiff of gossip attaching to either of them. Further, their large family suggests that their marriage was passionate as well as loving. Both parents were devoted to their children and, although in itself a minor incident, it is notable that despite his many interests and concerns, Sir James still found the time to accompany his son Basil to his lieutenant's examination in London, something very few other fathers did and which Basil records with pride and not a hint of embarrassment. Sir James's and Lady Helen's letters are full of family matters and they frequently travelled together to places such as London, Harrogate and Bath. Sir James's diary entries for June 1814 make clear just how united the family was, as it describes how he went to Harrogate to join Lady Helen and their daughters Helen and Magdalene. Following that, all four went to Bristol where they visited Elizabeth at her boarding school, and then to Bath, where they were joined by their sons, William and John, who travelled down from London to be with their family.[13]

It is also clear that Lady Helen was no quiet partner who confined herself to domestic tasks and to the social round. A formidable lady, she maintained a tight control on the villages on the estate, and so dynamic was her presence that she is talked of in Cockburnspath to this day.[14]

Magdalene Hall had a goodly heritage.

NOTES

1. Magdalene's great-uncle, Lieutenant-Colonel Robert Hall, had served, but as he died in 1764, Magdalene never met him.
2. Hutton's *Theory of the Earth* was originally published in summary form in 1785, in expanded form in 1788, and in full, as *Theory of the Earth with Proofs and Illustrations* in 1795.
3. One of the strongest advocates of the 'Picturesque' school, Price was strongly influenced by Burke's *Essay on the Sublime and Beautiful* which led him to write his own *'Essay on the Picturesque'* published in 1794.
4. The estate was sold by the Halls to the Usher family in 1918, in whose possession it remains. Sir James's grand house was demolished in the 1950s and was replaced by the present large, single-storey building.
5. Information supplied by Sally Smith, historian of Dunglass.
6. Scottish Record Office GD206/4/62 (Dunglass Muniments).
7. Scottish Record Office GD206/4/62 (Dunglass Muniments).
8. Text kindly provided by Sally Smith, historian of Dunglass.
9. Taken from the original manuscript of *Robert Burns Tour of the Borders: 5 May – 1 June 1787* now in the possession of John Murray & Co, and quoted with their kind permission.
10. Robert Burns to Robert Ainslie, Newcastle, 29 May, quoted in William Wallace, *The Life and Works of Robert Burns*, edited by Robert Chambers, revised by William Wallace, Edinburgh, 1896, 4 volumes.
11. The meeting took place on 23 October 1787 and is recorded in Burns' poem, 'Lines on Meeting with Lord Daer.'
12. It is only fair to add that Scott later prevaricated somewhat and denied that any one place was the model for either Ravenglass or Wolf's Crag.
13. Scottish Record Office GD 206/2/315/16 (Dunglass Muniments).
14. Information supplied by Sally Smith, historian of Dunglass.

CHAPTER IX

The Hall Children

The Hall children enjoyed a life of style and affluence, which revolved around devoted parents and, until 1804, Aunt Tibby. The most serious inconvenience in their lives was the rebuilding of Dunglass, during which Lady Hall and some of the older children lived in the new steward's house at Dunglass, which had been completed first for that purpose, while the younger children lived with a governess some miles away at Whitehall, a property inherited by Sir James from his Uncle William. Once the big new house was completed, however, they moved into what was then one of the grandest and most modern residences in the whole of Scotland. The surrounding countryside and sea could be wild, but indoors they had every contemporary convenience that money could buy, even though their mother tried to temper this coddling by insisting that the windows remain open at all times.

Various figures are given for the number of children, but the most authoritative statement is that of Basil, who, when discussing his family with Napoleon in 1817, was asked how many children there were and replied, 'Ten living',[1] which implies that there may have been some miscarriages, still-births or early deaths.[2] The four sons all began their education in Scotland at what was then the country's leading school, Edinburgh High School, but, with the exception of Basil, then moved south to London.

Sir John Hall, 5th Baronet

The Hall's first-born, John (1787–1860) had three responsibilities: to marry, to beget children and to take his turn in running the estate. He fulfilled all three, marrying Julia Walker in 1823, siring eight children, six of them boys (of whom no fewer than three subsequently succeeded to the title) and holding the baronetcy from his father's death in 1832 until his own in 1860. Like his father, he travelled widely and had scientific leanings, being elected a Fellow of the Royal Society (FRS), but he appears to have made little mark as an individual.

Captain Basil Hall, RN

The second son, Basil (1788–1844), was by far the most active and gifted of the Hall boys and is remembered long after the others have been forgotten. He was born during a violent thunderstorm at Dunglass on 31 December 1788, but his mother had insisted on the windows remaining open, resulting, so he claimed, in the sea being in his blood from his earliest memories. He considered his schooldays in Edinburgh to have been largely wasted, the terms constituting a series of deeply resented interludes between holidays, which were mainly devoted to going to sea with the fishermen from Cove, a hamlet on the coast below Dunglass. His sole, serious intellectual pursuit lay in reading Shakespeare, but only those plays with a significant nautical element, such as *The Tempest*, and when commenting on this later in life – by which time he was a very experienced sailor – Basil remarked that he considered the Bard's knowledge of seamanship to have been 'wonderfully correct'.

None of his ancestors had been interested in a naval career, but Basil's heart was set on the Royal Navy almost from birth and he joined his first ship, a frigate, HMS *Leander*, as a midshipman on 12 June 1802 at the tender age of 13 years and 5 months. His ship sailed the following month for the North American station and did not return to England until June 1808, when he immediately sat and passed the lieutenant's examination at his first attempt. He was then so excited by the prospect of commissioned service that he did not go home to Dunglass, but rushed to join his new ship, HMS *Leopard*, instead. After a very short period he transferred to HMS *Endymion*, which by 1808 was employed off the coast of Portugal in support of Sir John Moore's expedition. Throughout his life Basil never failed to seize the opportunity to see something new, and he went ashore to spend some time with the Army and claimed to have seen Sir John Moore being wounded and carried off the field. His ship then became one of the large force embarking the Army from Corunna and taking it back to England, and it was while engaged in this task that he met and shared a cabin with a young officer named William Howe De Lancey, as described in Chapter III.

Having taken the soldiers back to England, *Endymion* continued to operate in the Atlantic, and on 8 September 1811 Basil, seeing another opportunity for adventure, became one of the first men ever to clamber up the precipitous face of Rockall, a tiny island some 200 miles due west of St Kilda.[3] One part of this tiny rocky outcrop is known to this day as 'Hall's Ledge' in honour of that visit.[4]

In 1812 Hall transferred to HMS *Volage* in which he sailed to India, and in 1814 he was given command of a new ship, HMS *Victor*, which was being built by the well-known Indian company, Lowjee Wadia, in Bombay. He sailed *Victor* back to England in 1815, arriving in late June, just after the outcome of the Battle of Waterloo had been announced and managed to obtain a copy of Wellington's despatch from another ship, while sailing up the Channel. In that he read of the death of Sir William De Lancey, with whom he had shared a cabin in 1808, but it was not until he went ashore that he learned, to his considerable astonishment, that De Lancey had, for a short time, been his brother-in-law.

Hall then spent a few months in England – his first real spell ashore since 1802 – during which time he met Major-General Sir Hudson Lowe. This meeting was probably at the latter's marriage in London on 16 December 1815 to Sir William De Lancey's sister, Susan, whose first husband, Lieutenant-Colonel William Johnstone had died two years previously. Hall's stay in England was, however, relatively brief, and he sailed again on 9 February 1816 in command of HMS *Lyra*, sloop, on a most exciting voyage as the escort to Lord Amherst's mission to the Emperor of China. After many adventures in China, Korea and on the island of Okinawa (then known as Loo-Choo), Hall sailed back to England, but making two visits of significance to our story on the way.

The first was to Madras to deliver despatches. While there, Hall took aboard a passenger, Captain Henry Harvey, an Assistant Commissary-General in the Madras Army, who had recently learned that his father had died the previous year. As his father's heir, he needed to return to England to sort out the family's affairs and he sailed aboard *Lyra* on 1 June 1817. Basil broke the long voyage home with a second significant call, this time at the island of St Helena, which was reached on 11 August. There Hall stayed at Plantation House, the residence of the recently-promoted governor and his wife, Lieutenant-General Sir Hudson and Lady Lowe, whom he had met in London two years previously, but Basil's main aim, despite his youth and junior rank, was to visit the island's distinguished prisoner, Napoleon Buonaparte. Although the situation was complicated by the poor relationship between Lowe and the erstwhile emperor, it was difficult to thwart Basil when he had determined on a course of action, and the meeting was eventually organised by Dr O'Meara, Napoleon's personal physician.

At the meeting (although from Hall's respectful description of the former emperor it might more properly be described as an 'audience') Napoleon informed Basil that he had clear memories of his father, Sir James Hall, at Brienne, even to the detail that Sir James had attended the military college to learn mathematics and French. Basil expressed some surprise that Napoleon could remember one person so clearly from such a long time ago, whereupon Napoleon replied: 'Oh, it is not in the least extraordinary, because he was the first Englishman I ever saw, and I have recollected your father on that account ever since.'[5]

Basil then stretched the truth somewhat by telling Napoleon that Sir James also remembered him, whereupon Napoleon playfully suggested that, in that case, Basil's father might care to come out to St Helena to renew their acquaintance. The conversation then turned to Basil's recent experiences in Korea and China, and finally Napoleon allowed Basil to call Captain Harvey into the room and introduce him.

His object achieved, Basil sailed on, arriving at Portsmouth on 5 November 1817, where Harvey left for Bath, although we shall hear more of him later in our story. Basil was promoted post-captain on the following day – just over a month before his 30th birthday – and paid off *Lyra* on 13 November.[6] Despite his promotion, he then spent some two-and-a-half years ashore, most of which he devoted to travelling in Europe.

In the post-war era, commands for naval officers – even for such dedicated professionals as Basil – proved increasingly difficult to come by. Indeed, Basil commanded just one ship as a post-captain, HMS *Conway*, which he joined in 1820 and took to South America. He returned to England in 1823 and, as usual, produced a book about his experiences, but never went to sea in a serving capacity again. In 1825 he married Miss Margaret Hunter (1799–1876), daughter of Sir John Hunter, the British consul-general in Spain throughout the Peninsular War, and continued to travel and write, but now accompanied by his wife. Perhaps their most adventurous journey was to the United States, which resulted in a book about the habits and customs of that country's people, that caused offence in some quarters.[7]

Basil was a prolific author and had many works published on his various voyages, tours in the USA and Europe, and on scientific subjects. His style is rather didactic and rambling by later standards, but also contains a great deal of acute observation and sound common-sense. He was possessed of a superabundance of energy and one weary friend described how exhausting it was simply to watch Basil sightseeing. Further, his inquisitive mind was forever watching and questioning what was going on, and he not only listened to conversations but frequently made notes as they took place.

He was one of the Halls who befriended Sir Walter Scott, and visited the great man at Ashiestiel and Abbotsford regularly. He was also the instigator in obtaining government approval for Sir Walter to be taken to Malta aboard a Royal Navy frigate in 1831 for his health. Scott once expressed some concern when he noticed that Basil had a notebook open on his knee and was taking surreptitious notes of the conversation around the table, and there was more than a hint of fond exasperation in Scott's description of Basil:

> Sir Walter Scott, who, in his later years, owed much to the Captain's active friendship, describes him as 'that curious fellow, who takes charge of every one's business without neglecting his own'. Of acute and wakeful intellect, of wide and varied experience and culture, the interest of Basil Hall was intense in all that concerned Humanity.[8]

As we shall see, Basil was also close to his sister Magdalene and was of considerable help to her in overcoming the loss of her husband. He was admitted to the Royal Navy hospital at Haslar in 1842 and died there in 1844.

James Hall (1800–1854)

Sir James's and Lady Helen's youngest surviving son, James, had the intellectual interests characteristic of the family, but seems not to have pursued any one of them with sufficient application to achieve the distinction his talents deserved. Like his brothers he was educated in Scotland and England, following which he trained as an advocate, a career he actively pursued for only a few years; indeed, he set out on the Grand Tour the day after he qualified. He seems to have received funds from his parents, as he never undertook gainful employment, but was liberal in supporting bodies such as the British Institution and the Royal Academy. He stood as a Conservative candidate for the Dorset constituency of Taunton in the elections of 1841 and 1842, but failed on both occasions.

He had a wide circle of friends in artistic and literary circles and his greatest interest seems to have been in painting, which he studied at the Royal Academy in London. He was a friend and patron of many leading artists of the day, and exhibited his own work, both portraits and landscapes, and his sitters included the Duke of Wellington. He bought the manuscript of *Waverley* from Scott and also produced what is generally accepted to have been a notably bad portrait of Sir Walter.

He did not marry and was always said to be of a weak disposition. It was, perhaps, a typically sad note that he should have lost his patrimony in a 'get-rich-quick' scheme involving a new method of tanning leather, and he ended his days living with his sister, Lady Katherine Russel of Ashiestiel, dying at the relatively early age of 54.

Daughters

Sir James and Lady Helen Hall had six daughters. Elizabeth married the Reverend GP Boileau Pollen, while Katherine married Sir James Russel of Ashiestiel. Isabella died in infancy and two others died, unmarried, while still relatively young, Helen at 26 in 1817; and Frances at 28 in 1829. That left the principal character in our story, Magdalene.

Magdalene

Magdalene Hall was born in 1793 and there is nothing to suggest that she was anything other than a normal and healthy child, avoiding the sickness problems which seem to have affected some of her siblings. She was a keen horse rider and inherited some of her father's interest in rocks, since she discovered some curious stones on the beach below Dunglass.

There are two known portraits of Magdalene. The first, a miniature by the London-based artist, JCD Engelheart, has been dated from her dress and hairstyle as 1805–1810, when she would have been between 12 and 17 years old and a second, a watercolour, attributed to John Smart, which has been dated at late 1810 or early 1811.

Sir Walter Scott certainly knew Magdalene and it is a Hall family tradition, supported by the portraits, that the appearance and tempera-ment of the central character in Scott's novel, *The Bride of Lammermoor*, was based on Magdalene. Certainly, the girl in the portrait matches Scott's description:

> ... for Lucy Ashton's exquisitely beautiful, yet somewhat girlish features, were formed to express peace of mind, serenity, and indifference to the tinsel of worldly pleasure. Her locks, which were of shadowy gold, divided on a brow of exquisite whiteness, like a gleam of broken and pallid sunshine upon a hill of snow. The expression of the countenance was in the last degree gentle, soft, timid, and feminine, and seemed rather to shrink from the most casual look of a stranger, than to court his admiration. Something there was of the madonna cast, perhaps the result of delicate health, and of residence in a family, where the dispositions of the inmates were fiercer, more active, and energetic, than her own.[9]

It is not an exact description, of course, but near.

Magdalene's later life was almost as full of tragedy as that of the fictional Lucy Ashton, but she seems to have been a happy child, as Basil was to remember in later years:

> ... the days when she was a girl and I a boy – playing in the grass walks of Dunglass before I went back and then, again, when she was growing up and I returned from the coast of Spain, in the war, and found her and her sixteen (my greatest friend in those days) trigged up in Spanish hats by way of showing her national sympathy with the patriots.[10]

Magdalene resided alternately at Edinburgh and Dunglass, although much of her childhood was disrupted by going away to school and by the rebuilding of the family castle. She travelled only with her mother, although this included regular trips to London, where she was presented at Court, Harrogate and Bath.

She was heavily involved in her mother's social activities and it must have been at one of these in Edinburgh that she met the dashing Colonel William De Lancey, who had just returned from the long and arduous Peninsular campaign. Since De Lancey did not arrive in Edinburgh until November 1814 and Captain Hay saw them together at Dunglass in December, it would appear that the romance was sudden and intense, with Magdalene landing the greatest catch of the Edinburgh social season.

Curiously, Magdalene did not discover that her fiancé had met her brother, Basil, aboard HMS *Endymion*, until the day before the wedding, as Basil related:

> ... In 1814, probably, De Lancey came to Scotland on the Staff, became acquainted with our family & continued the acquaintance so far as to be actually on the eve of his marriage to my sister without his even having heard that she had a brother at sea or having heard my name mentioned! . . . So it was on the eve, I believe within 24 hours of the marriage, Sir William said 'I once knew an officer of your name – I wonder if he could be any relative? – I have lost sight of him though he was very kind to me.' A great shout and a laugh was now the answer to him upon his mentioning the Christian name of his old friend![11]

What followed the wedding can only be told in Magdalene's own words.

NOTES

1. 'He [Napoleon] next asked, "How many children my father had?" I said, "Nine alive."' quoted in Hall, Lady Sophie; 'The First Englishman Napoleon Ever Saw', *Nineteenth Century*, October 1912, pp 718–31. (This is the original manuscript of Basil Hall's meeting with Napoleon.)
2. The ten identified children are shown on the Hall family tree, although the dates of birth and death have not been firmly established in some cases.
3. HMS *Endymion*, Captain's Log, PRO ADM 51/2324.
4. A Hall family tradition that the name of the island is derived from the words 'Rock-Hall' in Basil's honour is more difficult to substantiate.
5. Lady Sophie Hall, 'The First Englishman Napoleon Ever Saw', p 724.
6. HMS *Lyra*, Muster Roll, PRO ADM 37/5903.
7. Hall, Captain Basil, RN, *Travels in North America in the years 1827 and 1828*, 3 volumes, Archibald Constable, Edinburgh, 1829.
8. Constable, Thomas, *Archibald Constable and his Literary Correspondents; A Memorial by His Son,* 1873 (Volume III), pp 471–472.
9. Scott, Sir Walter (ed Robinson, F), *The Bride of Lammermoor,* 'World Classics', Oxford University Press, pp 39–40.
10. Letter Basil Hall to Charles Dickens, Portsmouth 1 March 1841, Huntington Library.
11. Hall, *op cit.*

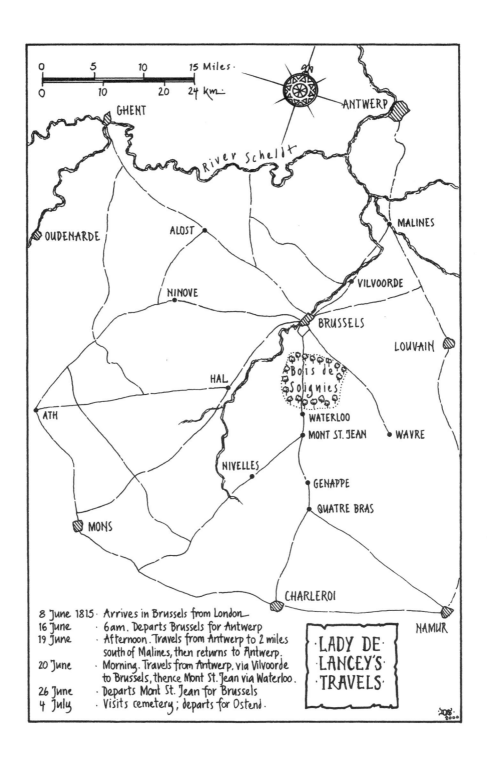

0 — 5 — 10 — 15 Miles
0 — 10 — 20 — 24 km

GHENT

ANTWERP

River Scheldt

OUDENARDE

ALOST

MALINES

NINOVE

VILVOORDE

BRUSSELS

LOUVAIN

Bois de Soignies

HAL

WATERLOO

ATH

MONT ST. JEAN

WAVRE

NIVELLES

GENAPPE

QUATRE BRAS

MONS

CHARLEROI

NAMUR

8 June 1815 · Arrives in Brussels from London
16 June · 6am. Departs Brussels for Antwerp
19 June · Afternoon. Travels from Antwerp to 2 miles
         south of Malines, then returns to Antwerp.
20 June · Morning. Travels from Antwerp, via Vilvoorde
         to Brussels, thence Mont St. Jean via Waterloo.
26 June · Departs Mont St. Jean for Brussels
4 July · Visits cemetery ; departs for Ostend.

·LADY DE·
·LANCEY'S·
·TRAVELS·

PART THREE

Lady De Lancey's Narrative

CHAPTER X
Lady De Lancey's Narrative

Lady De Lancey's Narrative[1]

Waterloo, 1815.

Thursday June 8th to Wednesday 14th

I left England to join my Husband, Sir W^m De Lancey and arrived at Bruxelles on Thursday 8th June 1815. I was much surprised at the peaceful appearance of that Town, and of the whole country from Ostend. We were billeted in the house of the Count de Lannoy[2] in the Park, which is a square of very beautiful houses with fine trees in the centre. The Count was very attentive, and we had an excellent suite of rooms, up four stories, which is the fashion in that country. It was amusing enough to see the people parading in the Park; I saw very little of the town, and still less of the inhabitants, for notwithstanding Sir William's belief that we should remain there quietly for a month at least, I have the comfort of remembering, that as there was a chance we might separate in a few days, I wasted no time in visiting or going to Balls, which I did not care for, and therefore I never went out, except for an hour or two to walk with Sir William. The people in general dined at 3, we dined at 6, & walked while others were at dinner, so that literally I never saw any body, except some gentlemen, two or three of whom dined with us every day Sir William's friends whom he brought to introduce to me.[3]

I never passed such a delightful time, for there was always enough of very pleasant society to keep us gay and merry, and the rest of the day was spent in peaceful happiness. Fortunately, my husband had scarcely any business to do, and he only went to the office for about an hour every day.[4] I then used to sit and think with astonishment of my being transported into such a scene of happiness, so perfect, so unalloyed, feeling that I was entirely enjoying life, not a moment was wasted. How active and how well I was! I scarcely knew what to do with all my health and spirits. Now and then a pang would cross my mind at the prospect of the approaching campaign, but I chased away the thought, resolved not to lose the present bliss by dwelling on the chance of future pain. Sir William promised to let me know as soon as he heard himself, every thing concerning the movement of the army, accordingly he gave me every thing to read to keep my mind easy. After some consideration, he decided that upon the commencement of hostilities I should go to Antwerp,[5] and there remain till the end of the campaign, which might last some months; he wished me not to think of going with him, as the rear of a great army was always dangerous, and an unfit situation for a woman; and he wished not to draw me into any danger, more than if I had remained in England.[6] He little thought that I should be in the midst of horrors I would not pass again, for any person now living and alas! the cautious anxiety he expressed, that I should not be shocked, only made me feel more desolate when I found myself in the midst of the most terrible scenes. Several other officers hearing that he designed sending me to Antwerp, fixed that their wives should go there also. It is a very strongly fortified town, and likewise having the sea to escape by if necessary, it was by far the safest place, and being only 25 miles from Bruxelles, it added so little to the time of hearing from Sir William that I acquiesced cheerfully. After this was arranged, we never thought more about it, and enjoyed each hour as it passed with no more anxiety than was sufficient to render time precious.

| **Wednesday June 14th** |

On the 14th, I had a little alarm in the evening by some public papers, and Sir William went out and returned in a short time. The alarm passed by so completely, that Thursday 15th June forenoon was the happiest time of my life. But I cannot recollect a day of my short married life that was not perfect. I shall never get on if I begin to talk of what my happiness was, but I dread to enter on the gloomy past, which I shudder to look back upon and I often wonder survived it. We little thought that Thursday was the last we were to pass together in peace, and that the storm would burst so soon.

| **Thursday June 15th** |

Sir William had to dine at the Spanish Ambassador's,[7] the first invitation he had accepted; he was unwilling to go, and delayed and still delayed, till at last when near 6 o'clock, I fastened all his crosses and medals on his coat, helped him to put it on, and he went off. I watched at the window till he was out of sight, and then I continued to muse upon my happy fate. I thought over all that had passed, how grateful I felt, I had no wish but that this might continue; I saw my husband loved and respected by every one. My life gliding on, like a gay dream.

When I had remained at the window nearly an hour, I saw an aide-de-camp ride under the gateway of our house, he sent to enquire where Sir William was dining, I wrote down the name and soon after I saw him gallop off in that direction. I did not like his appearance, but tried not to be afraid; a few minutes later, I saw Sir William ride past on the same horse to the Duke of Wellington's house which was just a few doors beyond ours.[8] He dismounted and ran into the house; I must confess my courage failed me then and the two succeeding hours, formed a contrast to the happy forenoon.

About 9 o'clock Sir William came in and seeing my wretched face he bid me not be foolish, for it would soon be all over. They expected a great battle on the morrow; he would send me to Antwerp in the morning, and desired I would be ready next morning at 6 o'clock. He said that though he expected the battle would be a decisive one and a conclusion of the business, he thought it best I should keep the plan of going to Antwerp, to avoid the alarms he knew would seize every one the moment the troops were gone – and he said he would probably join me there, or send for me to return the same evening. He said he would be writing all night, and wished me to prepare some strong green tea in case he came in, as the violent exertion of setting the whole army in motion quite stupefied him sometimes. He used sometimes to tell me that whenever the operations began, if he thought for 5 minutes on any other subject, he would be neglecting his duty. I therefore scrupulously avoided asking him any questions, or indeed speaking at all, and I moved up and down, as one stupefied myself. He went to the office and returned but he did not attempt to sleep. He went twice to the Duke's; the first time he found him standing looking over a map with a Prussian general, who was in full-dress uniform, with orders, etc.[9] The Duke was in dressing gown and slippers, preparing for the Duchess of Richmond's ball;[10] the two figures were quite admirable. The ball took place and the Reveille played through the streets the whole night. Many of the officers danced, and marched in the morning.

Friday June 16th

About 2 o'clock Sir William went to the Duke's; he was sound sleeping. At 3 the troops were all assembled in the Park, and Sir William and I leant over the window, seeing them march off – so few to return![11] It was a clear refreshing morning; the scene was

107

very solemn, and melancholy, the fifes playing alone, and the regiments one after another marched past, and I saw them melt away through the great gate at the end of the square. Shall I ever forget the tunes played on the shrill fifes and the buglehorns which disturbed that night?

At 6 in the morning, I went to Antwerp. Sir William gave me a letter to Captain Mitchell,[12] in the Qr-Master-General's department, requesting him to take charge of me; accordingly, soon after we arrived I was settled in a very comfortable apartment. I was at first an hour in the inn and lay down in a small back room.[13] In the course of the evening I sent my maid from the lodging to get some wine, when wandering in the passage of the Inn to find some one who understood English she opened the door of the room I had been in and she saw the body of the Duke of Brunswick on the very bed![14]

I was fortunate as to get a room to the back, so shut in with houses that I could not hear any noise in the street. Sir William had made me promise that I would believe no reports, nor on any account, to move without his written order for it. I thought it best not to listen to any stories, so I told my maid Emma not to tell me any, and to do her best not to be alarmed herself.[15] Captain Mitchell I found of great service; he is a very sensible man and seemingly good-hearted. There was a calmness in his manner, that was of infinite use to me, when I could not entirely get the better of my fears but too well founded. Though he was afterwards oppressed with business, night and day, he never failed to come to me when he had heard any accounts he could depend upon; but I may say I never saw so much kindness, and softness indeed, as during that miserable time.

The general and individual distress that rapidly followed the battles then fought, seemed quite to unman every body; and one grew accustomed to seeing men weep, without their attempting to conceal it. The same evening the Town Major, Machell,[16] called and brought Mrs— with him; he knew Sir William. The lady very kindly asked me to go and visit her in the country, about a mile off. I was much obliged to her, but said I hoped to return to Bruxelles so soon that I should not have time.

The town was now in a great bustle, though when I arrived it was perfectly quiet. Captain Mitchell told me that the battle had taken place, that the English had gained a victory, but he believed there was to be more fighting. He promised to send me any letter, or if he heard of Sir William. I sat up late, but none arrived.

Saturday June 17th

On Saturday, Antwerp was truly a scene of confusion, by the servant's account, for I would not stir out of my room. Not one of the ladies who had intended to come to Antwerp kept their resolution, and in consequence they got a great alarm, which was what my husband wished to avoid.

There was a great battle fought near Bruxelles on Saturday[17] and I was told, the noise of the cannon was tremendous and the houses shook with it. It was distinctly heard at Antwerp but I kept the windows shut, and tried not to hear. I only heard a rolling like the sea at a distance. Poor Emma, urged by curiosity, stood listening to terrible stories, seeing wounded men brought in, carriages full of women and children, all flying from Bruxelles, till she was completely terrified. She came and told me, that the ladies were hastening to England, for the French had taken Bruxelles. I saw that I must take my turn to alarm her, and said, "Well, Emma, you know that if the French were firing at this house, I would not move till I was ordered; but you have no such duty, therefore if you like, I daresay, any of the families will allow you to join them." Emma was shocked, at my supposing she would be so base as to desert me, and declared that tho' she was sure she would have to remain in a French prison for 5 years, she would not leave me. My reproof had all the effect I intended; for she brought me no more stories.

Though I had little reason to expect a letter from my husband, I sat up late in hopes. What was my joy at midnight to get a little note from him, written at Genappe, after the battle of the 16th.[18] He said he was safe, and in great spirits; they had given the French a tremendous beating. I wrote to him every day, and Captain Mitchell sent my letters, but he never received them.

On Sunday, Captain M. told me the last effort was to be made. I cannot describe the restless unhappy state I was in; for it had already continued so much longer than I had expected that I found it difficult to keep up my spirits, tho' I was infatuated enough to think it quite impossible that he could be hurt. I believe mine was not an uncommon case – but so it was – that I might be uneasy at the length of the separation, or anxious to hear from him; but the possibility of his being wounded never glanced into my mind, till I was told that he was killed.

Sunday June 18th

On Sunday there was a dreadful battle. It began at about 11 o'clock – about 3 when Sir William was riding beside the Duke, a cannon ball struck him on the back, at the right shoulder, and knocked him off his horse to several yards distance. The Duke at first thought he was killed; for he said afterwards, he never had in all the fighting he had been in seen a man rise again after such a wound. Seeing he was alive (for he bounded up again) the Duke went to him and stooping down, took him by the hand.

Sir William begged the Duke, as the last favour he would have it in his power to do him, to exert his authority to take away the crowd that gathered round him, and to let him have his last moments to himself. The Duke bade him farewell, and endeavoured to draw away his Staff, who oppressed him – they wanted to take leave of him, and wondered at his calmness. He was left, as they imagined, to die; but his cousin, De Lancey Barclay,[19] who had seen him fall, went to him instantly, and tried to prevail upon him to be removed to the rear, as he was in imminent danger of being crushed by the artillery, which was fast approaching the spot, and also there was a danger of his falling into the hands of the enemy. He entreated to be left on the ground, and said it was impossible he could live, that they might be of more use to others, and he only begged to be allowed to remain on the field, but as he spoke with ease, and Colonel Barclay, seeing that the ball had not entered, he insisted on moving him, and he took the opinion of a surgeon, who thought he might live, and got some soldiers to carry him in a blanket to a barn at the side of the road, a little to the rear. The wound was dressed, and then Colonel B. had to return to his division; but first he gave orders to have Sir William moved to the village; for that barn was in danger of being taken by the enemy. Before Colonel B. went, Sir William begged he would come quite close to him, and continued to give him messages for me, nothing else seemed to occupy his mind. He desired him to write to me at Antwerp; to say every thing kind, and to endeavour to soften this sad event and to break it to me as gently as he could. He then said that he might move him, as if he fancied it was to be his last effort. He was carried to the village of Waterloo, and left in a cottage, where he lay unheeded all night, and part of the next day. Many of his friends were in the village, and none of them knew where he was, or even that he was alive. It was by chance that an officer of the Staff found him next morning, and sent to inform Sir G. Scovell.[20] The evening before, the Duke had written the dispatches, and had inserted De Lancey as killed; interest was made that he should alter this, when he was told that he had been carried off the field alive. Some kindly thought this might be to benefit me; but I was not so fortunate. Sad scenes were passing in the meantime at Antwerp.

<table>
<tr><td>Monday
June 19th</td></tr>
</table>

On Monday morning Captain Mitchell came at nine o'clock to inform me, that the last battle was over, and the French were entirely beaten and that Sir W^m safe. I asked him repeatedly if he was sure, if he had seen any of his writing, or if he had heard from him. He had not – but he had read a list of the killed and wounded, and could assure me his name was not in it. Captn M was quite sincere; and was afterwards grieved that he had added much to the accumulation of misery, for this only made the dash down more severe. I now found how much I had really feared, by the wild spirits I got into. I walked up and down, for I could not rest, and was almost in a fever with happiness – and for two hours this went on.

At eleven a message came that Lady H–[21] wished to see me – I went down to the parlour, and found her and Mr James; I did not remark any thing in her countenance, but I think I never saw feeling and compassion more strongly marked than in his expression. I then said I hoped Lady Emily was well, he answered that she was so – with a tone of such misery that I was afraid something had happened, I knew not what – I looked at Lady H for explanation. She seemed too, a little agitated, and I said, "One is so selfish – I can attend to nothing, I am so rejoiced to find Sir W^m is safe." Mr James walked to the other end of the room, I did not know what to do, I feared my gay voice had grieved them, for I saw something had made them unhappy – little did I think the blow was falling on my own unfortunate head!

Lady H said, "Poor Mr James, he has lost a brother[22] and I a nephew; it was a dreadful battle, so many killed." – I thought it cruel of them to come to see me to tell all this, when I was so merry – but I tried to be polite and again apologised for appearing glad, on account of my own good fortune. Lady H. said, "Did you hear from him?" "No, but Captn Mitchell saw the list, and his name was not in it."

Mr James went out of the room; Lady H said, "He is gone to see it, I suppose" – and then began to talk of the list, and what were the first names in it, and a great deal about whether I had any friends in that country &c, &c, &c. She then asked what I intended to do if the fighting continued, and if I should go to England. I was a little surprised at these enquiries – but assured her that I would not move till Sir Willm came or sent for me. – She found me so obstinately confident that she began – and after a short time a suspicion darted into my mind – What a death-like feeling was that.

Lady H. confessed she had written the list and with a most mistaken kindness, had omitted several of the names – Sir W^m's among the rest. A General had come from the field and named them, and she, knowing I was in the country, had left his out, fearing that I should be suddenly informed – But such information could not be otherwise than a shock, whatever way it was told – and the previous account of his safety only tortured me the more – but it is needless to dwell upon it now and though I believe she thinks I never forgave her, I now recollect only the motive, which was kind. My difficulty then was to find out or rather to believe the truth. She assured me he was only wounded; I looked at her keenly, and said, "Lady H I can bear anything but suspense, let me know the very worst. Tell me, is he killed? I see! I see! You know it is so!" She then solemnly assured me he was only desperately wounded I shook my head and said "Ah it is very well to say so yes he must be wounded first, you know you say" and I walked round and around the room fast, "Yes, yes, you say so, but I cannot believe what you say now." – She was terrified for I could not shed a tear. She declared upon her word of honour that when Genl Alava left the field, he was alive, he was not expected to live. This I felt sounded like truth and I stood before her, and said, "Well, Lady H if this is so, and you really wish to serve me, help me to get to him instantly – I am sure Mr James will be so good as to hurry the servant. Oh! how much time has been lost already, if Captain Mitchell had but known, I should have gone at nine. Every minute may make me too late to see him alive." She was glad to do any thing for me, and was going. I stopped her at the door and said, "Now, if you are deceiving me, you may perhaps have my senses to answer for." She repeated her assurances, and I told her I would send my servant for the carriage, which was at the Town major's, if she would see any body to get horses, and I was ready – She said she would offer to go with me, but she knew it would oppress me. I said, "Oh! no, let me be alone," and I ran upstairs. No power can describe my sufferings for two hours before I could get away. Captn Mitchell requested a friend of his to ride forward to Bruxelles and to gallop back with information of where Sir W^m was, and whether it was of any avail still for me to proceed; he was expected to meet us half-way at Malines.[23]

We at last left Antwerp; but bribing the driver was in vain, it was not in his power to proceed; for the moment we passed the gates, we were entangled in a crowd of waggons, carts, horses, and wounded men, deserters, and all the rabble and confusion, the consequence of several battles. Every now and then we went several miles at a walk, and the temper of the people was so irritable that we feared to speak to them, and I had to caution my servant to be very guarded, because they were ready to draw their swords in a moment; two men got on the back of the carriage, and we dared not desire them to get off and this was no imaginary terror as I afterwards experienced. –

When we were a mile or two from Malines, the carriage stopped, and the servant said, "it is the Captain." I had drawn the blinds to avoid seeing the wretched objects we were passing – I hastily looked out, and saw Mr Hay.[24] When he saw me he turned his head away. I called out, "Mr Hay, do you know any thing?" He hesitated, then said, "I fear I have very bad news for you." I said, "Tell me at once, is he dead?" "It is all over" I sunk back into the carriage, and they took me back to Antwerp – When I had been a short time there, Mr Hay sent to know if I had any commands to Bruxelles, as he was going to return, and would do any thing for me there; at first I said I had none, and then I sent for him, and asked repeatedly if he was quite sure of what he said; if he had seen him fall. He had not been in the action, and of course was not near Sir Wm, "who was surrounded by Lord Wellington's Staff, – but in the middle of the action he was struck by a cannon ball, and instantly fell – the Duke went and leant over him and – he died like a soldier" – I then begged Mr Hay to make a point of seeing some one who had been near him, and if possible to learn if he had spoken, and if he had named me. Mr Hay promised this, and then asked if I would choose to go to England. I said, "instantly" – He then said if he had twelve hours to search the field once more, for his Brother was missing, he would be ready to take a passage for me, and to accompany me if I chose. (Mr Hay's Brother was never found, he was a young man of eighteen and this was his first campaign.)

He said Lady H and Mrs B[25] were below, anxious to be of use. I said I preferred greatly being alone, and was always much better alone. About half an hour after, Mrs B contrived to get into the room – I was terrified and called out, "Go away, go away, leave me to myself." She prayed and entreated me to hear her, and then said if I was ill would I send for her. I said, "Oh, yes, yes; but the only thing any body can do for me is to leave me alone." She was alarmed by my violent agitation, and went away – I locked the outer door and shut the inner one, so that no one could again intrude. They sent Emma to entreat I would be bled, but I was not reasonable enough for that, and would not comply. I wandered about the room, beseeching for mercy though I felt that now, even Heaven would not be merciful. – One is apt to fix on a situation just a little less wretched than one's own, and to dwell upon the idea that one could bear that better. I repeated over and over that if I had seen him alive for five minutes, I would not repine. At night Emma brought her bed into my room, as she feared I should be ill.

Tuesday June 20th

Towards morning I fancied I heard a sound of someone trying to get into the room. I had heard it a long while, but thinking it was someone coming to visit me, I made no answer – About two hours after, the attempt was repeated – I said to Emma, "There is a noise at the door, don't let Mrs B in, or Lady H." She went out and returning in a few minutes said, "I am desired to tell you cautiously." I said, "Emma go away, don't tell me any thing any way!" "Nay, but I must tell you, I have good news for you." "How can you be so inhuman! What is good for me now?" – "But – Sir William is not dead" – I started up and asked her what she was saying, for she would make me mad! She told me that Genl Mackenzie[26] was below, and had a message from Bruxelles, requesting him to inform me that Sir William was alive, and there was even hope of his recovery –

I ran down to Genl Mackenzie and began earnestly to persuade him, it must be impossible; I had suffered so much the day before, that I durst not hope for any thing now – His very voice faltered and his eyes filled with tears. He said, "Can you believe any man would bring such intelligence unless it were well-founded?" – He then gave me a letter from Sir G. Scovell, who had seen an officer of the Staff Corps, who had seen Sir William alive that morning who was anxious to see me; he was attended by a skilled surgeon, and he had been twice bled. This was on Monday evening at seven o'clock – I regretted the deal of time that had been lost, and said that yesterday morning was a long time ago, and was no argument for his being alive now – for it was often repeated in the letter not to raise my hopes.

I then asked Genl McK— to assist me in getting away; unfortunately I did not say I had a carriage. He said he was going to Bruxelles and would take me; I consented, and he went to get ready. I would not if I could describe the state I was in for two hours more. Then I lost all self-command; I would not allow Emma to put up any clothes, lest we should be detained. My anxiety and agitation increased – I had the dreadful idea haunting me that I would arrive perhaps half an hour too late.

This got the better of me, and I paced backwards and forwards in the parlour very fast and my breathing was like screaming – I went into the passage and sent Emma to see if the carriage was coming, and then sat down upon the stair, which was steep and dark. There Genl McK found me.

When he learnt I had a carriage, he sent the horses he had, for his carriage was not ready, and would not be for some time. When he saw what a state I was in, he roused me in a most sensible manner; he said, "Lady De Lancey, consider what you are doing. You are exhausting your strength and spirits to no purpose for your friends are endeavouring to forward your departure as soon as possible." I exclaimed "Oh, I shall never be there, he may be dying at this moment." – He took my hand, and said calmly and firmly, "My dear Madam, why fancy evil, you know what dreadful scenes you may have to go through at Waterloo; you will probably require all your courage, and must command yourself for his sake." I said no more, but quietly went to the parlour and remained waiting – such an immediate effect had his steady good sense on my fevered mind. I overheard him say, "No do not at present – she is unfit for it." I was alarmed and ran out, but I saw a lady retreating, and was grateful to him –

We left Antwerp between eight and nine o'clock, and had the same difficulties to encounter; but the road was not quite so much blocked up – Genl McK said he would ride after us in an hour, in case we should be detained; he also sent a dragoon before to order horses. When we were near Vilvorde,^{27} the driver attempted to pass a wagon, but the soldier who rode beside it would not move an inch to let us pass; the Waggon kept possession of the Chaussée the whole way, and we had to drive on the heavy road at the side. My servant got off the seat to endeavour to lead the horses past; this provoked the soldier, and a dispute began; I was alarmed and ordered the servant to get upon the carriage again – which he did. A Prussian officer who was enraged at our attempting to pass the Waggon which he was guarding, drew his sword, and made several cuts at the servant's legs, but did not reach him; he was preparing to get down again, but I looked from the opposite window and commanded him to sit still – and not to answer a word – or else to quit the carriage altogether, the driver now made a dash past the Waggon, and the Officer galloped after us and tried to wound the horses. This made me desperate, and I ventured on a most imprudent action; I drew up the blind, and holding out my hands, I petitioned him to let me pass – I exclaimed that my husband, a British officer, was dying, and if he detained me I might not see him – it had the desired effect, for without seeming to have heard me, he slackened his pace and was soon far behind.

When within ten miles of Bruxelles, the smell of Gunpowder was very perceptible – the heat was oppressive; as we came within a mile of Bruxelles, the multitude of wretched-looking people was great, as Emma told me, for I was both unwilling and unable to look out, I was so much worn with anxiety that I could scarcely sit up, as we entered Bruxelles we stopped, and I saw Mr Hay – I durst not speak, but he instantly said, "He is alive, I sent my servant to Waterloo this morning, he is just returned, and Sir W^m is better than they expected. I have horses standing harnessed, and you will soon be there, if the road is passable, though it was not yesterday for a horse."

We were soon out of Bruxelles and on the road to Waterloo. It is nine miles and we took three hours and a half – Mr Hay rode before us with his sword drawn, and obliged them to let us pass. We often stood still for ten minutes, the horses screamed at the smell of corruption, which in many places was offensive; at last when near the village, Mr Hay said he would ride forward, and find the house, and learn whether I should still proceed or not.

I hope no one will ever be able to say they can understand what my feelings must have been during the half hour that passed till he returned. How fervently and how sincerely did I resolve that if I saw him alive for one hour, I never would repine! I had almost lost my recollection, with the excess of anxiety and suspense, when Mr Hay called out, "All's well; I have seen him and he expects you." When we got to the village Sir G. Scovell met the carriage, and opening the door, said, "Stop one moment." "Is he alive?" "Yes, alive; and the surgeons are of the opinion that he may recover. We are so grieved for what you have suffered." "Oh! Never mind what I have suffered. Let me go to him now." He said I must wait one moment. I assured him I was quite composed indeed, he said, "I see you are, (with a smile) but I wish to warn you of one thing. You must be aware, that his life hangs on a very slender hold; and therefore any agitation would be injurious. Now we have not told him you had heard of his death; we thought it would affect him, therefore do not appear to have heard it." I promised, and he said, "Now come along" – I sat down for an instant in the outer room, while he went in, and when I heard my Husband say, "Let her come in, then," I was overpaid for all the misery – I was surprised at the strength of his voice, for I had expected to find him weak and dying; when I went into the room where he lay, he held out his hand and said, "Come Magdalene, this is a sad business, is it not?" – I could not speak, but sat down by him and took his hand. Though I found him better than I expected, I can scarcely say whether I hoped or feared the most at first – because I was so occupied by gathering comforts about him, that I had not time to think about the future. It was a dreadful preparation (but a sufficient one) being told of his death and then finding him alive but it was a sufficient one; for I was now ready to bear whatever might ensue without a murmur. I was so grateful for seeing him, once more, that I valued each hour as it passed, and as I had too much reason to fear that I should very soon have nothing left of happiness but what my reflections would afford me, I endeavoured, by suppressing feelings that would have made him[28] miserable, and myself unfit to serve him, to lay up no store of regret. He asked me if I was a good nurse; I told him I had not been much tried. He said he was sure he would be a good patient, for he would do whatever I bid him till he was convalescent; and then he knew he would grow very cross. I watched in vain for a cross word, all his endeavour seemed to be to leave none but pleasing impressions on my mind, and as he grew worse and suffered more, his smile was more sweet and his thanks more fervent for every thing that was done for him –

I endeavoured to find out from the surgeons the extent of the danger. They said that at present there were no bad symptoms, and after seeing him alive at all after such a wound, they would not despair; and if the fever could be kept off, there was a great chance of his recovery – with this in view, they wished to bleed him constantly; wishing also thereby to make the recovery more complete.

I knew they had no interest in me, and therefore would probably tell me the same as other people, so I continued to ask them after every visit, what they thought – But when by watching the symptoms myself, and also observing the surgeons' expressions, I saw what I must soon prepare for, I did not teaze them any more with questions, but tried not to give way, and endeavoured to keep up as long as it could be of consequence to him; for even, after all hope was gone and the disorder increased rapidly, I felt that if by agitating him I should afterwards imagine that I had shortened his life one hour, that reflection would embitter my whole life – I have the satisfaction of knowing I succeeded even better than I could have hoped – for towards the end of the week, when every symptom was bad, the surgeon (probably because I desisted from enquiring and did not appear agitated) doubtful what I thought yet, judging it right to tell me, asked Emma if she knew whether I was aware of the danger or not – She assured him that I had entirely given up hope for some time –

I found Emma of great service; her good will carried her through excessive fatigue, while at Waterloo and afterwards her excellent heart and superior judgement were quite a blessing to me. She told me that she was thankful she had been at Waterloo

– for it would do her good to have seen a little of what other people endure. She never before knew half the value of her peaceful comfortable home in London – where the absence of miserable objects, might alone be considered a benefit. I can hardly express what I felt, on returning to England, on seeing people surrounded with every luxury, unhappy at the want of the smallest comfort; I can fancy no better cure for all imaginary evils, than a week's residence at Waterloo.

Noise did not disturb Sir William fortunately, for the cottage was surrounded with roads[29] – one in front led to Nivelles, and every waggon going to and from the army, and all the wounded and prisoners, passed along that road; it was paved, and there was an unceasing noise for four days and nights: we were obliged to keep the windows open, and people used to pass close to that in his room, talking loud and sometimes looking in and speaking, but he never took any notice[30] – I never saw any body so patient. – The people to whom the cottage belonged, were luckily favourable to our cause, or they could have tormented us a good deal – instead of which, I never met with so much good nature, and tho' they never rested one moment helping the soldiers to water, and were constantly worn out with giving them assistance, we had only to tell them what to do, and they ran about to work for us. Their ménage was, I must allow, in a sad state, there was want of everything; I could not help thinking with envy, of the troublesome abundance, I had often seen in sick rooms, where there was far less need of it. However in a short time we got every thing he required, and I have the greatest comfort in recollecting that there was not one thing, which he expressed a wish for that we did not procure. I sent a servant constantly to Bruxelles, with a list of things we wanted, and once I recollect something was brought he had been very anxious for, naturally enough he was disappointed when it was not so good as he expected; but I was quite struck with his endeavour to praise it for fear I should be sorry. There was a languid melancholy about him, at the same time that he was calm and resigned, which would have made the most uninterested person grieved to see him suffering, and with such sweetness.

Emma once gave him some drink, and she told me that the tone of voice, and his smile when he thanked her, were like to break her heart, for he was in severe pain at the time.

He said the wound gave him no pain at all, but a little irritating cough caused excessive pain in his chest and side, which produced inflammation, and afterwards water on the chest, which was eventually the cause of his death. I suspect the Surgeons had never much hope, but they said there was a chance if the inflammation could have been stopped. – By constantly watching him, and gradually day after day observing the progress and increase of suffering and the elevated tone of his mind, along with fatigue and weakness, I was prepared for his final release in a manner that nothing but his firmness and composure could have effected. He had at first been bled in the outer room, which had two large windows to the road, and every one saw in. This he did not like, and he made the people move him to a small room, about 7 feet wide, with a bed across the end of it; they placed him so low and awkwardly in the bed, that when I first went in, I thought his legs were hurt, for he could not straighten his knees. After a day or two, he got shoved up by degrees, and then he could stretch his limbs. The bed was wretched, merely a wooden frame fastened to the walls, so that it could not be moved, which rendered it extremely difficult to bleed him, or to assist him in any way, as he could neither turn not raise his head an inch from the pillow, or rather sack of chaff, upon which he was laid. This was so full of dust that it made him cough; I soon removed it, and got a cushion out of the carriage instead. We had a clean blanket from Bruxelles, and at first we put on clean sheets every day; but latterly he grew so restless, that he preferred having only the blanket. I had purposely sent for a French cotton one – as I thought the flannel would teaze him. The bed was made tolerable at least, and tho' I could not be pleased with it, he was. – He repeated more than once, "What a thing it was for you, being in this country!" And I had the delight of hearing him say, that he did not know what he would have done without me – he said he was sure he could not have lived so long, for he would not have been so obedient to any one else I found he had been the worse for seeing some friends who had called the first day I was at Waterloo, so I told the servant afterwards never to let any body come into his room – I remember one day, an Officer called, and before he was out of sight I had his card converted into a teaspoon –

Sir W^m never eat any thing, except once or twice a morsel of toast out of the water; he drank a great deal of tea and lemonade. At first he had no milk for his tea, and he complained that it was very bad; but there was none to be had. I sent my servant to search for some, and he met some Prussian cows, and milked one, and brought a jug of fine milk. The different contrivances sometimes amused him; one day he wished to have the room fumigated, how was this to be done without fire-irons, or indeed without fire? We put some vinegar into a tumbler, and Emma went with a large pair of scissors and brought a piece of burning charcoal, and put it into the vinegar, and that made a great smoke. Every time we wanted any thing warmed or water boiled, Emma had to cross a court to make a fire, and then watch it, or someone would have run away with what she was cooking – meantime, I would call her ten different times, and this in wet or dry, night or day. I now regretted bringing so few clothes.

The day I went to Waterloo, Sir W^m told me the Duke had visited him that morning, he said he never had seen him so warm in his feelings. He had taken leave of him with little hope of seeing him again, I fancy. The Duke told him, he never wished to see another battle, this had been so shocking – it was too much to see such brave men, so equally matched, cutting each other to pieces, as they did. – Sir W^m said there had never been such fighting, that the Duke far surpassed any thing he had ever done before. – The general opinion seemed to be that it had been a particularly shocking battle: Sir W^m said he would never try it again, he was quite tired of the business; in speaking of his wound, he said, – "This might be the most fortunate event that could have happened for us both." – I looked at him for an explanation, – and he said, "Even if I recover completely, I should never think of serving again, nobody would ask such a thing, and we should settle down quietly at home for the rest of our lives." – The Evening after I went to Waterloo, Sir G. Scovell said he would take something to eat, and after seeing me fairly established he would go to the headquarters – he wrote a copy of return of rations, for which we were to send to Bruxelles; and also every other provisions must be got from thence, for the Village afforded nothing. – He left two sentinels, for fear there should be any disturbances, and we might feel unprotected. –

One night there was a great noise of people quarrelling in front of the house – the windows had no fastening whatever, but the people passed away without molesting us. – I was a little more seriously alarmed another day – some reports had reached us that the French were coming back, and were within nine miles – I thought it unlikely, but about 8 in the morning all the waggons that had passed for two hours, came back as fast as possible, horses trotting and men running. I was uneasy on Sir W$^{m's}$ account, his situation was so helpless. I leant forward to prevent people seeing him; I waited without saying any thing, till I learnt the cause of this bustle. I afterwards found that it was merely the waggons had gone several miles down the wrong road, and were hurrying back to make up for lost time.

From the time Sir G. Scovell left us, we scarcely saw any body, but the surgeons. It must add very much to the fatigue of their business, having every thing to do for the wounded whom they attend – Mr Powel,[31] who attended most constantly on Sir W^m, and evidently with great anxiety for his recovery, was sometimes quite knocked up, with walking many miles on the heavy road, to the fields and to cottages – at first he had some difficulty in considering me a useful person, and used to ask me to tell the servant to come; but he learnt to employ me very soon. The night I went, Sir W^m desired me to take some rest, for I looked ill. A portmanteau bed had been brought from Bruxelles for me, I left him reluctantly, for I grudged wasting any of such precious time; but he would not hear of my sitting up. I had just lain down with my clothes on; (for there was no blanket, and the floor was damp tiles,) I heard him call to his servant, who slept at the end of his room on a mattress; I jumped up and went to him, and did not leave him again. He wanted some drink, which I gave him, and then sat down beside him. He slept and woke every half hour, he was not restless, nor had he any pain, but he was constantly thirsty.

| Wednesday June 21st |

On Wednesday he wished to have leeches applied to his side where the bruise appeared; Mr Powel had no objection, and desired me to send for him when the leeches were brought from Bruxelles; I did so, but in the meantime, not knowing why he was sent for, I began as a matter of course to apply them; when he came, he apologised and thanked me; I was not at first aware, how I had obliged him; he said he was very tired and when he attempted to fix the leeches he did not succeed so well as I did. Next time they were to be applied, I asked him if I should send for him, he said I was as good at it as any hospital nurse could be, and as he had scarcely had an hour's rest any night since the battle, he would be greatly obliged to me if I would take the trouble. Sir W^m alleged that I grew vain of my skill in tormenting my poor husband with these animals.

The same day Dr Hume[32] called in passing to Bruxelles, for ten minutes; I was a little provoked at the gaiety of his manner, the gravity he assumed at Bruxelles would have suited the present scene. Though Sir W^m never complained, he was serious and seemed inclined to be quiet, and neither to speak nor to listen.

He generally lay thinking, often conversed with me, but seemed oppressed with general conversation, and would not listen when any one told him of the progress of the army; his thoughts were in a very different train. Dr Hume's rapid visit annoyed me much –

I did not feel the effects of having sat up on Tuesday night, till

next night, but I was resolved to fight against it; Sir W^m desired
me to go to rest, as he had done the night before – but I only
remained away till I had an excuse to return, and he always
forgot a second time to bid me go away – this was the only night
I had real difficulty to keep awake – the noise assisted me a
little,[33] – I counted the rushes of the chair for want of occupation
– some people said why did I not let my maid sit up, but that
showed they did not understand me, for if twenty people had sat
up, it would have made no difference to me. I frequently rejoiced
that I had no friend with me, who could exert authority to make
me take care of myself, when my only wish was to keep up as long
as he needed me.

| Thursday |
| June 22nd |

On Thursday he was not quite so well, before this
he had been making a gradual progress and
could move about with more ease – he spoke
much better than he did at first; his countenance
was animated; but I fear this was the beginning of the most
dangerous symptoms, and I saw that the Surgeon now became
uneasy at the appearance of the blood, and Mr Woodridge,[34] a
very eminent Surgeon, now constantly attended. Genl Dundas[35]
called this forenoon, he stayed only a minute, as Sir William was
not so well, and I was busy; after he was away, I recollected
having neglected to ask him to send a blanket and some wine; I
never had time to eat, and I always forgot to get wine, as I could
take a glass of that and a bit of bread in a moment, and my
strength was failing; I looked out and saw him still at the door; I
went out, and there were a number of people, Sir D. Hamilton
&c.[36] I told Genl Dundas that I had no blanket. "Bless me," every
one exclaimed, "no blanket!" I said it was not of much consequence, as I never lay down, but the floor was so damp that I was
afraid my maid would be ill, and her help was very essential; I
then asked for wine; both of which Genl Dundas sent down next
day. – That night I had no difficulty in keeping awake – Sir W^m
was restless and uncomfortable, his breathing was oppressed,
and I had constantly to raise him on the pillow; the pain in his
chest increased, and he was twice bled before morning.

He was very much better on Friday forenoon. Mr Woodridge
told us that every day since the battle the people of Bruxelles sent
down carriages to take the wounded to the hospitals; from 20 to
30 carriages every day.

<table>
<tr><td>Friday
June 23rd</td></tr>
</table>

On Friday Sir W^m was very feverish, and the appearance of the blood was very inflammatory; I had learnt to judge for myself now, as Mr Powel seeing how anxious I was, sometimes had the kindness to give me a little instruction. About 10 at night Mr Woodridge and Mr Powel came; while I told them how Sir W^m had been since their last visit, and mentioned several circumstances, I watched them, and saw they looked at each other; I guessed their thoughts. I turned away to the window and wept. They remained a little time, and I recovered myself; they lingered and seemed inclined to speak. But I was well aware of what they had to say; I felt unable to bear it then, and I shut the door instead of going out. – It was that night that Mr Powel asked Emma, if she knew what I thought – He desired to be sent for on the first appearance of change. –

<table>
<tr><td>Saturday
June 24th</td></tr>
</table>

At one in the morning, he was in great pain, and as I raised him that he might breathe more freely, he looked so <u>fixed</u> that I was afraid he was just expiring – His arms were round my neck to raise himself by, and I thought we should both have been killed by the exertion – he asked if Mr Powel had not talked of bleeding him again; I said I had sent for him, he bled him for the last time; from that moment, all the fever was gone; Mr Powel said it was of consequence to keep him quiet, and if he could sleep it would do him good. – At four in the morning, I was called out to see a Surgeon, sent from Mr Powel, who was ill in bed. He came to know how Sir W^m was; he had slept a little till three – but the oppression was returning.

This Surgeon told me, he had been anxious to speak to me several times – to tell me that it was he who had first seen him on the field, and who had given it as his opinion that he might live. He was grieved that it should fall to his lot to tell me that it was the opinion of the Surgeons that if I had any thing particular to say to Sir W^m, I should not delay long – I asked how long – he said they could not exactly tell – I said "Days or hours?" he answered the present symptoms would not prove fatal within 12 hours – I left him, and went softly into my Husband's room, for he was asleep – I sat down at the other end of the room, and continued looking at him, quite stupefied I could scarcely see. My mouth was so parched that when I touched it, it felt as dry as the back of my hand – I thought I was to die first – I then thought, what[37] would he do for want of me, for the remaining few hours he had to live – This idea roused me and I began to recollect our helpless situation, whatever happened, and I tried to think who I should inform of the circumstances. – I was not long in deciding on General Dundas – if he could be found and have time to come and take care of us both – I immediately wrote a long letter to him, telling how I was situated – and begged he would come after 12 hours. I said I hoped I should be calm and fit to act for myself; but as I had never been near such a scene before, I knew not what effect it might have upon me. I therefore explained what I wished might be done after all was over, with respect to every thing. I then sent the servant with the letter and orders to find Gen[l] Dundas, if he was within ten miles of Bruxelles. A few hours after I had a few lines from him saying he would be at Waterloo in the evening. After I had sent the letter, I sat down to consider what was next to be done. Though Sir W[m] was aware of his danger, I thought it my duty to tell him how immediate the Surgeons seemed to think it. I knew he was far from being the worse for such a communication, and I wished to know if he had any thing to say. – I sat thinking about it when he awoke and held out his hand, for me to take my station by his bed side. I went and told him – We talked for some time on the subject. He was not agitated, but his voice faltered a little, and he said it was sudden. This was the first day he felt well enough to begin to hope he should recover! He breathed freely and was entirely free from pain, and he said he had been thinking if he could be removed to Bruxelles, he would soon get well. I then asked him if he had any thing for me to do and any thing to say to any one. He reminded me of what he had told me, had engrossed his thoughts when he had imagined himself dying on the field. He said he felt exactly the same now – He said he felt at peace with all the world – he knew he was going to a better one, &c &c. He repeated most of what he had told me were his feelings before – that he had no sorrow but to part from his wife, and no regret but that of leaving her in misery – He seemed fatigued, and shutting his eyes desired me not to speak for a little. – I then determined not to introduce the subject again, nor to speak unless he seemed to wish it – as I had done all that was necessary.

In an hour or two he ate some breakfast – tea and toasted bread, with so much relish, that it almost overcame me – he observed that I must have caught cold, by sitting in a draught of air. I said I had – He felt so very much better that I was anxious the Surgeon should see him. He came in the evening. He was pleased to see Sir William free from pain – but said there was scarcely a possibility of his continuing so. He said that he might linger a day or two, but that every symptom was bad – he advised me to keep him as quiet and composed as possible. – I assured him no person had been in the room but the Surgeon whom he had brought to consult –, and I had sat beside him the whole day scarcely speaking. I said I had told Sir W^m his opinion of his case – he said it had evidently not agitated him, for his pulse was quite calm.

Mr Woodridge called in the afternoon, he was going to Bruxelles, and would do any thing there we wished – we had nothing for him to do and he was going when he repeated the question – Sir W^m looked at me earnestly, and said, "Magdalene, love – Genl Dundas." I answered "I wrote to him this morning," and no more passed. –

Late in the evening, when we were as calm and composed as could be, and I was sitting and looking at him, and holding his hand as usual, Mr Powel and D^r H— came in – the latter was even more cheerful than before – paid a rapid, noisy visit and away again – it disturbed our tranquillity not a little, but he is reckoned so skilful, we ought to have been glad to see him – He bade Sir W^m rouse up, felt his pulse, and said it would bear another bleed yet, if necessary –

The poor dying man raised his languid eyes, and said, "Oh no, I do not need it now; I am cool." D^r H— said he had no wish to bleed him, but would like to have his limbs fomented – he shook his head – I asked if he knew what it was – he said no, and he would like to try – I asked D^r H— if it would be advisable – He said he thought it might refresh him.

He went out and I followed to hear what he would say. He said to Mr Powel, "why do you give up a man with such a pulse, with such a good constitution too – you make them all sad and useless – it does no harm to be trying something" – he named several things: "Put a blister on his breast, and leeches after, if the pain is great on the side" – I looked at Mr Powel doubting, as I depended most on his opinion, as his constant attendance to the progress of the illness, gave it most weight. – I thought he looked sorry that my hopes should be removed – but of course he said nothing. – D^r H— said, "Oh, don't fear, he won't desert the cause" – I was angry at such nonsense, and said, "Be assured I do not fear that Mr Powel will desert the cause, but he said this morning there was no hope" – "Nay," said he, "not quite so much as that: I said there was little hope." I went away, and left them to discuss it themselves – Sir W^m said he wished to try what Dr H— was speaking about – and I went to order boiling water to be prepared – I made the people understand I wanted a great quantity in a tub: while I was speaking, Mr Powel returned – he had taken a turn with D^r H— who had, I fancy explained his opinion. He said he would go home and prepare a blister, and he believed he had leeches – I said, was it not a great pity to torment him; he said he would not pretend to say it – could be of much consequence, but for this reason he advised me to do it I was not aware how I should feel afterwards – and I might perhaps repent when it was too late, not having done every thing which a Physician of D^r H—'s eminence deemed advisable. He said that Sir W^m would not be at ease at any rate – and it would scarcely plague him – the fomentation would be pleasant to him and I might take the blister off in six hours if he wished it.

When I went to foment his limbs, I could not find a morsel of flannel – at last I thought of the servant's blanket, and tore it in two. Sir W^m said it was a most delightful thing and refreshed him much – he expressed a great wish to have a bit on his chest – I did not know what to do for flannel. I regretted now excessively, not having brought more clothes as I might have taken a flannel petticoat. This put me in mind of the one I had on, and I instantly tore a great piece out of it, and put it into the tub – the cottagers put up their hands, exclaiming, "Ah, Madame" – He said it did him good, and was delicious – unconscious where we had found the flannel; indeed he never was aware of the difficulty, for the tub was placed in the outer room.

Genl Dundas came. – Sir W^m heard me speaking to him, and asked who it was – I told him, and he asked if he were going to remain. I said he was – Sir W^m seemed gratified, but did not say anymore. Surely no earthly feeling can be superior to such perfect sympathy!

Sir W^m fell asleep, and I went out to see if there was any thing for Genl Dundas to eat – he told me he had got a very good room up stairs, and was willing to remain as long as I wished – his only request was that I should not mind him any more than if he was not there – but send for him when I wanted him. I opened the door of Sir W$^{m's}$ room and sat close to it, so as to hear if he moved or spoke – and I sat down to coffee – for the first meal I had had – and talked over several things necessary to be settled with Genl Dundas – I could not speak above a whisper, my voice was so faint – he entreated me to try if possible to take rest that night, for fear I should be ill before my husband could spare me. I promised – he then told me that Lady Hamilton had asked him to take me to her house when I should return to Bruxelles, and also the Count de Lannoy had prepared rooms, which he begged I would occupy as long as I pleased. I preferred going to the house we been in before, and I thought I should be more entirely alone there than in any other person's house which was what I wished, and knew would be best for me. – I was struck when I did return to

126

Bruxelles, with two marks of attention – I had a message from the Commissary to say, that orders were given that I was to draw rations and forage as long as I staid – and the other circumstance was this – On the letters I had sent from Antwerp I had neglected to write "Private," which is necessary when writing to a person in Office – I gave them up as lost, and was uncomfortable – after I had been three days at Bruxelles, they were all returned unopened, from Head-quarters.

Sir William called me; I sat a short time beside him, and after I had prepared drink for the night, I told him I was so very tired, I would go and lie down for a short time, if he would allow my maid to bring the medicine, which he took every four hours; he agreed, and asked if I did not always take plenty of sleep – I said, "Oh yes," – and was going – when he said the pain in his chest was returning – and perhaps leeches would do some good. This was the only time I hesitated to oblige him, for I really could hardly stand. – But of course I proceeded to apply the leeches, and in a few minutes the excessive drowsiness went off – so much so, that when, an hour after, I went to lie down, I could not sleep. I started every moment, thinking he called me. I desired Emma to waken me if he spoke or seemed uneasy. She gave him the medicine; he looked at her and asked where I was; she told him I was asleep: he said "that's right, quite right." The pain in his chest grew intolerable, and he depending upon my being asleep, yielded to complaint and groaned very much. Emma roused me and told me she feared he was suffering very much – I had slept half an hour – I went and stood near him, and he then ceased to complain, and said, "Oh it was only a little twitch" – I felt at that time, as if I was an oppression to him and I was going away, but he desired me to stay – I sat down and rubbed his chest, which dulled the pain, and towards morning I put on the blister.

Sunday June 25th	Between 5 & 6 he took some toasted bread and tea, about two inches of bread. Before he began, he entreated me to take off the blister, only for ten minutes, that he might eat in tolerable com-

fort – I said I would take it away entirely, and he was pleased. The Doctor came about 9; he was breathing then with great difficulty, and there was a rough sound in his throat – Mr Powel said the only thing to be done was to keep him quiet, as usual, and to prevent him speaking. He asked Mr Powel if he might not rise, for he might breathe easier at the window, and he was so tired of lying in bed. – Mr P. urged him not to think of it – he was not able, it would hurt him very much, &c. – About 11 o'Clock he sent me away for ten minutes, and with the help of his servant, he rose and went to the other end of the room. I was terrified when I heard he was up, and called Gen¹ Dundas, who went in and found him almost fainting – they placed him in bed again, and when I returned, he was much exhausted – I opened the window wide, and shutting the door, sat by him alone – in hopes he would go to sleep, and recover a little. He slept every now and then; he seemed much oppressed with the length of the day, for the first time; he asked me repeatedly what o'clock it was, he often asked if it was 3 yet. When I told him it was near 5, he seemed surprised. – At night he said he wished we could fall on some device to shorten the weary long night, he could not bear it – "so long" – I could not think of any plan – He said if I could lie down by him, it would cut off 5 or 6 hours. I said it was impossible for I was afraid to hurt – there was so little room – his mind seemed bent upon it – therefore I stood upon a chair and stepped over him, for he could not move an inch, and he lay at the outer edge. He was delighted, and it shortened the night indeed, for we both fell asleep.

| Monday June 26th |

At 5 in the morning I arose; he was very anxious to have his wound dressed – It had never been looked at – he said there was a little pain, merely a trifle, but it teazed him – Mr Powel objected; he said it would fatigue him too much that day – he consented to delay –

I then washed his face and hands, and brushed his hair, after which I gave him his breakfast – he again wished to rise, but I persuaded him not to do it – he said he would not do anything I was averse to, and he said, "See what control your poor husband is under;" he smiled and drew me close to him, so that he could touch my face, and continued stroking it with his hand for some time – Towards 11 he grew more uneasy – he was restless and uncomfortable, his breathing was like choking – and as I sat gazing at him, I could distinctly hear the water rattling in his throat – I opened the door and window to make a thorough draft – I desired the people to leave the outer room, so that his might be as quiet as usual, and then I sat down to watch the melancholy progress of the water in his chest, which I saw would soon be fatal.

About 3 Dʳ H— and Mʳ Powel came; I must do the former the justice to say he was grave enough now. – Sir William repeated his request to have the wound dressed. Dʳ H— consented, and they went away to prepare something to wash it with; they remained away about half an hour – I sat down by my husband, and took his hand; he said he wished I would not look so unhappy

– I wept – and he spoke to me with so much affection. He repeated every[38] endearing expression – he bid me kiss him – he called me his dear Wife. –

The Surgeons returned – my husband turned on his side with great difficulty – it seemed to give much pain. After I had brought every thing the Surgeons wanted, I went into another room; I could not bear to see him suffering –

Mr Powel saw a change in his countenance – he looked out and desired Emma to call me – to tell me instantly Sir William wanted me; I hastened to him. I stood near my husband – he looked up to me and said, "Magdalene, my love, the spirits" – I stooped down close to him, and held the bottle of lavender to him – I also sprinkled some near him and he looked pleased.

He gave a little gulp, as if something was in his throat – the Doctor said "Ah, poor De Lancey, he is gone" – I pressed my lips to his and left the room –

I went upstairs where I remained unconscious of what was passing – till Emma came to me and said the carriage was ready, and Genl Dundas advised me to go to Bruxelles that evening – but that I need not hurry myself –

I asked her if the room below was empty – she assured me it was, and I went down and remained sometime beside the body – There was such perfect peace and placid calm sweetness in his countenance that I envied him not a little that he was released – I was left to suffer – I then thought I should not suffer long – as I bent over him, I felt as if violent grief would disturb his tranquil rest –

These moments that I passed by his lifeless body were awful and instructive; their impression will influence my whole life.[39]

I left Waterloo with feelings so different from those I had on going to it! Then all was anxious terror that I would not be there in time to see one look, or hear one word. – Now there was nothing imaginary – All was real misery – there now remained not even a chance of happiness but that which depended on the retrospect – of better days and of duties fulfilled. As I drove rapidly along the same road, I could not but recall the irritated state I had been in, when I had been there before – and the fervent and sincere resolutions I then made that if I saw him alive, I would never repine.

Since that time I have suffered every shade of sorrow – but can safely affirm, that except the first few days, I have never felt that my lot was unbearable – I do not forget the perfection of my happiness – while it lasted – and I believe there are not many who after a long life can say that they have felt so much of it –

As I expressed some uneasiness to Gen[l] Dundas at leaving the body with none but servants, Colonel Grant[40] at his request, went to Waterloo, the same evening, and remained till it was brought up the next day to Bruxelles –

Wednesday **June 28th**

General Dundas then kindly executed all my orders, with respect to the funeral &c – which took place on Wednesday 28th, in the Cemetery of the Reformed Church.[41] It is about a mile from Bruxelles, on the road to Louvain –

I had a stone placed with simply his name and the circumstances of his death

Tuesday **July 4th**

I visited his grave on the 4th July – The burying-ground is in a sweet, quiet retired spot – a narrow path leads to it from the road – it is quite out of sight, among the fields – and no house but that of the grave-digger's cottage is near it – Seeing my interest in that grave, he begged me to let him plant rose bushes round it – and promised I should see it nicely kept when I should return –

I am pleased that I saw the grave and the stone;[42] there were nearly forty other new graves and not another stone. – At 11 o'Clock the same day, I set out for England. –

That day, <u>three</u> months before, I was married.

M. De L.

1816

NOTES

1. This text is exactly as in Lady De Lancey's own monogrammed copy of her 'Narrative,' whose provenance is given at Appendix A. It should be noted that:

    a. Lady De Lancey sometimes spells proper names in full, sometimes uses the initial capital followed by a period; and on other occasions the initial capital followed by a dash; eg, Lady H—. One lady, Mrs B., she never identifies and her maid is never referred to other than by her Christian name, Emma. I have retained all such names in the way Lady De Lancey spelt them.

    b. The punctuation is also exactly as she wrote it.

    c. The dates in the margin are as in the original.

2. The Count was a Belgian nobleman and his house was in the Impasse du Parc.

3. For example, Lieutenant-Colonel Sir Augustus Frazer, Commander Royal Horse Artillery reports in a letter dated 15 June 'I find on my table an invitation to dine with De Lancey tomorrow; his lady is here; this will be a pleasanter way of passing the day than marching to Mons.' Unfortunately, it was an appointment he was never to keep. Frazer, *Letters*, p 534

4. Some comments have been passed on this apparent idleness. Sir William was, as other events proved, no stranger to hard work and there can be no doubt that his subordinates not only did all that had to be done, but also persuaded their newly-married chief that, until military matters became more urgent, his first loyalty lay with his wife. [See also remarks in Chapter VI].

5. Antwerp had been selected by Wellington as the main port for the arrival of British troops and for the evacuation of the British Army, should that become necessary.

6. It was by no means impossible for officers' wives to accompany their husbands on campaign. For example, Lieutenant-Colonel Scovell, an Assistant Quartermaster-General at Wellington's headquarters during the Peninsular War, was accompanied by Mrs Scovell. Similarly, the redoubtable Juana accompanied her husband, Captain Harry Smith of the Rifles, in the Peninsula from 1812 to 1814 and throughout the Waterloo campaign.

7. The Minister Plenipotentiary from Spain to the King of the Netherlands was Major-General Don Miguel D'Alava. This officer, who was popular and highly respected by his British colleagues, had served for several years as the Spanish liaison officer at Wellington's headquarters during the Peninsular War. Earlier in his career he had served in the Spanish Navy and commanded a line-of-battle ship, *Santa Anna,* at Trafalgar and was the only known person to have been present at both that battle and Waterloo.

8. Wellington was residing at a house on the corner of the Rue de la Montagne du Parc and the Rue Royale, next door to the Hôtel de France.

9. Without a doubt, this was Major-General Baron von Müffling, the Prussian liaison officer at Wellington's headquarters. This was almost certainly the meeting described by von Müffling as 'towards midnight' (*Passages from my Life,* p 230).

10. The Duke and Duchess of Richmond had taken a house in Brussels. The Duchess threw the Ball on the night of 15 June, to which Sir William and Lady De Lancey received invitations. As Lady De Lancey made no preparations to attend, it would seem that they had no intention of going, even before De Lancey was suddenly involved in working on the 'routes'.

11. This was Major-General Picton's 5th British Division, consisting of the British 8th and 9th Brigades and the 5th Hanoverian Brigade. The British units were battalions of: 1st Foot (Royal Scots); 28th Foot (Gloucester Regiment); 32nd (Duke of Cornwall's Light Infantry); 42nd Foot (The Black Watch) (Royal Highlanders); 44th Foot (Essex Regiment); 79th (Queen's Own Cameron Highlanders); 92nd (Gordon Highlanders); 95th Rifles (Rifle Brigade).

12. This was Captain JJ Mitchell, 25th Foot.

13. The inn was Le Grand Laboureur.

14. Lady De Lancey may have muddled the days. The Duke of Brunswick was killed at the Battle of Quatre Bras on the afternoon of Friday 16 June and it seems highly unlikely that his body could have reached Antwerp before the following day, at the earliest.

15. Nothing is known about Emma, except that she came from London and was employed as Lady De Lancey's maid.

16. This was Captain R Machell, 2nd Battalion, 30th Foot, who was detached for duty as Town Major in Antwerp (Monthly Returns, Southampton University; WP 9/7/1). Machell was from Beverley, Yorkshire, and may well have known De Lancey when they were both boys in that town in the 1780s.

17. Lady De Lancey was mistaken about the day and in later copies this is amended to the correct day, Friday 16 June.

18. Wellington's headquarters on the night 16/17 June were in the Roi d'Espagne (King of Spain) inn at Genappe.
19. Captain and Lieutenant-Colonel Henry Delancey Barclay of the 1st Foot Guards, served on the Adjutant-General's staff at Waterloo. He was the son of Susan De Lancey and Major Barclay who had settled in Annapolis, Nova Scotia after the American Revolution. He was William De Lancey's second cousin.
20. Lieutenant-Colonel Sir George Scovell, KCB, served in the QMG's department in the Peninsula from 1808 to the end of the campaign and thus knew De Lancey very well. In the Peninsula he commanded the Corps of Guides and was in charge of the postal and communications service until 1813 when he took command of the Staff Corps of Cavalry. In the Waterloo campaign he served as AQMG and in command of the Staff Corps of Cavalry.
21. Lady Jane Hamilton, wife of Sir Hew Dalrymple Hamilton, 4th baronet. When *Lady De Lancey's Narrative* was published in the New York *Century Magazine* the editor mis-identified this lady, illustrating the article with a portrait of Lady Emma Hamilton, Admiral Nelson's paramour.
22. There were four officers named James at Waterloo: Ensign John James, 30th Foot; John Haddy James, assistant-surgeon, 1st Life Guards; Cornet Philip Haughton James, 11th Light Dragoons; and Ensign William James, 3rd Foot Guards. Of these, the only one killed was Ensign John James, 30th Foot, so it must be presumed that this was his brother.
23. Now known as Mechelen, this is a small town approximately half-way (15 miles [25 km]) between Antwerp and Bruxelles.
24. Mr William Hay of Duns Castle had been in the 16th Light Dragoons in the Peninsular War and had come from England a few days before to see his old friends and to introduce his newly commissioned young brother, Cornet Alexander Hay, aged 18, to his old regiment. Mr Hay was on the battlefield during the early part of the battle and early next morning he revisited the field, trying to find some trace of his brother, who had been killed late on the previous evening while the 16th Light Dragoons were in pursuit of the enemy; his body was never found.
25. It has not proved possible to identify this lady.
26. This was almost certainly Lieutenant-General John Mackenzie, who was in command of the British troops in Antwerp.
27. Correctly spelled Vilvoorde, this village is about 5 miles (8 km) north of Bruxelles.
28. Underlined in the original.
29. The fact that '. . . the cottage was surrounded with roads' tends to confirm that the cottage was immediately south of the junction of the Nivelles and Charleroi *chaussées* in the village of Mont St Jean and not in the village of Waterloo itself.
30. Keeping the windows open would have been no hardship for Lady Magdalene who had been trained from childhood by her mother to do so, regardless of the weather.
31. James Powell was a Surgeon in the Ordnance Medical Department, which had three grades: Surgeon, Assistant-Surgeon, and 2nd Assistant Surgeon. Thus, he was a senior and experienced man. Lady De Lancey consistently spells his name as 'Powel'.
32. Doctor John Robert Hume (1781–1857) was a Deputy-Inspector on the Army Medical Staff. He studied at Glasgow and Edinburgh and then went straight into the Army Medical Department and to the Peninsula in (about) 1808. He

became a particular friend of the Duke of Wellington, who appointed him his personal physician. He was the man to whom Wellington said after the battle: 'Well, thank God, I don't know what it is to lose a battle, but certainly nothing can be more painful than to gain one with the loss of so many of one's friends.' On his return to England, Hume had a distinguished civil career and was the surgeon in attendance on Wellington at his duel with the Earl of Winchelsea on 21 March 1829.

33. In other versions of *The Narrative* this reads: '. . . the noise of the carts assisted . . .'.

34. Lady De Lancey consistently refers to this man as 'Woodridge' but his name was actually Woolriche. Stephen Woolriche was a Deputy-Inspector in the Ordnance Medical Department.

35. There were two general officers named Dundas in the British Army in 1815, both full generals in rank. Neither of them appears in 'Waterloo Roll Call' or the 'List of Officers in the Netherlands, 1815' and Lady De Lancey does not identify which one this was. General Sir David Dundas was married to Sir William De Lancey's aunt Charlotte, and thus had a close family tie, but was 80 years old in 1815 and is most unlikely to have been in Belgium. The other was General Francis Dundas, who was somewhat younger and certainly was in Belgium at this time as he subsequently submitted a report on the battle (B.Lib ADD 19,590 f25 'Papers relating to the Battle of Waterloo'). Unfortunately, that report does not mention his involvement with the De Lanceys. The name of the 'Hon General Dundas' is also included on the list of those attending the Duchess of Richmond's Ball. Francis Dundas had not served in the Peninsula and the only place where he and De Lancey are known to have served together is the Cape of Good Hope from August to December 1796, although at that time Dundas was the governor and De Lancey a very junior officer. But, as will become clear, he devoted a considerable amount of time to helping Magdalene.

36. Sir Hew Dalrymple Hamilton, 4th Baronet.

37. The word 'what' is repeated in the original. The second appearance is then crossed through with a pencil line and the word 'would' (also in pencil) added above it.

38. In the original the word 'every' is repeated and the second entry crossed out in pencil.

39. The official Army 'Monthly return' confirms De Lancey's death as 26 June 1815. WP 9/7/1.

40. Probably Lieutenant-Colonel Colquoun Grant, 11th Foot, one of the AQMGs on De Lancey's staff. They had served together in the Peninsula.

41. This was the St Josse Ten Noode Cemetery on the south side of the Chaussée de Louvain, where a number of officers killed at Waterloo were buried. The inscription on the stone erected at Lady Magdalene's request read:

> THIS STONE IS PLACED TO MARK WHERE THE BODY OF
> COL. SIR W. HOWE DE LANCEY,
> QUARTERMASTER-GENERAL,
> IS INTERRED.
> HE WAS WOUNDED AT THE BATTLE OF
> BELLE ALLIANCE (WATERLOO)
> ON THE 18TH JUNE 1815.

42. The bodies of many of the British officers killed at Waterloo were buried in

various cemeteries in the area, some of them being subsequently removed to England by their families. The remainder, including that of Colonel De Lancey, were moved to a new collective grave in the cemetery in Everre, three miles north-east of Bruxelles in 1889. The burial vault is topped by the Waterloo Monument, which consists of a bronze angel looking down over a dying soldier, flanked by a pair of sprawling lions. The vault contains the remains of sixteen British officers and one sergeant-major. Over the entrance to the vault is a brass plate, inscribed:

IN MEMORY
OF THE BRITISH OFFICERS, NON-COMMISSIONED OFFICERS
AND MEN WHO FELL DURING THE WATERLOO CAMPAIGN IN 1815
AND WHOSE REMAINS WERE TRANSFERRED TO THIS CEMETERY IN
1889. THIS MONUMENT IS ERECTED BY HER BRITANNIC MAJESTY
QUEEN VICTORIA EMPRESS OF INDIA AND BY THEIR COUNTRYMEN
ON A SITE GENEROUSLY PRESENTED BY THE CITY OF BRUXELLES.

CHAPTER XI
Magdalene

After her harrowing experiences, Magdalene left Brussels for England on 4 July 1815 and, since she had already written to her parents at Bath, her mother was waiting for her in London. Then, when both were ready, they made their way northwards to Dunglass, where Magdalene was reunited with her father and sisters. News of Magdalene's terrible experience had, however, preceded her and she was given much sympathy in London, Edinburgh and on the Dunglass estate.[1] Sir Walter Scott, joined in the tributes:

> . . . Thou saws't in seas of gore expire
> Redoubted Picton's soul of fire,
> Saws't in the mingled carnage lie
> All that of Ponsonby could die,
> De Lancey change Love's bridal wreath
> For laurels from the hand of Death . . .[2]

Magdalene had practical matters to attend to, including swearing out an administration on her husband's estate on 7 August, being '. . . the lawful widow and relict . . .'[3] The value of that estate cannot now be established, but financial help came from an unexpected quarter, the Waterloo Fund, which had been set up to administer the public subscriptions that flowed in after the Allied victory. In a letter to the Duke of Wellington dated 17 November 1815, Thomas Rowcroft, who administered the fund, gave details of the initial disbursements, which included £1,500 (£66,000) to 'the widow of Colonel De Lancey,' by far the largest sum given to any dependent.[4] Lady Magdalene also became entitled to a colonel's widow's pension from the government of £280 (£10,600) a year.

As mentioned in her 'Narrative', Magdalene had ensured that a stone was erected on her husband's grave before she left the Netherlands, but she now decided that he should be commemorated at Dunglass, as well. The Collegiate church, which stood beside Dunglass House, was ideal and one wing of the building was cleared so that it could be used as a repository for simple plaques commemorating members of the family. Thus, in late 1815 the first plaque was unveiled and it is not difficult to envisage the tears which accompanied the ceremony or the memories which flashed through Magdalene's mind as she read the words:

Sacred
To The Memory of
COLONEL Sir Wm de Lancey
Knight Commander of the Bath
and
Acting Quartermaster-General
at the Battle of WATERLOO
in which he was mortally wounded
on 18th of June 1815.
He died there on the 26th of June
attended by his wife MAGDALENE
Daughter of Sir JAMES HALL, Bart.
His body was laid in the
ground allotted to Protestants
near Brussels

The family rallied round to help assuage Magdalene's grief. On 12 November 1815 Lady Helen wrote to her eldest son, John, that: '. . . Poor Magdalene has gone up [to London] to live in the neighbourhood of her husband's friends, who have shown her great kindness, and your sister Helen keeps her company.' This was followed by another letter on 23 November 1815 in which she reported that:

Magdalene has determined to fix her residence for a time at Chelsea where are most of De Lancey's relations she talked of it as a temporary measure so that it always remained in her own favour to stay longer or shorter as she found it agreeable . . . Basil came home & immediately got an appointment to command the *Lyra*, a sloop accompanying the embassy to China. His acceptance of the post meant that Basil was obliged to leave Dunglass after having been there for only twelve days so Magdalene thought she would like to come up with him & as his ship was at Deptford see more of him by that means than any other. It had been previously arranged that I was to accompany her whenever she came & to stay with her some time, so we all came together. Until she can get some lodgings in Charles St, she has taken some in Smith Street, Chelsea, No 33 we expect to get into it in less than a fortnight.

One of the De Lanceys that Magdalene met in Chelsea was her sister-in-law, Susan Johnstone (née De Lancey), also a widow, her husband having died in 1813 and left her with two daughters, Charlotte (b. 1800) and

Susannah (b.1802). Susan suddenly found herself being courted by Major-General Sir Hudson Lowe, the man who had been displaced by William De Lancey in Brussels in May and who had just returned from the Mediterranean, prior to his departure to take up his appointment as Governor of the island of St Helena and *ex officio* gaoler to the exiled Napoleon Buonaparte. Susan seems to have been a good catch for the somewhat dour major-general and an army doctor, who dined at Government House in St Helena in 1818, has left a surprisingly detailed inventory of Lady Lowe's charms:

> Nobody seems disposed to like Sir Hudson, but we were all delighted with his wife. Lady Lowe was not a good figure, but she had a fine face, laughing eyes, much talking talent, a fair and beautiful neck, and lovely arms. In short she presided at her own table with much grace and brilliancy and was altogether a very captivating woman.[5]

The Lowes were married in December and the new Lady Lowe found herself faced with a difficult problem, since her daughter Charlotte was in poor health and unable to face an arduous voyage, let alone a stay of years on such a remote island. An unexpected solution was, however, found when Magdalene offered to look after her niece, thus providing her with a good home and enabling the newly wed couple to sail with the other daughter, Susannah, to St Helena, as planned.

In May 1816 Magdalene returned with Charlotte to Scotland, where they went to live at Whitehall, near Chirnside, a house inherited by Sir James from her Uncle William. According to her mother, Magdalene '... requires peace & quiet & country air', although she also '... takes pleasure in the thoughts of the easy intercourse with us as neighbours'. Magdalene took the opportunity to consult doctors in Edinburgh about her niece, to be told that 'nothing but judicious care could save her life for three months'. Undeterred, Magdalene gradually coaxed Charlotte back to health and then found herself looking after the '... active, healthy & the happiest little woman that ever breathed so completely obedient & attentive that I have never needed any governess'.[6]

At this time Lady Helen still had four daughters at home, Katherine, Elizabeth, Helen and Frances, and when in late 1816 Helen was found to be terminally ill with what appears to have been tuberculosis, the person who took responsibility for her was, once again, Magdalene.[7] She nursed Helen devotedly in Edinburgh and then took her back to Dunglass, where, after much suffering, she died with Magdalene at her side on 16 March 1817.

Magdalene's oldest brother, John, was in Paris from late 1815 onwards, and he wrote to Magdalene in 1816 suggesting that she might like to join him, but she demurred, explaining in her reply that she and Sir William had often discussed the prospect of foreign travel and that such an undertaking so soon after his death would be 'too fanciful'. In any case, she had first Charlotte and then Helen to look after. Following Helen's death, however, Magdalene decided that travel abroad was just what she and her niece needed and not only did they both go, but, characteristically, Magdalene faced up to the greatest of challenges and made Brussels her first port-of-call, where some personal ghosts were laid to rest. September 1817 found her in Paris, from where she reported to her mother that she was 'highly enjoying' her stay. She was there again the following year, this time with her beloved brother, Basil, as the latter reported when he wrote to Sir Hudson Lowe (now a lieutenant-general) in far-off St Helena:

Paris 26 July 1818

My Dear Sir

I received your letter of the 4th of May only 2 days ago. I was very happy to find that you had at last received my letter about Miss Charlotte Johnstone and that you were satisfied with what had been done. Lady De Lancey who is here is writing to Lady Lowe in reply to her letter of 17 May and Charlotte is also writing. Therefore I need say nothing about things. Except that they are both in excellent health and Charlotte, poor thing, is in great delight at the prospect of seeing you again. Her heart is very much at St Helena and I have been exceedingly pleased to observe the pains which Magdalene has taken to keep Charlotte's affections steadily and almost exclusively towards her parents. I think you will be pleased with Charlotte who has made excellent use of her time and great opportunities. I have no doubt we shall be able to arrange everything about her passage in a satisfactory way and that in a few months you will have her safe and snug in your island . . . [8]

Basil and Magdalene duly despatched Charlotte to St Helena where she joined her mother and step-father in late 1818.[9] Then, her duty to her niece admirably discharged, Magdalene returned with Basil to Scotland, where her life took a sudden and completely unexpected turn.

After Helen's death Magdalene had said that she would never again allow herself to become too close to another human being, as being so involved in the deaths of two people she loved dearly within two years had drained her, both physically and emotionally. But, at some time in late 1818 she fell passionately – very passionately – in love for a second time, the denouement being faithfully chronicled (as always) by the *Gentleman's Magazine*, with the somewhat surprising announcement that a marriage had taken place on 27 March 1819:

Henry Harvey, esq, Madras Army, to the widow of the late Sir Wm De Lancey, KCB, eldest daughter of Sir James Hall, Bart.[10]

Captain Henry Harvey

Henry was not the first romantic in his family, since his father, Doctor Robert Harvey MD, had eloped with a minor, Miss Mary Read of Bradford, Wiltshire, and, having succeeded in evading her parents, they arrived safely in Gretna Green, Scotland, where they were married on 5 May 1777. The newly weds duly returned south, where they remarried in Exeter in December of that year, this time in church, presumably to satisfy the proprieties and Mary having passed her 21st birthday.[11] They had two children, a girl, Elizabeth, and a boy, Henry, the latter being baptised at St Katherine's Chapel in Holt, Wiltshire on 13 July 1783. He was educated in Winchester before going up to Trinity College, Cambridge, although he is not recorded as having been awarded a Bachelor of Arts degree.[12] It appears that he left early as he was gazetted an Ensign in the Madras Army of the Honourable East India Company Army on 8 July 1801. His first unit was the 12th Madras Native Infantry in which he took part in the Second Maratha War (1803–5), including the Battle of Assaye (23 September 1803), where he received a wound that was to trouble him for the remainder of his life. Promotion was slow and he did not reach the rank of captain until 13 July 1811 and then, either because regimental life was beginning to pall or due to his wound, he transferred to the Commissariat, becoming an Assistant Commissary-General.

When Henry's father, Robert, died in 1816 he left small annuities to his widow and daughter, but the bulk of his estate, amounting to several thousand pounds and a house, was bequeathed to his only son, Henry. News of the death took many months to arrive in Madras and the first opportunity to secure a passage home arose when, by chance, the sloop, HMS *Lyra*, Lieutenant Basil Hall, RN, in command, called in, having recently delivered despatches from Lord Amherst to the Governor-General in Calcutta. Harvey found a berth as the personal guest of *Lyra's* amiable captain and they sailed from Madras on 1 June 1817, proceeding via the Ile de France (Mauritius) and enjoying 'a prosperous and pleasant voyage round the Cape of Good Hope' until they arrived at the island of St Helena on 11 August, where Harvey accompanied Basil on his visit to Napoleon. Having achieved his object in St Helena, Basil sailed on to England, although bad weather in the Channel meant that he had to divert to Gantry Bay in Ireland, where arriving on 15 October[13] whence Harvey left to deal with his family business.

Magdalene's Second Marriage

In late 1818 Henry Harvey went to Edinburgh to stay with Basil Hall, where he was introduced to his old shipmate's sister, the widowed Lady Magdalene De Lancey.[14] They appear to have fallen in love at first sight and by December 1818 they were engaged, with the wedding date set for the end of March 1819. But first Henry had to go south to organise his business affairs and arrange a house for his bride. He left Edinburgh on 26 January and his journey took him to London, Bath and Cheltenham, but, wherever he was, he received a constant stream of letters from Magdalene – forty in all – every one of them reflecting a burning passion.[15]

Such passion did not, however, remove the need for hard-headed financial matters and the document upon which their marriage settlement was based still exists, showing them describing their assets in great detail.[16] Henry was worth some £14,000 (£55,000), of which no less than £10,000 (£40,000) was in India, suggesting that, for the doctor's son from Bath, the period spent in the East had not been without profit. Magdalene was equally open about her assets and income, and, although much less well-off than Henry, she considered herself to be very comfortably placed. The outcome was that Harvey and Magdalene were married from Dunglass House on 27 March 1819, the actual ceremony taking place in the church at Oldhamstocks, a hamlet some six miles away.

After their wedding, Henry Harvey did not return to India and formally retired from the Madras Army on half-pay on 28 November 1821, one reason for which must have been to devote more time to his rapidly growing family. Immediately after the wedding they had set out for a 'Grand Tour' and Magdalene gave birth to their first child in Rome on 1 January 1820, a bare nine months after the wedding. She was named Helen, after both her grandmother and her mother's beloved sister, who had died so tragically two years earlier. The next child, Robert, was born on 5 December 1820 in Edinburgh, but then they took up residence in Worcester, where their third child, Frances, was born in March 1822.

It would appear, however, that all was not well, since Magdalene's sisters, Katherine (now Lady Russel) and Frances, came south to be with her during the confinement. Shortly after the birth Henry Harvey took them all to the tiny seaside spa of Salcombe Regis on the south coast, just eight miles from Sidmouth, for the sea air, but this failed to have any effect and on 17 July Frances reported to a friend, that:

> You will not be surprised after the letter I wrote to you some days ago to hear the melancholy news I have now to tell. Poor Magdalene is relieved from her sufferings she expired on Friday the 12th without a struggle. She passed from a heavy sleep to death without waking – she breathed slower & slower by degrees & then no more. She took her leave of her children on Sunday and received the sacrament on Wednesday. Nothing would be more peaceful & easy than her death and we are glad that she had not to linger longer in suffering but oh it is a dreadful stroke when it comes.[17]

Magdalene was buried in the peaceful graveyard of the Salcombe Regis parish church of St Mary and St Peter[18], and Lady Katherine made several watercolours of the graveyard, which she took back to the grieving Lady Helen in Scotland.[19] Katherine may also have been responsible for the unusual note added against the entry in the parish burial register, that Magdalene was: '. . . Wife of Captain Harvey – formerly the widow of Sir William Howe De Lancey Quarter Master General of the Army under the Duke of Wellington.'[20] Magdalene was 28 years old when she died, and had travelled farther and experienced more of life than many of her contemporaries. She was a product of the Scottish Enlightenment: well-educated, intelligent, and, through her parents' wealth, used to virtually all the comforts that contemporary society could provide. Despite this, and probably due to her remarkable mother, she had an inner core of steel and, despite being totally ignorant of military affairs, she held her own with her husband's colleagues in Brussels and overcame the perils of the chaotic conditions immediately following the Battle of Waterloo to find her husband. She then provided him with all the nursing care he needed, neither cavilling at applying leeches nor hesitating to change his soiled bandages. She also coped with his death, helping her husband firmly but tenderly as his life slipped away. Perhaps the most extraordinary act during those ten days came on the last night, when she lay down beside him so that they could sleep together, bringing him greater comfort than is the lot of most men on the verge of death.

She then went through the whole experience of attending the death bed of someone else that she loved with her sister Helen, but her letter describing that episode to her brother John is indicative of her approach to life. The first half of the letter is devoted to a detailed and moving description of Helen's illness and death. Then, the final scene described, she draws a line firmly across the page and the remainder of the letter is happy and cheerful in tone, devoted entirely to the future, and mainly concerns the proposal that she and Charlotte should join John on the Continent; what had happened could not be undone, but life was for living. Similarly, although her love for William De Lancey was something which she clearly treasured, that did not stop her from falling in love a second time and giving herself completely to another man.

Magdalene's 'Narrative' is a lasting memorial to her first husband, which is what she meant it to be, but it is also, quite unintentionally, a remembrance of a lively and high-spirited young woman who was suddenly faced with the brutal realities of the battlefield and of death. Her descriptions of her inner thoughts and doubts, the utterly honest descriptions of her moments of weakness in Antwerp, her dealings with the brutal Prussian officer, her sudden surges of anger at the unfeeling surgeon, and the lying beside her husband on the night before his death provide a unique insight into the mind and behaviour of a young woman. That indomitable spirit did not die with her, however, and was to be passed down through succeeding generations, as will now be seen.

NOTES

1. In fact, the sympathy eventually proved somewhat onerous and three years later Magdalene told a friend in a letter that whenever she entered a room full of people many of the women would stop talking out of a mistaken respect for her bereavement and which she found rather trying.
2. Scott, Sir Walter, 'The Field of Waterloo, A Poem', Stanza XXI.
3. 'On the seventh day Admon of all and singular the Goods Chattels and Credits of Sir William Howe De Lancey late a Colonel in the Army and a Knight Commander of the Bath deceased was Granted to Magdalene De Lancey the lawful Widow and Relict of the said deceased having been first sworn by [?] duly to Admon.' Families Record Centre 'Admons' August 1815.
4. *Supplementary Despatches*, Volume XI, p 239. Rowcroft was, in fact, responding to a suggestion by Wellington that the two generals' widows were well looked after, but that Colonels De Lancey, Ompteda and Du Plat 'must have left their families in great distress; and the Committee would be pleased to have an opportunity of increasing the provision made for them.' [Dispatches, Vol XII, pp 650–651]
5. Staff Surgeon, A (Dr Henry, 66th Foot); *Trifles from my Portfolio, etc . . .* , Vol I, pp 210–11.
6. Letter, Magdalene to her eldest brother, John Hall, dated 16 May 1817.
7. I am indebted to Dr East of Kingskerswell, Devon, for this diagnosis, which is based on reading the available letters.
8. Basil Hall to Sir Hudson Lowe (British Library ADD 45.517 folio 47).
9. The young and vivacious Charlotte, well educated and straight from Paris, appears to have had a devastating effect on the small community in St Helena. In 1820, at the age of 18, she married the Russian Commissioner, who represented the Tsar in supervising Napoleon's imprisonment, Count Aleksandr Antonovich Balmain. Dr Henry, the ever-observant 'Staff Surgeon' described the pair: 'She was young and handsome, and the gentleman neither the one nor the other.' The newly weds then departed for Europe; their subsequent fate is not known, but presumably they went to Russia.
10. *Gentleman's Magazine*, Volume LXXXIX, Part 1, Jun-Jul 1819, p 368.
11. The wedding took place in St Stephen's parish church Exeter on 23 December 1777, where the vicar clearly, if somewhat drily, marked the register: 'The said Parties having been previously married in Scotland during the minority of the said Mary Read.' Devon Record Office, Exeter, St Stephen's MF–1.
12. In *Alumni Cambriensis* Harvey is listed as having been at school 'at Winchester'. The historian of Winchester College can find no student of that name, but states that there were a number of boarding schools in the town at that time and that Harvey might have attended one of those (letter to author).
13. Letter, Hall to Admiralty, Gantry Bay, 15 October 1817. PRO AM 1/1954.
14. Basil was certainly in Edinburgh in early 1819, as he wrote to Sir Hudson Lowe from there on 7 February (BL Add 15729 f 102). It is an unusual coincidence that Basil Hall met both Magdalene's husbands before she did, and brought both back to England from foreign parts: De Lancey from Corunna in 1809 and Harvey from Madras in 1817.
15. These letters still exist, carefully preserved, each annotated, presumably by Henry Harvey, with the date and place of receipt. It is clear from these letters that Harvey was sending a constant stream to Magdalene in Scotland, but unfortunately these have not been kept. Private collection.
16. Manuscript memo signed by Henry Harvey to Lady De Lancey's solicitor,

John Tod, dated January 1819. Private collection.
17. Letter Frances Hall to Catherine Johnston, Hutton Hall, Acton; Dunglass 17 July 1822. Private collection.
18. She lies in grave number 58 on the south side of the church.
19. There is no firm medical evidence as to the cause of death, but, again, Dr East suggests that it was most probably tuberculosis.
20. Devon County Record Office, Exeter: Salome Regis Register MF2. Entry #60.

CHAPTER XII
Magdalene's Descendants

Magdalene had numerous descendants, but it is intended to trace the fortunes of just one particular branch to its end in 1940, for reasons which will become apparent. Following Magdalene's death in 1822, Henry Harvey returned to Worcester where he found himself a widower with three infant children to look after. Two years later he had the most immense – and, it would appear, totally unexpected – stroke of good fortune, when a distant relative, Miss Christiana Balch, died, leaving him a large estate at St Audrie's, on the west Somerset coast, near Bridgwater.[1]

Henry Harvey thus became a member of the 'landed gentry' and when he had the estate valued in 1827 he found that he owned some 2,100 acres, two mansions and several villages, as well as numerous farms and quarries, the whole being valued at £33,966 (£1,500,000) and bringing him an annual income of £1,303 (£6,500).[2] This, coupled with his £10,000 in India, made him a man of considerable substance and he quickly bought himself a house in the capital (12 Devonshire Place, a wealthy area in central London), but he took some interest in his estate and made a number of improvements. He also remarried, his new wife being Agnes Ramsay, who presented him with a third daughter, Mary Elizabeth, in 1827.

As if to offset such good fortune, disaster struck a double blow in 1828. The first came in June, while they were staying with Magdalene's sister, Elizabeth, and her husband, the Reverend George Boileau Pollen, at the rectory in Little Bookham, Surrey,[3] when Henry's and Magdalene's only son Robert died, aged 8.[4] Then, only four months later, Agnes died in Paris while giving birth to her second daughter, Agnes Rosina, leaving Henry a widower for the second time, but now with four young daughters to look after, the eldest of them just 8 years old. He soon married for the third time, his new bride being Emily Duncan Stewart, although there were to be no more children. Meanwhile, country life appears not to have suited Henry and in 1831 he sold most of the St Audrie's estate, gaining £35,000 (£1,800,000) from the deal[5] and took up permanent residence in London, whilst also acquiring a second home in Brighton.[6]

Henry remained in close contact with the Halls. In 1824 he joined Sir James and Basil in becoming founder-members of the Athenaeum, an exclusive gentleman's club in London.[7] As has been seen, Henry stayed with his sister-in-law in 1828 and then, when Lady Helen Hall died in 1837, she remembered him and Magdalene's two daughters with great affection in her Will, bequeathing six engravings to Henry, while Frances, the younger of Magdalene's two daughters, received a pair of brooches. Helen, however, was proudly described as 'my first grandchild' and received more: two engravings, which had been made from her Aunt Katherine's drawings of the churchyard where Magdalene was buried, a brooch and a gold bracelet. The two girls also received a 'Japan-topped work table' each.[8]

Henry continued to prosper and by 1840 the family had moved from Devonshire Place to Streatham, although by his death in 1853 they had returned to central London, with a house in an even more exclusive area, at Number One, Cambridge Square, near Hyde Park, and he died still a wealthy man, his estate being worth some £30,000 (£1,800,000) and his family were well provided for.

Frances married an up-and-coming naval officer, Commander Francis Scott, RN, in 1842, while, of his two daughters by Agnes Ramsay, Mary married an East India Company chaplain, the Rev. John Whiting, and Agnes Rosina married Lieutenant Robert Carmichael-Smyth, 93rd Highlanders, by coincidence the grandson of the Chief Royal Engineer at the Battle of Waterloo who had known De Lancey well. The first of Henry's daughters to wed, however, was Helen, who married an Army officer, Captain John Williams Reynolds, a man whose name was known the length and breadth of the kingdom as the victim of the 'Black Bottle' Affair.

The Reynolds Family

John's father, Lieutenant-General Charles Reynolds (1756–1819), was the son of a London baker who went to India at the age of 14, obtained a commission in the East India Company army in 1774, and became the first Surveyor-General before retiring as a colonel in 1807 and returning to England.[9] At the age of 55 he married Mary Hunter, the 22 year-old eldest daughter of Sir John Hunter, British Consul-General in Spain, and when he died in 1819 Reynolds left his widow with four children, one of whom was John Williams, born in 1817. Henry Harvey was a friend of the much older Charles Reynolds and was appointed John's guardian.

Henry Harvey supervised John Reynolds' education at Eton and then helped him to obtain a commission in a particularly fashionable cavalry regiment, the 11th Light Dragoons, which he joined in Cawnpore, India, in mid–1835. Life in the regiment changed forever on 23 October 1837 when a new commanding officer, Lieutenant-Colonel Lord James Brudenell (1797–1868), arrived. The following year he succeeded his father to become the 7th Earl of Cardigan, inheriting huge estates and an income of some £40,000 (£2 million) a year.

The Black Bottle

The regiment returned to England in 1839, where it was stationed at Canterbury, and quickly became known as 'smart', its reputation being further enhanced when, having escorted Prince Albert on his arrival in England to marry Queen Victoria, it was renamed 11th Prince Albert's Own Hussars. But in May 1840 the regiment's image was tarnished when it became embroiled in a major scandal, with Henry Harvey's ward, Captain John Reynolds, at its centre. The problem started at a formal dinner, when John was asked by a guest for some Moselle, which the waiter neglected to decant, placing the bottle on the table. Cardigan's eagle eye caught sight of the black bottle among the regimental silver and he was so incensed by what he considered to be both a major breach of etiquette and a deliberate flouting of his order, that on the following morning he sent the President of the Mess Committee to deliver a formal rebuke.[10] As rows over such trivial matters tend to do, this quickly escalated into a major controversy, with Reynolds protesting to Cardigan, Cardigan placing Reynolds under arrest, and both of them applying to the Commander-in-Chief for support.

Henry Harvey entered the fray in support of his ward, obtaining interviews with the Adjutant-General and the Commander-in-Chief, and writing letters to all and sundry, including the Prime Minister, the Secretary-at-War and Prince Albert (as colonel of the regiment). He also obtained the support of his old friend and noted author, Captain Basil Hall RN.[11] Up to this point all had been gentlemanly and in private, but when Cardigan court-martialled another officer[12] and fought a duel with a former officer of the regiment, the correspondence was published in *The Globe*, a national newspaper of the day, and then repeated in *The Times* on 17/18 September. Harvey denied responsibility for such a leak[13], although the completeness of the documentation and the detailed description of events in the commentary suggest otherwise. This was a devastating public attack on some pillars of the British Establishment and the fact that Harvey launched it from the haven of the Athenaeum, with the pen his chosen weapon and the letters column of *The Times* his battlefield does not detract from the courage of his campaign.

John Reynolds

The affair eventually simmered down and John Reynolds remained with the 11th Hussars until December 1840, when he applied to attend the staff officers' course at the Senior Department of the Royal Military College, which had moved to Camberley in Surrey since De Lancey's day. His application required the commanding officer's recommendation, which Cardigan refused, whereupon Reynolds applied to the Horse Guards for permission to sell his commission. Alarmed at the thought of further bad publicity, the Military Secretary summoned Captain Basil Hall to a meeting, although why this should have been with Hall rather than Harvey, is not now clear. John Reynolds then went to see the Military Secretary, where, despite being very junior, he sought to impose a number of conditions, including a retraction of the censure, six months' leave, attendance at the Staff College, and a promise that he would never again have to serve under Lord Cardigan. Somewhat surprisingly, he appears to have succeeded with at least the last three of these conditions.

Meanwhile, a happier event took place on 2 January 1841 when John married his guardian's (and Magdalene's) eldest daughter, Helen, in St Leonard's church, Streatham. His bride was four years younger than John and it may be imagined that she had nursed a *tendresse* for the dashing John during their childhood and had entertained a loving anxiety during his absence in India. She would also have been privy to John's problems with Lord Cardigan and to her father's involvement (which she may even have inspired) and now was the time to demonstrate that she stood by him.

Having completed the Staff College course, Reynolds was placed on half-pay, but he was by no means idle, becoming a student and then a researcher at the Chemical Society[14] and contributing significantly to the growing but then little understood science of organic chemistry. He is credited, for example, with the discovery of the hydrocarbon, propylene[15], and his work led to election as a Fellow of the Chemical Society, an honour bestowed on few cavalry officers of the British Army. Then, perhaps due to a feeling that he had been hard done by, the Army brought him back to full pay, promoted him to lieutenant-colonel (he had been promoted major in 1851) and sent him to Jamaica as deputy adjutant-general, where he served from 1856 until the mid–1860s. Promotion to colonel followed in 1861 and in 1866 he undertook his final military posting at Headquarters Northern Command, being promoted to major-general in 1874.

There was, however, a surprising sequel to the 'Black Bottle Affair', when in 1865 Reynolds and Cardigan both happened to attend an 11th Hussars' regimental dinner. The senior officer present was encouraged to persuade the two old antagonists to make up their quarrel, and the pregnant silence as Reynolds approached Cardigan may be imagined. To everyone's astonishment, the two men were so overcome by emotion that they were unable to speak and had just grasped each other by the hand when dinner was announced, whereupon, still holding hands, they led the others to the table and sat down together.[16] The following year John Reynolds was one of the distinguished guests at Cardigan's farewell parade with the 11th Hussars, the regiment that both of them had loved so much, which was off to India. John Reynolds, who was described by a young officer of the 11th Hussars as 'a handsome and particularly courteous old gentleman', died at Koblenz in 1875. His widow, Helen, then moved to the Mediterranean, where she stayed in various hotels until her own death in Naples in 1887.

Magdalene's Grandchildren

As described above, Magdalene's youngest daughter, Frances Harvey, married Commander Francis Scott (1820–75) in 1842. He led an active naval career, eventually reaching the rank of vice-admiral and retiring to his native Cumberland where he became Deputy Lord Lieutenant. They had no children and, following her husband's death, Frances moved to London, where she resided until her death in 1881.

Magdalene's eldest daughter, Helen, and her husband, John Reynolds of the 11th Hussars, had three children: a son, Henry Charles, born in 1841, and two daughters, Edith Magdalene and Katherine Helen, whose second names perpetuated those of their grandmother and great-grandmother, respectively. Henry followed his father, first to Eton[17] and then into the Army, but, perhaps not surprisingly, did not choose his father's old regiment, selecting, instead, the Royal Engineers, into which he was commissioned from the Royal Military Academy, Woolwich in December 1862. He served as an Executive Engineer in various postings in England and India before transferring to the Survey Branch in 1876, possibly influenced by the map-making activities of his grandfather, Lieutenant-General Charles Reynolds. Once back in England, Henry was posted to Bristol where he married Sarah Goodwyn in Clifton on 17 April 1877, the service being conducted by the Bishop of Bristol, which suggests a degree of social status. Sarah's father had served for many years in the Indian Civil Service, where he was a judge in the Madras Supreme Court, and Sarah herself was born in Calicut, so it could well be that they had met in India but decided to marry in England. Henry had one more Army posting, to Belfast, Ireland in 1882, but then retired on health grounds with the brevet rank of lieutenant-colonel in July 1883.

This gave Henry the opportunity to follow in his father's footsteps and take up the serious study of chemistry. He worked in the laboratory of University College, Bristol for five years before moving to Cheltenham in 1889, where he set up his own private laboratory. His particular interest was the study of atomic weights, but his health deteriorated, partly as a result of malaria contracted in the East, and he died in 1899, leaving an estate valued at £49,000 (£3 million).[18]

Helen's two daughters, Edith and Katherine, lived with their Aunt Frances in London from 1875 until her death in 1881. Frances had no children of her own, so she split her fortune between her nephew, Henry, and her two nieces, Edith and Katherine, ensuring in the latter two cases that (shades of Lady Helen Hall!) any future husbands would never be able to get their hands on the money.

Major Douglas Reynolds VC

Henry and Sarah Reynolds had four children and it is Douglas, their third child and second son, who leads us towards the finale of this story. Douglas was born in Clifton, Bristol in 1881 and was educated at Cheltenham College and the Royal Military Academy, Woolwich, from where he was commissioned into the Royal Field Artillery (RFA) in 1899. He volunteered for service in South Africa in the Boer War, but did not reach the front until some four months before the conflict ended. He then went to India and later to Ireland, but when the First World War broke out in August 1914 he immediately went to France with the 37th Howitzer Battery, RFA, part of the 5th Division of II Corps of the British Expeditionary Force (BEF), the body dubbed by Kaiser Wilhelm II as 'The Contemptible Little Army'.

Aged 32, Douglas took part in the advance into Belgium, the Battle of Mons and the subsequent withdrawal, but after three days of trekking back into France, 37 Battery, with the rest of 5th Division, turned on the pursuing Germans and stood at Le Cateau on Wednesday 26 August 1914. Throughout that morning 37 Battery provided direct supporting fire for the infantry, firing against hordes of German infantry on the opposite side of the valley, but enemy fire was also intense and the battery commander was wounded and then captured in the morning, leaving Douglas Reynolds in command. Eventually the enemy pressure became so great that 37 Battery was forced to withdraw, but they had insufficient horses to take the last two howitzers with them. Losing his guns was something no Gunner worth his salt would accept lightly, and in the nearby village of Reumont Reynolds chanced upon two teams of horses and quickly found more than sufficient volunteers to man them. Having obtained permission from the Commander Royal Artillery (CRA) to make an attempt to recover the guns he and his men galloped towards the enemy.

They were under constant fire from German artillery and infantry – the latter no more than 100 yards from the guns – and one of the teams was cut down but the other, comprising Douglas Reynolds and Drivers Job Drain, Godley and Frederick Luke, limbered up their gun. As they set out to return to the British lines Driver Godley was killed, but Reynolds and the other two galloped the gun to safety. The second team was not so fortunate and, when two of the horses were killed and the other injured, they had to abandon the gun. For this action, Captain Reynolds and Drivers Drain and Luke were each awarded the Victoria Cross, while the officer commanding the second team was awarded the Distinguished Service Order.

As if this was not enough, during the Battle of the Marne (September 1914), Reynolds spotted an enemy artillery battery which was holding up the advance and carried out a reconnaissance which brought him within short range of the battery, enabling him to direct the fire which silenced it.

Reynolds was then severely wounded at the Battle of the Aisne (15 September 1914), a piece of shrapnel entering his side and working its way up to his chest, where it remained. He was promoted to major and trained a new battery, taking time off to marry Miss Marie Dolores (Doris) Petersen in March 1915.[19]

Immediately after the wedding, Douglas returned to France to take his new battery into action, where, just before Christmas 1915, he became a victim of a gas attack. He returned to England for the birth of his son, also named Douglas (but always known as Peter) on 26 January 1916, then, despite feeling unwell, he insisted on returning to France. Soon after landing he was taken ill and admitted to Number 1 Red Cross Hospital at Le Touquet, where he died of 'septicaemia from gas poisoning' on 23 February 1916.[20] In *The Story of the Victoria Cross*, a book which is, by definition, full of heroes, the author (himself a holder of the VC) offers a fitting epitaph: 'Surely there can be few examples of more enduring bravery than that displayed by Captain Reynolds.'

Lieutenant Peter Reynolds, Irish Guards
Unfortunately, war had not finished with Magdalene's descendants. Douglas's widow, Doris, remarried in 1919, her new husband being Major John Crocker Bulteel, who had won both the Distinguished Service Order and the Military Cross in the Great War. The family settled in the Bulteel family home in the beautiful Devon village of Holberton and in due course the young Peter went away to boarding school at Eton. There he was very well liked and respected, becoming a fine athlete and captain of his house, and being elected to membership of the exclusive Eton Society (a twenty-strong body, known as 'Pop'). He was also academically successful, gaining entry to Cambridge, where he read law at Magdalene College.

Peter had a serious side as well, and travel on the Continent convinced him of the looming danger of war, as a result of which he volunteered for the Army Supplementary Reserve, being commissioned into the Irish Guards on 16 May 1936. He attended training camps every year until the outbreak of war and was mobilised on 2 September 1939 for service in the regiment's second battalion. His first taste of action came in an ill-fated expedition to the Hook of Holland, where the battalion landed on 12 May 1940 and departed in haste three days later, just ahead of the victorious Germans.

Like De Lancey and the 80th Foot so many years earlier, Peter and his battalion were allowed only the shortest stay in England, re-embarking five days later, this time heading for France to take part in an action whose fame has been overshadowed by that of Dunkirk. The battalion landed in Boulogne at 6.30 am on Wednesday 22 May 1940 and was immediately thrown into the defence of that port, being allocated a sector just beyond the village of Outreau. The guardsmen were in their position by mid-day and, having learned their lesson about the threat from German dive-bombers during their brief stay in the Netherlands, they immediately started to dig-in, which was just as well, since German artillery started shelling them at 3.30 pm.

Peter Reynolds was commanding a rifle platoon in Number 4 Company, but was selected by the commanding officer to carry out a reconnaissance that afternoon, whose aim was to try to find the French forces rumoured to be in the vicinity. The patrol consisted of Peter and three guardsmen in a motorcar accompanied by two motor-cyclists, but they failed to find the French and, having come under German fire on several occasions, they returned with a negative report. Back with his platoon, Peter was subjected to air attacks and artillery shelling throughout the night, with infantry attacks coming in from 10 pm onwards, which hit Number 1 Company, immediately to his left, particularly hard.

It would be an understatement to say that the Irish Guards were in a poor situation, albeit through no fault of their own: they had been rushed into a defensive position in a totally strange area; the position was overlooked by the Germans; they had no mortar, artillery or air support; and they even lacked a proper supply of grenades, mines and barbed wire. To add to their problems, the position was so wide that the commanding officer had no choice but to place all four rifle companies in the line, leaving him with no reserve other than the carrier platoon. Then, to cap it all, communications both within the battalion and from the battalion back to brigade headquarters were by motor-cyclist or runner, since they had been provided with neither radios nor telephone lines.

Peter Reynolds' platoon was sited on a knoll overlooking a reservoir, and from the start had been slightly out on a limb, but when the platoon on its left was over-run during the night, it was left totally isolated. There was no time to put this right, however, since on the morning of Thursday 23 May the platoon was subjected to heavy and sustained attacks from 7 am onwards. The platoon was quickly surrounded by German infantry, which was supported, first, by artillery and later by tanks – both of them military luxuries not available to the British – but still Peter and his guardsmen held them at bay with rifles and light machine-guns. The company commander wanted to tell Peter to withdraw, but was unable to communicate with him, so the young lieutenant, just 24 years old, appears to have taken the decision that, in the absence of orders to the contrary, it was his responsibility to defend the position to the last man and the last round. Such an unequal struggle could not last for long and at about 9 am the position was totally over-run; not one man escaped, the few not killed being captured.

The remnants of 2nd Battalion Irish Guards were forced back into Boulogne that afternoon and re-embarked after dark, the battalion's second withdrawal under fire in the space of ten days and, not surprisingly, it was difficult to sort out what had happened to those who had not returned. One unfortunate result was that Doris Bulteel was officially informed that her son was 'missing' but was then appalled to read an announcement in *The Times* on Saturday 22 June 1940 that he had been killed. Quite where *The Times* had obtained this story is not clear, because it amended its report to 'Missing' on the following Monday morning. That was how it remained for Peter's family for the rest of the war, with their hopes kept alive by intermittent reports of supposed sightings in various prisoner-of-war camps. In 1945, however, it became clear that these reports, although doubtless well-intentioned, were untrue and, to the distress of his family and many friends, it was finally established that Peter had died during the final stages of the German attack on his position at Outreau.[21]

In his last battle, Peter Reynolds showed great courage, proving that he was cast in the same mould as his father, and he is buried in the cemetery at Outreau, the village he died defending. His grave is just twenty miles from his father's at Etaples and both are some 150 miles from Waterloo, where Magdalene nursed the dying De Lancey in 1815.

Magdalene would, naturally, have been infinitely saddened by the tragic deaths of her great-grandson and great-great-grandson, two such promising, popular and respected young men. But, it is not too fanciful to imagine that Magdalene, whose courage, determination and indomitable spirit were beyond all doubt, would have been as proud of them as she was of the two husbands she loved so well.

NOTES

1. The St Audrie's estate was bought by Robert Balch Senior in 1753. When he died in 1779 he passed the estate to his eldest son, Robert Junior, and when he died unmarried in 1799, the estate passed to the second brother, George, the last remaining male member of the Balch family. When he also died unmarried in 1814, Christiana, the only remaining child of Robert Balch Senior then inherited, but when she died in 1823 she, too, was unmarried. Henry Harvey was the only living male descendant of a marriage between a Balch and a Harvey some 150 years previously, making him Christiana Balch's cousin several times removed. Since Henry made no mention of the possibility of such an inheritance in his marriage settlement with Magdalene it is presumed that this must have been unexpected. (Somerset County Record Office DD/AH/40/1; information from the Curator, Admiral Blake Museum, Bridgwater]

2. Henry had the estate surveyed in November 1827. Somerset County Record Office D/Pc/qua.w 3/1/1.

3. Elizabeth married Reverend George Boileau Pollen (1798–1847) in 1824. Boileau Pollen had inherited the Lordship of the Manor from his uncle and was also the rector of the parish church; he remained at Little Bookham until his death in 1847.(*Alumni Oxiensis*)

4. Robert's interment is recorded in the All Saints, Little Bookham Burial Register (Entry No 42, 23 June 1828) and is signed by the rector, Rev GPB Pollen. He lies in Plot Number 178 in the north-west corner of the graveyard in the shade of an ancient yew tree. As was customary at the time, the cause of death was neither given in the register, nor recorded on the headstone; it could have been through either illness or accident. I am indebted to NJ Carr, Esq, Churchwarden, for this information.

5. The new owner was Rev. Elias Webb, and the contract and conveyance are in the Somerset County Record Office (DD/AH/40/1). Harvey did not, however, sell everything at once, retaining the *advowson* (the right to nominate the new vicar) until 1836 and the second mansion for even longer.

6. I am indebted to DPS Stafford Esq., of West Quantoxhead for his help in identifying the link between Henry Harvey and St Audrie's. The house that Henry owned still stands. Rev. Elias Webb sold it in 1836 to Sir Peregrine Fuller-Palmer-Acland; it was a school from 1934 to 1991; and is now a Buddhist retreat centre.

7. All three names appear on the first membership list, published on 22 June 1824. Information kindly supplied by Sarah Dodgson, Librarian, The Athenaeum.

8. The Will, dated 6 May 1837, is now in the Scottish Record Office in the Dunglass Muniments (GD 206/4/23).

9. Despite having retired, he continued to be promoted, becoming a major-general in 1810 and a lieutenant-general in 1814.

10. Cardigan had issued an edict that porter (a form of stout) was not to be drunk in the Officers' Mess and appears to have mistaken the black wine bottle for a similarly coloured bottle of the forbidden porter.

11. Basil's involvement was due only in part to his friendship with Harvey, but he was also John Reynolds' uncle, having married Sir John Hunter's younger daughter, Margaret, in 1825.

12. Captain Richard Reynolds, John's cousin, but the offence was entirely unrelated to the 'Black Bottle Affair'.

13. Letter to *The Times*, 7 October 1840.

14. Later the Royal Society of Chemistry.

15. One acclaimed paper was titled *On Propylene, a New Carbohydrogen of the C_aH_a Series*, published in the *Journal of the Royal Chemistry Society*, 1851, Part III. Propylene (C_3H_6) is now widely used as the basis for substances varying in application from aircraft de-icing to instant coffee.

16. Williams, Godfrey, *The Historical Records of the Eleventh Hussars, Prince Albert's Own*, p 306.

17. Henry attended Eton from summer 1855 to summer 1859, boarding with Mr Vidal. Letter to author from Penelope Hadfield, College Archivist, 30 November 1999.

18. *Journal of the Chemical Society*, Volume 77, 1900, pp 596–7.

19. She was the daughter of a wealthy shipping magnate, William Petersen, a Dane who took British citizenship and was later knighted for his services during the war.

20. Douglas Reynolds' son, Peter, was born on 26 January 1916. Douglas signed his Will in his house at Cherkley Court, Leatherhead, Surrey on 6 February 1916 and died in the military hospital at Le Touquet, France on 23 February 1916.

21. I am indebted to Peter Reynolds' sister, Mrs Mary Birch Reynardson, for her recollections of her brother.

Appendices

The History of
'Lady De Lancey's Narrative'

'Lady De Lancey's Narrative' exists in two versions: the 'Full Narrative', some 15,000 words long, of which nine copies have been identified and seven located; and the 'Abridged Narrative', some 2,800 words in length, of which one copy has been identified, but none located. These copies, all in manuscript, were seen by a limited number of people between 1816 and 1888, when the 'Abridged Narrative' was published in a British magazine; following which the 'Full Narrative' was published twice in 1906: first, in a New York magazine and, secondly, in book form, in London, as will be explained.

THE FULL NARRATIVE

Origins

Two explanations for Lady De Lancey committing her experiences to paper have been given. One comes from a note signed by Lady Katherine Russel, Magdalene's sister, attached to one of the copies, which states that:

> This journal was written some months after the Battle of Waterloo (18th June) where [Sir William De Lancey] was mortally wounded. [Magdalene] had returned to Scotland, & wrote down her narrative for the information of a friend who was residing with her.[1]

The second, in *The Century Magazine*, states that it was '. . . written by her for the information of her brother, Captain Basil Hall, R.N., the noted author . . .'[2] No evidence to confirm or refute either of these explanations has been found.

Magdalene returned to Dunglass in August 1815, went up to London with Basil in November and returned once again to Scotland with her niece, Charlotte Johnstone, in May 1816. She stayed at Chirnside for a short period before taking responsibility for her dying sister, Helen, first in Edinburgh and later at Dunglass. All copies seen by this author are signed 'M De L, 1816' and it therefore appears most likely that she wrote the 'Full Narrative' in mid–1816 at Chirnside.

Lady De Lancey's Volume

A bound manuscript copy of *Lady De Lancey's Narrative* has been found in a trunk owned by Magdalene's great-great-great grandson, together with two portraits of Magdalene as a young woman and some forty letters from her to her second husband. The volume is bound in hard covers, covered in blue velvet with the initials 'M DE L' in gold on the front and consists of 140 pages, of which 102 contain text, the others being blank. The pages are of high quality paper, which is watermarked, but not dated. The writing, entirely in manuscript, uses copperplate script and was clearly written with great care, although there are a few instances of words repeated and one word has been erased and replaced.

The text is headed 'Lady De Lancey's Narrative' (i.e., it does not bear the words 'copy of . . .') and is signed 'M De L' in the same hand as the main text. Since Magdalene would not have used those initials after her second wedding (27 March 1819), it seems a reasonable assumption that she wrote it, that it is her own copy and that it passed to Captain Henry Harvey on her death, following which it was passed down through her descendants.[3] It also seems reasonable to conclude that Lady Magdalene would have regarded this as being the authentic wording.

Copies

Once the existence of *Lady de Lancey's Narrative* became known, Magdalene received numerous requests for copies, some of which she produced herself, while others were made by her sisters; all are headed 'Copy of Lady De Lancey's Narrative at Waterloo 1815'. Two types of copy have been found: the first on grey-coloured paper, measuring 8.5 x 5.5in (21.6 x 14mm), tied together by a leather lace, one of which is watermarked with the date '1817', while others bear a watermark, but no date. A second type of copy is on foolscap-sized (17 x 13.5in [43 x 34cm]) paper; these appear to have been made later, one example consisting of pages with the watermark dates 1840 and 1841, while another is dated 1860.

Nine copies have been identified in the course of research and, for convenience in identification in this book, these have been allocated numbers; such numbers do not, however, necessarily relate to the sequence in which they were produced and there may also be duplication in some cases.

- Copy #1, originally in the Hall family papers at Dunglass, was presented to the Scottish Record Office in 1949 by Lady Sophie Hall.[4] It is held in the 'Dunglass Muniments'.[5]

- Copy #2, also from the Hall family papers, was presented by Lady Sophie Hall to the 7th Duke of Wellington in October 1949; it remains in the possession of the current Duke. It is annotated as having been copied by Magdalene's sister, Frances (1801–29) and has a covering note from Lady Russel to her daughter. The paper is watermarked 'C Willmott 1817'.[6]

- Copy #3 was shown by Magdalene's brother, Basil to Constable, the Edinburgh publisher, in 1819, to Sir Walter Scott in 1824 and to Charles Dickens in 1841. Presumably this was the same copy on each occasion, and it would appear from a letter Hall sent to Dickens in 1841 that he only had the one copy.[7] The present whereabouts of this copy are unknown.

- Copy #4 was made by Basil's wife, Margaret (1799–1876), probably from Copy #3, and probably after their return from North America in 1832. This was inherited by their grand-daughter, Lady Parsons in 1906, and was the copy used by Major Ward in his 1906 book, *A Week at Waterloo*. Its present whereabouts are unknown.

- Copy #5 was found by Major Ward in 1905 in the possession of 'W Arthur Sharpe, Esq of Highgate N'. This had originally been owned by Samuel Rogers (1763–1855), a wealthy man, who wrote numerous books and poems, and accumulated a large collection of books and paintings; he was a friend of Basil Hall, who may have either given or sold him a copy. Rogers' sister Sarah (1796–1851) married her first cousin, Samuel Sharpe (1799–1881) in 1827, and W Arthur Sharpe was one of their grandchildren, so presumably the copy of *Lady De Lancey's Narrative'* seen by Ward had been passed directly or indirectly from Samuel Rogers to his grand-nephew. This copy cannot now be located.

- Copy #6 is a much later document, annotated as having been copied from a copy which had been made by Magdalene's sister, Lady Katherine Russel and bears a copy of the same note as Copy #2. It would appear to have been made at Dunglass, by persons unknown, and is now in the possession of a descendant of the Hall family; it has been seen by this author.

- Copy #7 is the only one listed by the Royal Commission on Historical Manuscripts and is in private (not family) hands; this author has been unable to see it.

- Copies #8 and #9 are held by Lady Magdalene's great-great-great-grandson in the same box as Lady De Lancey's Volume and have been seen by this author. One is of the earlier, smaller size on watermarked but undated paper; the second is foolscap size, watermarked 1840 and 1841.

Wording
There are many small variations in wording and punctuation between different copies of the 'Full Narrative'. In his book, Major Ward remarked on minor differences between Copies #4 and #5, while this author has compared Major Ward's text (Copy #4) word by word with that of Lady De Lancey's Volume and Copy #1, and has noticed many minor differences. Some of these probably result from the drudgery of copying out such a long document, although others may have been due to Lady Magdalene continually searching for just the right word or phrase, a practice familiar to most authors.

Publication
The earliest known attempt to publish 'Lady De Lancey's Narrative' came from the Scottish bookseller, Archibald Constable, as described by his son:

> Shortly after this [16 November 1819] my father received a special token of friendship and confidence, in being permitted to read a narrative that deeply interested all who were privileged to see it, but which, from feelings of delicacy had hitherto been confined within a very narrow circle. This narrative, as had been anticipated, deeply interested my father – so deeply indeed that he proposed at a later period that it should be included in an edition of 'Paul's Letters to His Kinfolk', and, had the decision rested with Captain Hall, permission certainly would have been granted, for he writes, – 'I am equally desirous with you that it should be', but despite this and the following solicitation from Sir Walter Scott it was withheld.[8]

The 'following solicitation' referred to was a letter written by Sir Walter Scott to Captain Hall, not long after Magdalene's death (to whom he refers as 'Mrs Harvey'):

> MY DEAR CAPTAIN HALL,
> . . . Constable proposed a thing to me which was of so much delicacy that I scarce know how to set about it, and thought of leaving it till you and I meet.
> It relates to that most interesting and affecting journal kept by my regretted and amiable friend, Mrs Harvey, during poor De Lancey's illness. He thought with great truth that it would add very great interest as an addition to the letters which I wrote from Paris soon after Waterloo, and certainly I would consider it as one of the most valuable and important documents which could be published as illustrative of the woes of war. But whether this could be done without injury to the feelings of survivors is a question not for me to decide, and indeed I feel unaffected pain in even submitting it to your

friendly ear who I know will put no harsh construction upon my motive which can be no other than such as would do honour to the amiable and lamented authoress. I never read anything which affected my own feelings more strongly or which I am sure would have a deeper interest on those of the public. Still the work is of a domestic nature, and its publication, however honourable to all concerned, might perhaps give pain when God knows I should be sorry any proposal of mine should awaken the distresses which time may have in some degree abated. You are the only person who can judge of this with any certainty or at least who can easily gain the means of ascertaining it, and as Constable seemed to think there was a possibility that after the lapse of so much time it might be regarded as a matter of history and as a record of the amiable character of your accomplished sister, and seemed to suppose there was some probability of such a favour being granted, you will consider me as putting the question on his suggestion. It could be printed as the Journal of a lady during the last illness of a General officer of distinction during her attendance upon his last illness, or something to that purpose. Perhaps it may be my own high admiration of the contents of this heartrending diary which makes me suppose a possibility that after such a lapse of years, the publication may possibly (as that which cannot but do the highest honour to the memory of the amiable authoress) may not be judged altogether inadmissible. You may and will, of course, act in this matter with your natural feeling of consideration, and ascertain whether that which cannot but do honour to the memory of those who are gone can be made public with the sacred regard due to the feelings of survivors. Lady Scott begs to add the pleasure she must have in seeing Mrs Hall and you at Abbotsford and in speedy expectation of that honour I am always,

    dear Sir,
       most truly yours,
        [Walter Scott]
ABBOTSFORD, 13th October 1825[9]

This letter from such a distinguished author (and family friend) spurred Basil into making another effort, as recorded by Thomas Constable:

On December 6th 1825 Captain Hall makes a final allusion to the subject in a letter to my father:– 'I am extremely sorry to tell you, that after using every proper argument with the person chiefly concerned, I have totally failed in obtaining leave to print the Narrative which you were so anxious to obtain, and which I was equally anxious should see the light. I regret much that it is totally out of the question.

> There can be no more done or said on that point, and I have only to assure you that I did all that I could'.[10]

Even as late as 1841, Basil still had publication in mind, as he explained to Charles Dickens:

> I send you the narrative of which I spoke to you, written by my sister, the late Lady De Lancey at Waterloo. I feel certain that the plain truth & singular composition of this melancholy story will not touch you less deeply than your felicitous scenes have touched others. I have only to repeat that I do not wish you to show it beyond your own fireside circle & that you enjoin those who do read it or hear it read not to speak of it – as it has always been the anxious wish of the family to keep it out of sight. In this feeling I do not at all participate – I mean that I should have wished to publish it – but, of course, I must do as others wish.[11]

Basil gives no name, but it must be assumed that it was Henry who refused the permission, since Magdalene had died intestate in 1822 and Henry Harvey had sworn out the administration of her estate. This would have included the right to publication of *Lady De Lancey's Narrative* and whatever Henry's reasons were, they must have been strongly held, since Basil was a most persuasive man.

The full version of *Lady De Lancey's Narrative* was eventually published in 1906.[12] On the death of Frances Emily Christian (1829–1905), one of Basil's three children and Magdalene's niece, her papers passed to her daughter, Margaret Eliza, Lady Parsons (1863–1945), wife of Major-General Sir Charles Parsons (1855–1923), who found the copy of *Lady De Lancey's Narrative* and realised its literary value. At the time Lady Parsons' husband was commanding British troops in Eastern Canada, with his headquarters at Halifax, Nova Scotia, and she happened to mention the document at a dinner party where one of the guests was Major Bernard Rowland Ward, Royal Engineers. Ward had recently had a book published, *Notes on Fortifications with Synoptical Chart* (John Murray, London, 1902), which, one must presume, made him the resident literary expert in military circles in Halifax, and he then cooperated with Lady Parsons in getting the document into print.

Through what appears to have been a mixture of inexperience, misunderstandings and naïveté rather than of low cunning or greed, these two people made something of a hash of things, since the document was published twice in the same year, for which they received two separate payments. It was first offered to *The Century Magazine*, a New York journal, which had no hesitation in accepting it, publishing it in their April 1906 issue, the preamble explaining that:

This manuscript account by Lady De Lancey of her tragic experiences during and immediately after the battle of Waterloo, revealing her devotion as a nurse to her wounded husband, Colonel Sir William Howe De Lancey, was written by her for the information of her brother, Captain Basil Hall, RN, the well-known author, and is here printed from the copy in possession of his grand-daughter, Lady Parsons . . .[13]

This was the first time the full narrative had been published and also included not only the full text of the letters from Sir Walter Scott and Charles Dickens (see below), but also photographs of the letters themselves. For this, Lady Parsons was paid $US750 (approximately £153 [£9,000 at 2000 prices]), of which she gave Major Ward £25 (£1,500).

Meanwhile, in July 1905 Major Ward offered the manuscript to a number of London publishers simultaneously, an action which aroused the ire of at least one of them, John Murray, who wrote to Ward telling him that such an 'auction' was not the way to do business. Despite this, Murray accepted the proposal and Major Ward set to work to write an introduction and to assemble supporting notes and illustrations. This book was duly published in June 1906 by Murray, and is today to be found in a few libraries and is sometimes listed in the bibliographies of books concerning Waterloo or Wellington.

Novel
The story of the De Lanceys formed the basis of an historical novel, *In Love and War*[14] by the Canadian writer, James B Lamb. He took the basic story as recounted in Ward's book, carried out considerable additional research and added conversations to recreate this romantic and ultimately tragic story.

Literary Comment
As to the literary value of *Lady De Lancey's Narrative*, this author leaves it to far more distinguished writers to comment. First, Thomas Moore:

A note early from Lord Lansdowne, to say that Captain Basil Hall, who is at Bowood, wishes much to see me; and that if I cannot come over to-day to either luncheon or dinner, he will call upon me to-morrow. Answered that I would come to dinner to-day . . . Hall gave me before I came away, a journal written by his sister, Lady De Lancey, containing an account of the death of her husband at Waterloo, and her attendance upon him there, they having been but three months married. Walked home; took the narrative to bed with me to read a page or two, but found it so deeply interesting, that I read it until near two o'clock, and finished it; made myself quite miserable and went to sleep, I believe, crying.[15]

And second, Charles Dickens:

DEVONSHIRE TERRACE
Tuesday evening,
16th March 1841.

MY DEAR HALL,

For I see it must be '*juniores priores*' and that I must demolish the ice at a blow. I have not had courage until last night to read Lady De Lancey's narrative, and, but for your letter, I should not have mastered it even then. One glance at it, when through your kindness it first arrived, had impressed me with a foreboding of its terrible truth, and I really have shrunk from it in pure lack of heart.

After working at Barnaby all day, and wandering about the most wretched and distressful streets for a couple of hours in the evening – searching for some pictures I wished to build upon – I went at it, at about ten o'clock. To say that the reading that most astonishing and tremendous account has constituted an epoch in my life – that I shall never forget the lightest word of it – that I cannot throw the impassion aside, and never saw anything so real, so touching, and so actually present before my eyes, is nothing. I am husband and wife, dead man and living woman, Emma and General Dundas, doctor and bedstead – everything and everybody (but the Prussian officer – damn him) all in one. What I have always looked upon as masterpieces of powerful and affecting description, seem as nothing in my eyes. If I live for fifty years, I shall dream of it every now and then, from this hour to the day of my death, with the most frightful reality. The slightest mention of a battle will bring the whole thing before me. I shall never think of the Duke any more, but as he stood in his shirt with the officer in full-dress uniform, or as he dismounted from his horse when the gallant man was struck down.

It is a striking proof of the power of that most extraordinary man Defoe that I seem to recognise in every line of the narrative something of him. Has this occurred to you? The going to Waterloo with that unconsciousness of everything in the road, but the obstacles to getting on – the shutting herself up in her room and determining not to hear – the not going to the door when the knocking came – the finding out by her wild spirits when she heard he was safe, how much she had feared when in doubt and anxiety – the desperate desire to move towards him – the whole description of the cottage, and its condition; and their daily shifts and contrivances; and the lying down beside him in the bed and both falling asleep; and his resolving not to serve any more, but to live quietly thenceforth; and her sorrow when she saw him eating with an appetite so soon before his death; and his death itself – all these are matters of truth, which only that astonishing creature, as I think, could have told in fiction.

Of all the beautiful and tender passages – the thinking every day how happy and blest she was – the decorating him for the dinner – the standing in the balcony at night and seeing the troops melt away through the gate – the rejoining him in the sick bed – I say not a word. They are God's own, and should be sacred. But let me say again, with an earnestness which pen and ink can convey no more than toast and water, in thanking you heartily for the perusal of this paper, that its impression on me can never be told; that the ground she travelled (which I know well) is holy ground to me from this day; and that please Heaven I will tread its every foot this very next summer, to have the softened recollection of this sad story on the very earth where it was acted.

You won't smile at this, I know. When my enthusiasms are awakened by such things they don't wear out.

Have you ever thought within yourself of that part where, having suffered so much by the news of his death, she will not believe he is alive? I should have supposed that unnatural if I had seen it in fiction.

I shall never dismiss the subject from my mind, but with these hasty and very imperfect words I shall dismiss it from my paper, with two additional remarks – firstly, that Kate has been grievously putting me out by sobbing over it, while I have been writing this, and has just retired in an agony of grief; and, secondly, that if a time should ever come when you would not object to letting a friend copy it for himself, I hope you will bear me in your thoughts . . .

. . . I don't know how it is, but I am celebrated either for writing no letters at all or for the briefest specimens of epistolary correspondence in existence, and here I am – in writing to you – on the sixth side! I won't make it a seventh anyway; so with love to all your home circle, and from all mine, I am now and always,

Faithfully yours,

(Signed) CHARLES DICKENS[16]

THE ABRIDGED NARRATIVE

At an unknown date, but presumably between 1816 (when she wrote the full-length version) and 1819 (when she re-married), Magdalene prepared a much shorter version, principally in order to make copying easier, as she explained in the preamble:

Knowing that many of my friends are desirous to have an account of the distressing scenes I have passed through, and finding the subject too painful to be renewed by writing frequently on these scenes, I have determined to form a short narrative which may be given to those who desire the information.[17]

165

This 'Abridged Narrative' is some 2,800 words long, being produced by deleting virtually all matter of a personal nature; the full text is given at Appendix B. There are a number of minor discrepancies between the two versions but none is a matter of any importance. The 'Abridged Narrative' does, however, include some literary touches not present in the original, most notably, the very poignant: 'I stood with my husband at a window of the house, which overlooked a gate of the city, and saw the whole army go out. Regiment after regiment passed through and melted away in the mist of the morning.'

The 'Abridged Narrative' was published in *The Illustrated Naval and Military Magazine* of June 1888, long after everyone involved had died, Mrs De Lancey Lowe[18] explaining in the preamble that:

> While looking over the papers of my late husband Major-General E. W. De Lancey Lowe, I found the following narrative, written, in now faded characters, by his aunt, Lady De Lancey. It recounts the curious and painful experiences of the only woman, with the exception of the maid who accompanied her, who is known to have visited the field of Waterloo immediately after the battle.[19] Its pathos and tenderness are touching in their simplicity, and, though those loving hearts have long since been reunited where war is not, we can still sympathize with the poor young bride (she was only nineteen) who lost her all in the great struggle that gave liberty to Europe . . . So much sympathy was felt for her at the time, that when the rejoicings and illuminations took place, the street in Edinburgh in which she had lived was purposely left in total darkness. – A. L. R. E.[20]

There must have been numerous copies of the 'Abridged Narrative' but none has been found during the research for this book. However, it would only have been about ten pages long and if, like the copies of the 'Full Narrative,' it lacked a cover sheet, it may not have appeared to later owners to be a significant or valuable document.

THE BATHURST PRECIS

A further variation is contained in a small notebook now in the National Army Museum, in the front of which is an inscription to: 'Lady Emily Charlotte Bathurst, the gift of an unworthy friend and cousin, A.D. 1817.'[21] The only contents of this notebook is a précis of *Lady De Lancey's Narrative*, which was clearly taken from the original full version (not the 'Abridged Version') and gives the gist of the story, although with rather greater attention to the earlier events in Brussels and Antwerp than to those which occurred later in Waterloo village, possibly because the copyist's dedication to his or her task declined as the work progressed. It seems possible that this may have been the copy read by the Duke of Wellington and to which he referred in his conversation with Thomas Moore.

NOTES

1. Manuscript note attached to the copy of Lady De Lancey's Narrative in the possession of the Duke of Wellington. (Copy #2). A copy of the same note is attached to Copy #7.
2. 'A Week at Waterloo', The Century Magazine, Vol LXXI, April 1906, No 6, p 821.
3. Major Ward remarked in 1906 (p 24) that '. . . The original manuscript has been lost track of . . .' suggesting that Magdalene's descendants of the time, who were certainly in contact with the publisher, John Murray, either chose not to reveal it to him, or were unaware of its existence.
4. Lady Sophie Hall (d.1952) was the widow of Sir John Hall, 9th Baronet (1865–1928).
5. Scottish Record Office, GD206/4/48.
6. Information supplied by Hon. Georgina Stonor, O St J, archivist to the Duke of Wellington, KG.
7. Letter Hall to Dickens, Portsmouth, 12 March 1841. 'Pray let me have Lady De Lancey's Narrative when you have done with it, as a friend here wishes to see it.' Henry E Huntington Library, Hall letter #58.
8. Thomas Constable, Archibald Constable and his Literary Correspondents, pp 473–4.
9. Letter Sir Walter Scott to Captain Basil Hall RN, reproduced in A Week at Waterloo, RB Ward, pp 121–4. A photograph of this letter appeared in Ward's book; it was thus in existence in 1906, but cannot now be found.
10. Thomas Constable, op cit, p 475
11. Hall to Dickens, Portsmouth, 13 February 1841, Henry E Hartington Library, Hall letter #57.
12. The details of how Lady Parsons and Major Ward handled the publication of Lady De Lancey's Narrative have been reconstructed from original letters in the archives of the publisher John Murray of London.
13. The Century Magazine, Volume LXXI, No 6, April 1906, pp 821–45.
14. In Love and War, James B Lamb, Hutchinson of Canada, 1988.
15. Thomas Moore's diary for 29 August 1824, taken from Memoirs, Journal and Correspondence of Thomas Moore edited by Lord John Russell, Volume IV, p 239.
16. Ward, BR, A Week at Waterloo, John Murray, 1906; pp 124–30. As with the Scott letter (note 9 above) this letter existed in 1906 but cannot now be found.
17. De Lancey, Lady Magdalene, 'Lady De Lancey: A Story of Waterloo,' The Illustrated Naval and Military Magazine, Volume VIII, No 48, June 1841, p 88.
18. Major General Edward De Lancey Lowe (1820–80) was the second son of Sir William Howe De Lancey's sister, Susan (1780–1832) by her second husband, Lieutenant-General Sir Hudson Lowe (1769–1844).
19. This was not correct. There were many soldiers' wives searching for their loved ones and many Belgian peasant women searching for anything of value. In addition, the redoubtable Juana Smith rode across the battlefield on the way to find her husband, Harry Smith.
20. The Illustrated Naval and Military Magazine, June 1888, pp 414–16. Her maiden name was Anne Louise Russell (A.L.R) but the reason for the additional 'E' is not known.
21. National Army Museum (NAM) 6305/122/1.

APPENDIX B
The Abridged Version

Lady De Lancey: A Story of Waterloo[1]

Knowing that many of my friends are desirous to have an account of the distressing scenes I have passed through, and finding the subject too painful to be renewed by writing frequently on these scenes, I have determined to form a short narrative which may be given to those who desire the information.

I was married in March 1815. At that time Sir William De Lancey held an appointment on the staff in Scotland. Peace appeared established, and I had no apprehension of the trials that awaited me. While we were spending the first week of our marriage at Dunglass, the accounts of the return of Bonaparte from Elba arrived, and Sir William was summoned to London, and soon afterward ordered to join the army at Bruxelles as Adjutant-Quartermaster-General.[2] I entreated to accompany him, and my happiness in his society continued to increase with every day. I found him everything my affection had imagined, and the esteem and regard testified towards him by all ranks proved to me that I might confide entirely in the sterling worth of his character and principles.

We withdrew as much as possible from the gaiety then offered us in Bruxelles, where the numerous English families appeared to consider the arrival of the army as the commencement of a series of entertainments. Ten days we passed almost entirely together; Sir William occupied part of the morning with the business of his situation, but was so quick and regular in his method of arranging, that he found time to show me every object of attention at Bruxelles; our evenings were spent in tranquil enjoyment, nothing was known of the advance of the French, and there was no idea of immediate danger.

On Thursday the 15th of June we had spent a particularly happy morning, my dear husband gave me many interesting anecdotes of his former life, and I traced in every one some trait of his amiable and generous mind; never had I felt so perfectly content, so grateful for the blessing of his love. He was to dine at the Spanish Ambassador's; it was the first time he had left me to spend an evening away since our marriage. When the hour approached he was most unwilling to go; I laughed at him, insisting on helping to dress him, put on the ribbons and orders he wore,

169

and at last sent him away; he turned back at the door, and looked at me with a smile of happiness and peace. It was the last!

A short time after a message came from the Duke of Wellington to Sir William. He returned from the dinner and told me that news had been received of the near approach of the French, and that a battle was to be expected immediately, and that he had all the orders and arrangements to write as the army was to leave Bruxelles at daybreak. I entreated to remain in the room with him, promising not to speak. He wrote for several hours without any interruption but the entrance and departure of various messengers who were to take the orders. Every now and then I gave him a cup of green tea, which was the only refreshment he would take, and he rewarded me by a silent look. My feelings during these hours I cannot attempt to describe, but I preserved perfect outward tranquillity.

Sir William told me that when he went to the Duke of Wellington he found him in his shirt, dressing for the Duchess of Richmond's ball, and a Prussian officer stood by him in full dress, to whom he was giving orders in case of an engagement with the French before the main body of the army joined. How many attended the ball that evening, who were stretched on the field of battle so soon after.

The *reveille* was beat all night, and the troops actively prepared for their march. I stood with my husband at a window of the house, which overlooked a gate of the city, and saw the whole army go out. Regiment after regiment passed through and melted away in the mist of the morning. At length my husband was summoned. He had ordered everything ready for my removal to Antwerp, thinking Bruxelles too near the probable field of battle, and he charged me to remain as much as possible alone, to hear no reports nor to move till he sent to me. He endeavoured to cheer me by saying he thought the action would be a decisive one in favour of our troops, and that he should see me in a day or two.

When he had gone I felt stupefied, and had but one wish, to do all that he had desired. I went to Antwerp, and found the hotel there so crowded, that I could only obtain one small room for my maid and myself, and it was at the top of the house. I remained entirely within, and desired my maid not to tell me what she might hear in the hotel respecting the army. On the 18th, however, I could not avoid the conviction that the battle was going on; the anxious faces in the street, the frequent messengers I saw passing by, were sufficient proof that important intelligence was expected, and as I sat at the open window I heard the firing of artillery, like the distant roaring of the sea as I had so often heard it at Dunglass. How the contrast of my former tranquil life there was pressed upon me at that moment!

I felt little fear respecting my husband, as I persuaded myself his post would be near the Duke of Wellington, and less exposed than in the midst of the battle. He was struck by a cannon-ball as he rode by the Duke's side; the ball was a spent one, yet the shock was so violent, that he was thrown a considerable distance, and fell with such a force that he rebounded from the ground again. There was no visible contusion, but the internal injury was too great to be surmounted. He was able to speak in a short time after the fall, and when the Duke of Wellington took his hand and asked how he felt, he begged to be taken from the crowd that he might die in peace, and gave a message to me.

After the battle was concluded, all those whose duty it was to send in returns being killed or wounded, Lady H—, who was at Antwerp, was employed by her husband, General H—, to write the returns as they came in. Knowing I was in Antwerp, she purposely omitted Sir William's name in the list of the wounded, and a friend of Sir William's, seeing the return, came to me to tell me he was safe.

I was delighted and felt that I could not be grateful enough. I was told then that General and Lady H— desired to see me. I ran to meet them with joy, but being struck by the melancholy expression of their countenances, I thought they had probably lost friends, and checked myself.[3] General H— looked at me and turned to the window, and then suddenly left the room. Lady H—, with great kindness, informed me that Sir William was severely wounded. Having been deceived before, my first impression was that he was killed. I refused to believe the contrary, and became almost distracted with grief; and I entreated to be left alone, and locked myself in. I remained some hours, scarcely conscious of anything but the feeling that I should see my dear husband no more.

A messenger came from Bruxelles later to say Sir William was better, that hopes were entertained that he might recover, and to desire me to come to him. Lady H— and my maid came to the door to tell me. It was some time before they could make me understand that they had good news to give; then I admitted them, and my feelings changed to an eager desire to be gone. After taking the refreshments Lady H— insisted upon, I ran up and down to hasten the preparations for my departure, until General Mackenzie, who had come to see me, recalled me to myself by a few calm and kind words. He said my friends were doing all they could, that I should have great calls for exertion when I reached Waterloo, and I ought to spare myself beforehand. I sat down and waited patiently, and thought if I could only see my husband alive, even if it were but for a few hours, I should never repine again.

The journey was dreadful; the roads were filled with waggons, carts, and litters bringing the wounded; with detachments of troops; with crowds of people; it seemed impossible to get on. The people were brutal in the extreme, particularly the Prussian soldiers. I had the greatest difficulty to prevent my servant who was on the box from losing his temper. I spoke to him from the carriage, begging him not to return the abusive language they gave us, and to remember we were unable to oblige them to let us pass. Once a Prussian rode up to the carriage with his sword drawn and refused to let it proceed, and even cut at the servant's legs. I had kept the blinds down, but I then drew them up, and implored him with my gestures to let us go on. He drew back, and the look of pity on his before fierce countenance proved what effect the appearance of real distress will have on even the most hardened.

We were a night and two days on the road.[4] General H— had put a bottle of wine and a loaf into the carriage, and upon a few mouthfuls of these we were supported. The horses could never move beyond a foot-pace, and we were often detained for a long time in the same spot. When we came to the field of battle, which we were obliged to cross, the sight of the dead terrified the horses so much, that it was with great difficulty they were forced on, and frequently they *screamed* with fright; the sound was a most piercing one, and such as I can never forget.

The hovel where Sir William lay was on the further side of Waterloo, near the high road. When I got to the door, the officer, who had rode by the side of my carriage across the field, went in and told Sir William I was there. I heard his voice, clear as usual, say: "Let her come in directly," and the sound nearly overpowered me. I found him unable to move, or even to turn his head, and suffering at times great pain; but he was perfectly collected and cheerful, and he expressed the greatest comfort at my presence.

Nothing could be more wretched than the hovel, it had been plundered and set on fire by the French, and was destitute of everything. The surgical attendance was the very best, and nothing could exceed the kindness of all towards us. It was scarcely possible to procure food or necessaries, but all that could be found was brought to us. My maid proved an excellent nurse, and prepared everything that Sir William ate, but he could take but little. The cottage had two rooms, in one of which we cooked his food, and I had the inexpressible comfort of knowing that he had all that he wished for.

I passed the greatest part of the ten days his life lasted sitting by him and holding his hand; he could not speak much, but all he said was kind, soothing, and perfectly resigned. He often desired me to go and lie down in the other room; but if I returned in a few moments he forgot to send me away again. I fear he concealed his sufferings out of consideration for me, for sometimes, when I was out of his sight, I heard him groan deeply. The road, which was immediately near the cottage, was the only one by which all the waggons passed; but he did not appear to mind the noise. I think I slept but once during the ten days, and that was when he had fallen into a doze, and I leaned my head on his pillow; when I awoke he was looking at me and said it had done him good to see me sleep.

The first night I was there an officer, hearing I had no blanket, sent me one, and this was of the greatest use to us in fomenting Sir William's limbs and chest, it relieved the pain; having torn the blanket into pieces, as well as my own petticoat and my maid's, we were able to continue the fomentations for a considerable time. The surgeons were sometimes so exhausted, that when they came in the evening, they were nearly fainting and unable to speak. I applied the leeches, dressed the blisters, which had been ordered on his breast, and he often said I did it more gently than the surgeons.

One day we had an alarm that the French were returning; I prepared myself for it, and only prayed that I might die with my husband. Sir William noticed every little circumstance which occurred, and was amused at the ingenuity which I exerted to procure him comforts. An officer, who called to inquire after him, left a card which was directly made into a spoon to feed him. At one time he really appeared better, and said he thought he might recover, and that then it would be the happiest event of his life, for no one could expect him to continue in the army after such an injury as this, and he might retire and live with me.

Two days before the last, as no hope of saving his life remained, I was told that he could not live more than a very short time as water had formed on his chest. I thought it my duty to tell him; he bore it with the greatest firmness, and resignation to the will of God; but said that it was almost sudden to him as he had felt so much easier for several hours. He said many things at intervals to me respecting my return to England, and the comfort I should have in thinking over the time I had passed with him, and he prayed with me and for me.

I can scarcely recall the circumstances of the last twenty-four hours. He suffered much at times from oppression of the breath, and the advances of death, though slow, were very visible. He sunk into a lethargy and expired without a struggle. Two of the medical men were in the next room during the last day, and General D— was waiting in a house near; but they did not interrupt us.[5] When all was over, and I saw my dear husband lying dead, so calm and with such a peaceful expression on his countenance, I felt what a blessed change he had made from this world of trouble and suffering.

General D— took me with him to Bruxelles. Sir William was buried near Bruxelles, in the same place with many other officers. I wished to have attended, but was advised not to do so. I received the greatest kindness from many whose names I did not know before.

As I sat alone on the day of the funeral, reflecting on what had passed, I remembered it was three months that very day since my wedding.

NOTES

1. This text is as given in *The Illustrated Naval and Military Magazine*, No 48, Volume VIII, June 1888, pp 414–16. This author has been unable to find a manuscript copy of the original.
2. His post was Quartermaster-General and there was no such appointment as 'Adjutant-Quartermaster-General'. This error may have appeared in the original through an ignorance of the military niceties or may have been introduced when making copies.
3. This differs from the 'Full Narrative' in which the people she meets are 'Lady H— and Mr James.'
4. In the 'Full Narrative' the journey was completed in one day.
5. General D— was General Francis Dundas.

THE MILITARY SERVICE OF
COLONEL SIR WILLIAM HOWE DE LANCEY KCB

Dates	Event	Rank	Place	Unit	Remarks
7 Jul 1792	Commissioned	Cornet	England	16th Light Dragoons	
26 Feb 1793	Promoted	Lieutenant			
25 Mar 1794	Purchased command of Independent Company			Independent Company	
Oct 1794	Joined first unit		Netherlands	80th (Staffordshire) Foot	British campaign in the Netherlands
Apr 1795	Returned to England		England		Unit recovering and recruiting
Jul - Aug 1795	Embarked for the coast of France		France		Quiberon expedition. Returned after three weeks at sea
Aug 1795 - Jan 1796	Operations on French coast				La Vendée expedition
12 Apr 1796	Sailed to the Cape of Good Hope		Cape of Good Hope		Four months in Cape. Took part in Saldanha Bay operation
20 Oct 1796	Promoted	Captain		17th Light Dragoons	Uncle was colonel of the regiment
Dec 1796	Sailed from Cape to India				

Dates	Event	Rank	Place	Unit	Remarks
Early 1797	Arrived at Madras; thence to Trincomallee, Ceylon		India/Ceylon		British had taken Ceylon from Dutch in 1796
1797	Appointed ADC to Maj-Gen St Leger				St Leger was Col of 17th Lt Dragoons
1797	Expedition against the Manila islands		India/Malay peninsula; reached Penang		Abortive expedition against Spanish possessions in the Philippines.
Jan 1798	Returned to Calcutta		India		
Late 1798 ?	Sailed to England	Captain		17th Light Dragoons	
Sept 1799	Joined Regiment at Canterbury		England		
17 October 1799	Promoted to Major	Major		45th (Nottinghamshire) Foot	Regiment in West Indies; allowed to stay in England
1801	Entered the Senior Division at High Wycombe; joined regiment during vacation				Student #53 on Staff College roll
Nov 1801 - Jan 1802	Served with 45th Foot during vacation				
Summer 1802	Employed on a survey of the coast from Rye to Sandwich				Staff College training

Dates	Event	Rank	Place	Unit	Remarks
Nov 1802 - Jan 1803	During the vacation of 1802 went to France		France		Short peace from 27 Mar 02 to 16 May 03
26 May 1803	Appointed 'Extra Permanent Adjutant in QMG's Department'			QMG's Department	Major in Army, major in QMG dept. One of first professional staff officers
1803	Posted to Yorkshire District		England		
1 Jan 1805	Promoted Lt Col in Army	Lt Col (Army)			Remained major in QMG dept
Mar 1806	Posted to HQ in Ireland as AQMG		Ireland		His superior was Col Murray
1807	Promoted	Lt Col (QMG Dept)	Ireland		
April 1808	With Lt Gen Sir John Moore to Sweden		Sweden		Lt Gen Hope's division. Murray was QMG
July 1808	With Moore to Portugal		Portugal		Lt Gen Hope's division
16 Jan 1809	Departed Corunna			QMG's Department	One of last to embark. Aboard HMS *Endymion*
Mar 1809	Embarked at Cove of Cork	Lt Col (QMG Dept)	Ireland		

Dates	Event	Rank	Place	Unit	Remarks
Apr 1809	Appointed DQMG to Army under Lt Gen Sir A Wellesley		Peninsula		Wellington's HQ. Chief was Col Murray
Dec 1811	Acting QMG				Wellington's HQ. On posting of Murray
Aug 1812	Reverted to DQMG				Wellington's HQ. On arrival of Gordon
Dec 1812	Acting QMG				Wellington's HQ. On departure of Gordon
4 Jan 1813	Promoted	Colonel			
17 Mar 1813	Reverted to DQMG				Wellington's HQ. On Murray's return
1813	DQMG with Left Wing of the Army				Under Lt Gen Hill, then Lt Gen Hope
Jul/Aug 1814	Departed Peninsula				Still in France in Jul 1814
Late 1814	To Army HQ in North Britain		Edinburgh, Scotland	QMG's Department	In post late Nov
Apr 1815	To Wellington's headquarters in Brussels		Netherlands	QMG's Department	Arrived late May
18 Jun 1815	Wounded				Waterloo
28 Jun 1815	Died				Mont St Jean

BATTLES IN WHICH COLONEL DE LANCEY TOOK PART

Date	Battle	Country	Appointment	Remarks
31 Dec 1794	Thuyle	Netherlands	80th Foot	Classified as an 'affair'
16 Jan 1809	Lugo, the Battle of Corunna	Spain	QMG staff officer	Classified as an 'affair'
12 May 1809	Passage of the Douro	Portugal	DQMG	
27-28 Jul 1809	Talavera	Spain	DQMG	
27 Sep 1810	Busaco	Portugal	DQMG	
5 May 1811	Fuentes de Oñoro	Portugal	DQMG	
6 Apr 1812	Badajoz	Spain	Acting QMG	
22 Jul 1812	Salamanca	Spain	Acting QMG	
21 Jun 1813	Vittoria	Spain	DQMG	
25 Jul - 31 Aug 1813	San Sebastian	Spain	DQMG with Lt Gen Hill's corps	Negotiated terms with French commander
10 Nov 1813	Passage of the Nive	France	DQMG	
16 Jun 1815	Quatre Bras	Netherlands	QMG	
18 Jun 1815	Waterloo	Netherlands	QMG	Wounded at about 3pm

Sources:
1. 1794-1809. De Lancey Record of Service as completed by him at Headquarters Badajoz, 8 October 1809. PRO WO 25/745
2. 1809-1815. Reconstructed from Army List (various years) 1809-1815; Peninsula Medal List, Wellington's *Dispatches*, etc.

MAJOR WILLIAM HOWE DE LANCEY:
RECORD AT ROYAL MILITARY COLLEGE, HIGH WYCOMBE

1. **Number.** 53
2. **Name.** Wm H De Lancey
3. **Rank.** Major
4. **Regt.** 45th Regt
5. **When started on studies.** 23 May 1801
6. **State of knowledge on entering**:
   a. **French.** 3
   b. **Maths.** 1
   c. **Drawing.** 1
7. **Period of entering on each class**:
   a. **First.** 1801. May 23
   b. **Second.** 1801. Jun 30
   c. **Third.** 1801. Jul 30
   d. **Fourth.** 1801. Oct 17
   e. **Fifth.** 1802. May 23
8. **State of Improvement on Quitting the Establishment.**
   a. **French.** Competent
   b. **Maths.** 5
   c. **Drawing.** Competent
   d. **German.** 2
   e. **General Jarry's Instructions.** 1
9. **Period of leaving the Establishment.** 14 Sep 1802.
10. **References.** Assistant Quarter Master General; killed at Waterloo.

SOURCE:

Royal Military College: Register of the Officers of the First Department. Entry # 53.. Bold headings are verbatim as in original ledger. Held at the former Army Staff College, Camberley.

APPENDIX D
The De Lancey Controversies

Two issues concerning the Battle of Waterloo bear De Lancey's name and impinge upon his military reputation. The first is the whereabouts of a group of documents, the 'De Lancey Papers', the second a particular item known as the 'De Lancey Memorandum'.

I. THE DE LANCEY PAPERS

The papers of the QMG's Department, covering the period 15–18 June 1815, have never been found, a circumstance which some historians regard with suspicion, their views ranging from 'carelessness' to accusations of a deliberate cover-up intended to conceal incompetence or duplicity, or both. Others regard this as an unavoidable, albeit regrettable, outcome of the confusion of battle and the destruction inevitably associated with it.

These papers might answer some unresolved questions, including what intelligence Wellington received on 15 June and at what time, and, secondly, the time and content of instructions issued by the headquarters between 15 and 18 June. De Lancey's name is involved because he was the head of department during the period concerned, but also because of two contradictory remarks made by Lieutenant-Colonel Gurwood (1790–1845), editor of the first edition (1838) of *Wellington's Dispatches.* In Volume XII of that work Gurwood states that: 'The original instructions issued to Colonel De Lancey were lost with that officer's papers . . .'[1], and there the matter might have rested had he not, in the same year, sent a letter to Captain William Siborne[2] stating that: '. . . the orders of movement &c, from the registers of the QMG's dept, which of course were never mislaid, even at the unfortunate moment of Col De Lancey's death. I should think Col Freeth might give you some hint where these are to be found . . .'[3]

The Army Headquarters at Waterloo

Wellington's field headquarters consisted of a large number of officers, clerks and orderlies[4] whose administration (i.e., moves, quarters, baggage, etc.) was the responsibility of the headquarters commandant, Colonel Sir Colin Campbell, assisted by the supervising officer, Major Dawson Kelly, who was graded an Assistant Quartermaster General.[5] The headquarters comprised two elements: the field headquarters, which accompanied Wellington; and a rear element which followed the army in waggons and met the field element at nightfall, whenever possible. Although some details remain obscure, the operation of the headquarters was sophisticated, with movement and the issuing of orders being well-polished drills. Wherever feasible, use was made of modern technology, one example being the mobile printing press, which was mounted in three purpose-built carts supplied by the Royal Waggon Train (a corps directly controlled by the QMG Department) and operated by a sergeant.[6] Indeed, this was so important that the press and its operator were among the first reinforcements summoned from England when setting up the new headquarters in Brussels in April 1815.[7]

The field element was a large body, which included Wellington, his Military Secretary and aides-de-camp, the officers of the Quartermaster-General's and Adjutant-General's departments, the commanders of the specialist arms (Commander Royal Horse Artillery and Commander Royal Engineers), and a number of orderlies and, possibly, clerks. In addition, there were a number of foreign officers attached, plus their aides-de-camp. This formed a large and colourful body, probably some forty to fifty strong, although a number would always have been away obtaining information or delivering messages. The body was usually divided into two groups, one very small, consisting of Wellington and his immediate staff (Military Secretary, QMG and a very few ADCs), with the remainder a short distance (probably several hundred yards) to the rear.

Wellington was almost always within the range of the enemy artillery and headquarters' losses at the Battle of Waterloo were considerable, with three senior officers seriously wounded while within a few feet of the commander: De Lancey (about 3pm), Somerset (about 5pm) and Uxbridge (about 7pm). Two of Wellington's ADCs (Canning and Gordon) and one AG staff officer (Curzon) were killed during the battle, and fifteen officers of the AG and QMG staff wounded. Lieutenant-Colonel Sir Augustus Frazer, the Commander Royal Horse Artillery, who was close to Wellington for most of the day, had one horse shot in the neck and killed, while his second horse rolled over him after being hit by a case shot. Losses among the clerks and orderlies are more difficult to establish, but Frazer records that the orderly carrying Wellington's documents box was killed, while his own orderly had a horse killed under him.[8]

By the end of the day, the situation within the headquarters was very disorganised, with the three principal staff officers, the Adjutant-General, the Quartermaster-General and the Military Secretary, all seriously wounded, and matters were not helped by the sudden departure of Major Kelly. Dawson Kelly's regiment, 73rd Highlanders, suffered appalling losses in the course of the day, and by late afternoon all officers still alive were seriously wounded and only fifty men out of an original six hundred remained unwounded. At this point a sergeant was despatched to the HQ to explain the position to Kelly, and for him there was no question as to where his duty lay – he departed immediately to take command of his battered regiment.

Nor were matters for the rear headquarters any better, with conditions in and around the Forêt de Soignes equally chaotic, and the vast military traffic, including the army's baggage train, ammunition supplies and reserves, swollen by hordes of deserters and refugees. There are repeated reports of traffic jams, and of carts, carriages and horses being forced off the road, stolen or simply destroyed in the crush.

Office Procedures
Although documents still exist describing some of the duties of the QMG staff, there are none covering office procedures themselves, i.e., the minutiae of work within the headquarters in battle. Obviously, when all concerned were inside a building there were both time and resources for clerical procedures to be followed, with support available from other officers and orderlies, particularly for the vital but time-consuming activity of copying documents. Once deployed, however, facilities were spartan, with commanders and staff officers spending virtually all day on horseback, where the facilities for carrying 'writing tackle' were strictly limited, making writing difficult, particularly at night or in the rain. This is not to say that written documents were not produced; Wellington is known to have produced a number of letters and Frazer wrote a letter to his wife on the morning of the battle: the first part (some 400 words) at 3 am and the second (a further 200) at 9 am.[9] These were, however, written in moments of relative tranquillity, possibly under cover, and certainly not at the height of battle. Some officers were less well prepared and Lieutenant-Colonel Scovell relates how he was returning to Waterloo village on the afternoon of 18 June when he observed a Hanoverian cavalry regiment withdrawing from the battlefield. Having failed to halt them he decided that a written instruction was required, but, despite being an experienced staff officer, he had nothing to write with and had to go to the Waterloo Inn, where he borrowed the necessary items from Colonel Cathcart (AQMG with the Cavalry).[10]

Staff departments retained a copy of outgoing correspondence, which was eventually filed in a document known as a 'Letter Book', and those seen by this author are virtually identical in appearance and size, consisting of up to 500 pages, bound in heavy leather covers, the whole measuring 17 inches long by 11 inches wide and 2½ inches deep (43 x 28 x 6 cm), and weighing no less than 10¼ lb (4.65 kg).[11] Such a heavy, bulky document could never have been carried on a battlefield; it might just possibly have been carried in a saddle-bag, but never in a jacket pocket. Further, even if such a book had been carried, it would seem that using it to enter copies would have been very difficult, partly due to the inconvenience of holding such a document on horseback and writing in it (which would have required a quill pen and an ink-pot), but also because of the simple shortage of time and the pressure of events.

Lieutenant-Colonel Sir Charles Vere Broke, a senior AQMG under De Lancey's department, took over after De Lancey was wounded and documents issued by him during the advance to Paris are all loose sheets, suggesting that the custom might have been to take loose sheets into battle, using some for the outgoing messages and others for the duplicate copies, and to collate the latter and bind them as and when the opportunity arose. Wellington's letter book registers were compiled at the end of each month in alphabetical and chronological order and it seems reasonable to suggest that the QMG's documents were treated similarly.

De Lancey's Involvement
A post-mortem examination carried out very shortly after De Lancey's death by Wellington's personal surgeon, Dr John Hume of the Army Medical Department, recorded that 'eight ribs were forced from the spine, one totally broken to pieces, and part of it in the lungs.'[12] The pain from such a massive injury must have been immense – scarcely imaginable to someone who has not experienced it – and it is not surprising that De Lancey was convinced that he was about to die. He was then carried to the rear in a blanket, which must have added to the agony, spent the night on his own and was then moved to the cottage, where, as Lady Magdalene testifies, he was in continuous pain. Like his fellow officers who suffered amputation without a murmur, De Lancey preserved a stoic demeanour throughout, but in such circumstances, it is entirely understandable that he showed little interest in the fate of any papers.

There is, however, another explanation for this apparent lack of concern about the papers; that the matter had already been resolved. We know that someone (his name is unrecorded) retrieved the Royal Engineers' map from the breast pocket of De Lancey's jacket. The sequence of events is described on the copy of the map in the Raglan Papers in the Gwent County Record Office, where a long manuscript note, signed by Lieutenant-Colonel Carmichael Smyth on 31 January 1845, states that the original map:

> . . . was on the person of Sir William De Lancey when that officer was killed; it was recovered for Lieutenant-Colonel Carmichael Smyth by Brigade-Major Oldfield from Lieutenant-Colonel Sir Charles V Broke, Deputy Quartermaster-General, at Cateau Cambrances on the advance upon Paris in June 1815 . . .[13]

Broke handed the map to Oldfield because it belonged to the Royal Engineers, but he would have had no reason to hand over any other documents, since they had nothing to do with that corps. The reason that there is no other report about removing the map (or any other documents) from the wounded De Lancey could well be that this was considered such a routine task that it was simply not worth mentioning.

Anyone who has attempted it will know that carrying a wounded man across rough ground in a stretcher is a particularly strenuous task and when the conveyance was a blanket and the ground littered with bodies, it must have been physically very demanding. Thus, it is highly unlikely that the four soldiers who carried De Lancey to the rear would have included any documents or other heavy impedimenta to add to their load. Even if they did and the documents were still with De Lancey in the cottage, it seems improbable that Scovell, who was with him when Lady Magdalene arrived, would not have taken them with him when he left.

Where Else Might The Documents Have Been?
Some of De Lancey's documents may have been on his horse rather than in a pocket or sabretache. None of the eyewitness reports of De Lancey being wounded make any mention of the horse also being hit and the animal would almost certainly have been purloined by one of the many officers and cavalrymen whose own horses had been wounded or killed. Confirmation that such riderless horses were commandeered can be found in several General Orders issued in July, demanding the return of such horses to their rightful owners.[14]

It is, however, probable that anything required at short notice would have been carried by an orderly, also on horseback,[15] while any bulky documents, particularly those more than a few days old, would have been carried in an office waggon, which was never on the battlefield, but may have been swept up in the mayhem that transpired on the lines of communication.

De Lancey's papers were by no means the only ones to be lost, as Lieutenant-Colonel Sir Augustus Frazer, an eyewitness to these events, describes:

> ... Talking of books and papers, the Duke's red box containing his papers was lost in the field. The orderly who carried it was killed, which I well recollect, my own orderly's horse having been killed at about the same time. Poor Canning [a senior ADC] then took the box, but he being also killed his horse galloped off and was lost in the mêlée; and neither horse nor box has been found since.[16]

Nor was this the first occasion upon which some of Wellington's papers had been lost, since his Peninsular papers were sent back to England aboard a ship which sank in the River Tagus. Many documents were saved, but some, including those covering from December 1810 to mid-1811 were never recovered.

Colonel Freeth

In his letter quoted above, Gurwood told Siborne that Colonel Freeth '... might give you some hint where these [papers] are to be found ...' The only officer of that name in that year's (1838) Army List was Lieutenant-Colonel James Freeth, Royal Staff Corps, who was at that time Assistant Quartermaster-General at the Horse Guards under the Quartermaster-General, Lieutenant-General Sir James Willoughby Gordon.[17] If there were, indeed, papers from the QMG's department at Waterloo hidden away, then the deputy at the QMG's office at Whitehall seems a likely person to have known where they were. Few documents written by that officer have been found, however, and none with any bearing on De Lancey or Waterloo.

If those documents did, indeed, exist in 1838 then it is not totally impossible that they still exist today and it is indisputable that documents concerning Waterloo are still being found, the original of 'Lady De Lancey's Narrative' being a case in point. The Waterloo documents might be in some official repository, where they are either badly catalogued or their significance unrecognised, or in a private collection, where the present owner is either unaware of them, shuns publicity, or wishes to avoid being pestered by researchers.

Conclusions

In the absence of hard evidence, the fate of the QMG's documents can only be a matter for conjecture. However:

- It is odd that Gurwood should have chosen to tell Siborne, a junior and unknown officer, that the documents still existed in 1838 and, as far as is known, he never told anyone else. Assuming, however, that he was correct and that Lieutenant-Colonel Freeth was a party to the secret, not the slightest indication has been found suggesting where the documents might be today.

- De Lancey would have had the minimum of documents actually with him at the time he was wounded and it is probable that all those were passed to Lieutenant Colonel Broke, together with the Waterloo Map. Broke returned the map to the Royal Engineers during the advance to Paris, but would have had no reason to give them any other documents.

- From the time that De Lancey was wounded (about 3 pm) to the end of the day, there was a non-stop sequence of dramatic events, with the headquarters under constant threat. Thus, if De Lancey's papers were not taken over by Broke, they may simply have been lost or destroyed, as was the case with Wellington's documents.

- Whatever may have been the fate of the 'missing' papers, there is no justification in the suggestion that the fatally wounded De Lancey was responsible, either by commission or default, for their disappearance.

II : THE 'DE LANCEY MEMORANDUM'

At some time following publication of the first edition of *Wellington's Dispatches*, the editor, Gurwood, met Colonel Sir De Lacy Evans (1787–1870), who had just returned from two years in Spain. Evans handed over a number of documents, as explained in a footnote to the 1852 edition of *Dispatches*:

> The original instructions of the 15th, 16th and 17th June, in the handwriting of the Duke of Wellington, for Colonel De Lancey, D.Q.M.G., were lost, with the papers of that officer after his death. Original copies, however, preserved by Col Sir De Lacy Evans, who was with Col De Lancey when they were issued and despatched to the different corps of the army, have been handed by Sir De Lacy Evans to the compiler. The memorandum of movements detailed by the D.Q.M.G. to the officers in command of corps and divisions have been compared, and are in conformity with the instructions contained in the original copies.[18]

Among these papers was one totally new document, headed 'Disposition of the British Army at 7 o'clock a.m. 16th June,' (see page 189) and to clarify its meaning Evans added a footnote, which he signed (see page 190). This 'De Lancey Memorandum' also appeared in the *Supplementary Despatches* published in 1863, which included De Lacy Evans' footnote, but not that written by the 1852 editor.[19]

The controversy caused by this document continues to this day and among the allegations are that it contains factual errors, that it is a poor piece of staff work, even that it is a forgery. Unless some undiscovered documents come to light, however, a definitive explanation cannot be given, but comments on its purpose and content can be offered, although since this book is about the De Lanceys and not military operations it is not proposed to consider its tactical implications.

Maps

In 1815 maps were in short supply, and even those that did exist were usually inaccurate and incomplete. Lieutenant-Colonel Frazer, for example, remarked in a letter dated 16 June that he had '. . . just learned that the Duke moves in half an hour. Wood thinks to Waterloo, which we cannot find on the map: this is the old story over again.'[20] Those few maps that were available were so valuable that it was not the custom (so far as is known) for them to be marked to show locations and unit moves, as would be done on any modern battlefield, and the map which De Lancey used to plan the new position at Waterloo (and which is now in the RE Museum, Chatham) is unmarked, apart from a few faint pencilled lines. Thus, if commanders and staff officers were unable to mark their maps, they would have had to rely on their memories, written documents or oral briefings from others to know where units were located and to where they were moving. This would have been a particular problem on 15–16 June 1815 when the whole of a large army was on the move and the enemy situation was constantly changing as new information arrived.

Wellington and De Lancey
De Lancey and Wellington had known each other from the 1790s onwards and worked closely from 1809 to 1814. Wellington was a hard task-master who did not hesitate to get rid of those whose standards failed to meet his requirements (for example, Willoughby Gordon), but he repeatedly praised De Lancey in his dispatches from the Peninsula and, knowing that Murray would take several months to arrive, he requested De Lancey by name in April 1815. It would thus appear that De Lancey fully met the commander's requirements.

It also seems reasonable to assume that they knew each other as well as any two men in such a position could, and that De Lancey would have had detailed knowledge of precisely how Wellington operated and the manner in which he required his written work to be presented. It is also common for men in such positions to develop less formal methods of working; thus, in a crisis documents between the two may well have been prepared in note form, with the very minimum of 'frills' or formalities.

The Nature of the Document
The only evidence of the 'De Lancey Memorandum' is the printed version and the explanatory notes that appear in the 1852 *Dispatches*. Evans' copy appears to have been returned to him and cannot now be traced, so that it is impossible to prove or disprove that the original was in Evans' hand, although Gurwood says that it was. Examination of the document without Evans' footnote shows it to be set out in the baldest possible terms, with not a single unnecessary word. It has a single heading indicating the purpose of the information, while the lack of column headings suggest that it was either intended to be handed over to Wellington with an oral explanation, or that it followed a standard format which had been used before and which both Wellington and De Lancey understood. A third possibility is that, in making his copy, Evans was simply in such a rush that he omitted the column headings, salutations and signature, contenting himself with getting the gist of the information down on paper.

THE 'DE LANCEY MEMORANDUM'

DISPOSITION OF THE
BRITISH ARMY AT 7 o'clock A.M. 16th JUNE

1st Division	Braine le Comte	marching to Nivelles and Quatre Bras
2nd Division	Braine le Comte	marching to Nivelles
3rd Division	Nivelles	marching to Quatre Bras
4th Division	Audenarde	marching to Braine le Comte
5th Division	beyond Waterloo	marching to Genappe
6th Division	Assche	marching to Genappe and Quatre Bras
5th Hanoverian Brigade	Hal	marching to Genappe and Quatre Bras
4th Hanoverian Brigade	beyond Waterloo	marching to Genappe and Quatre Bras
2nd Division, 3rd Division, Army of the Low Countries		at Nivelles and Quatre Bras
1st Division, Indian Brigade, Army of the Low Countries	Sotteghem	marching to Enghien
Major-General Dornberg's Brigade and Cumberland Hussars	beyond Waterloo	marching to Genappe and Quatre Bras
Remainder of the Cavalry	Braine le Comte	marching to Nivelles and Quatre Bras
Duke of Brunswick's Corps	beyond Waterloo	marching to Genappe
Nassau Corps	beyond Waterloo	marching to Genappe

MANUSCRIPT NOTE ADDED TO THE
'THE DE LANCEY MEMORANDUM' SIGNED (BUT NOT DATED)
BY COLONEL DE LACY EVANS

> The above disposition written out for the information of the Commander of the Forces by Colonel Sir W. De Lancey. The centre column of names indicates the places at which the troops had arrived or were moving on. The column on the right of the paper indicates the places the troops were ordered to proceed to at 7 o/clock A.M. 16th June, previous to any attack on the British.
>
> (Signed) De Lacy Evans

Current Whereabouts

Major-General Robinson, author of several books on Wellington's campaigns, wrote in 1910 that:

> The original, lost at Waterloo, we can of course scarcely now hope to see; and Sir De Lacy Evans's copy seems also now to have disappeared. It is not among the documents at Apsley House: Colonel Gurwood is said to have returned all MSS to the owners; and Sir De Lacy Evans's papers have not, it is understood, been preserved.[21]

Searches of the known Evans documents by this author have failed to find the 'De Lancey Memorandum'.

Sir De Lacy Evans

Evans (1787–1870) is inevitably at the centre of questions about the 'De Lancey Memorandum'. He served in the Peninsula from 1812 onwards, mainly with the 3rd Dragoons although he also spent a brief period as a DAQMG (March–May 1814), working directly to the QMG, Major-General Murray. He went to North America in 1814 on the QMG staff, but then rushed back to take part in the Waterloo campaign, arriving in the Netherlands in June 1815. He left no detailed description of his activities prior to being involved in events at Quatre Bras, making any reconstruction, at best, speculative.

Evans' arrival in the Netherlands was not expected, so he would not have had a post to go to. It therefore seems reasonable to assume that he went straight to Brussels, where it would have been natural for him to report to the QMG's department, since he knew it was at the hub of affairs and he was himself an experienced QMG officer.

Evans told Gurwood that he had been 'with Colonel De Lancey when they [the orders] were issued and despatched to the different Corps of the Army'. This suggests that he was roped in to help on the evening of 15 June, at a time when, as Jackson has explained, every available QMG staff officer was required to produce the necessary copies of the movement orders. The next firm information on Evans' whereabouts is in his letters to Siborne[22] where Evans describes how, on 17 June he was sent, together with another officer, to reconnoitre the defile at Genappe but 'chiefly to select a position on the high ground above it towards the Waterloo side, for the whole of the Heavy Cavalry and some Horse Artillery to form on immediately they should clear Genappe. This was under the orders of Lord Angelsey . . .' Since the formation he was tasked to site was the Heavy Cavalry, this confirms that he had joined Ponsonby's Brigade by this stage and it could well be that Ponsonby selected Evans for this task because, first, as an 'extra ADC' he could be spared and, secondly, with his previous experience as a QMG officer, he knew what was required. In his description of the events on 18 June Evans does not mention going elsewhere (for example, to Wellington's headquarters), so it can be assumed that he spent the whole day of the battle with Ponsonby's Brigade.

Evans became a Member of Parliament in 1831, but took time off in 1835 to command a mercenary force known as the British Legion in the Spanish Carlist War, returning to England in June 1837, when official approval of his activities was shown by promotion to colonel (June 1837), followed by a knighthood (August 1837). De Lacy Evans was thus a very experienced and respected soldier as well as an MP at the time he submitted the 'De Lancey Memorandum' to Gurwood, and he later went on to command a British division in the Crimean War. He was promoted to general in 1861 and died in 1870. It is also worth pointing out that Evans was no favourite of Wellington's (and vice versa), was not a member of the 'charmed circle' and, indeed, believed that the Duke had held back his promotion. It therefore seems highly improbable that Evans would have taken part in any attempt to support Wellington.

In *Wellington's Dispatches* it is made quite clear that Evans had signed the explanatory note, which was either at the foot of or attached to the 'De Lancey Memorandum'. It is considered self-evident that had Evans disagreed with either document as eventually published he would have asked the editor or the publisher of the 1852 edition to issue a correction, or, if that was not forthcoming, to take some action to protect his reputation; he certainly had plenty of time to do so, since he did not die until 1870.

A Fraud?

Could the 'De Lancey Memorandum' have been a fraud, intended in some way to bolster Wellington's reputation? To achieve this, it would have been necessary for Wellington and Gurwood, either separately or in combination, to be active parties in a deliberate fraud, or for some third party to have perpetrated a hoax which has then fooled many people for some sixty years.

However, *Dispatches* were widely read at the time, and when the second edition appeared in 1852, many men who had served at the headquarters during the Battle of Waterloo and who had known De Lancey personally were still alive. For example, Lord Fitzroy Somerset (d. 1855), who was Wellington's Military Secretary in 1815 and saw all his correspondence, was also renowned for his honesty and integrity; thus, despite his known loyalty to Wellington, it seems improbable that he would have remained silent, had he felt there to be anything suspicious about the document. There were also a number of men alive who had been on De Lancey's staff at the battle – Abercromby (d. 1853), Gomm (d. 1875), Greenock (d. 1859), Scovell (d. 1861), and Woodford (d. 1879) – and these, too, would have had to remain silent for a fraud to have succeeded. Thus, if the document was a forgery the possibility of discovery was considerable and the two men most intimately involved – Wellington and Evans (Gurwood had died in 1845) – both had considerable public reputations to protect and for either of them to have been involved in a fraud would have been the most absurd folly.

Conclusions

It is, therefore, concluded that:

- The document was an internal 'staff paper' written by Colonel De Lancey for Wellington's information.

- The details of moves and locations were those known to Colonel De Lancey at the time he wrote it, and if it contains inaccuracies, these are due to the limitations of communications, maps and staff procedures of the time.

- There is no evidence of fraud.

- In the absence of any conclusive evidence to the contrary, the 'De Lancey Memorandum' must be considered to be authentic.

NOTES

1. Gurwood, *Dispatches* (1838), Volume XII, p 474, footnote.
2. Captain William Siborne was the author of *History of the War in France and Belgium in 1815*, which was first published in 1844. Many of the letters he received from participants in the battle when researching for his book were later assembled and published by his son, Major-General HT Siborne, as *Waterloo Letters* in 1891.
3. Gurwood to Siborne, letter dated Paris, 23 March 1838. British Library Add MS 34.706, folio 460. The name has been carefully examined and is definitely 'Freeth'.
4. For example, a General Order issued at Badajoz (11 September 1809) instructed that HQ clerks would receive 2s 6d in addition to their soldier's pay. (University of Southampton, WP9/1/2/1 f 84.). Clerks were permanent elements of the HQ, while orderlies were attached from regiments and rotated at regular intervals.
5. See General Order, Brussels, 4 June 1815.
6. The press was transported in carts supplied by the Royal Waggon Train (*Supplementary Despatches*, p 431) and was operated by Sgt Buchan of the 3rd Guards (*Supplementary Despatches*, p 540).
7. Letter Major-General Barnes, AG in Brussels, Volume XIV, pp 540–1.
8. Major-General Willoughby Gordon, QMG in London, dated 13 April 1815. *Supplementary Despatches*. Wellington had been accompanied by an 'Orderly Dragoon' throughout the Peninsular War (Browne, THB, *The Napoleonic War Journal of Captain Thomas Henry Browne*, ed. Buckley, Bodley Head, p 156).
9. Frazer, *Letters of Colonel Sir Augustus Frazer*, ed. Sabine, Longman, Brown, London, 1859, pp 543–6.
10. Scovell, *Copy of Memorandum of Service at the Battle of Waterloo*, PRO WO/37/12
11. One such is the Adjutant-General's Letter Book at the University of Southampton, WP 9/5/2.
12. Frazer, *op cit*, p 582.
13. Gwent County Record Office, Raglan Papers 'Wellington C. Nos 130–155. Misc Letters and Memoranda'. The Gwent map has a footnote stating that 'This is a copy of a copy made from the original sketches. The pencil lines on the original sketches are supposed to be those the Duke of Wellington made on the morning of the 17th June 1815'. This footnote is signed by Oldfield and dated 'Dublin, December 15th 1852'.
14. *Supplementary Despatches*, Volume XIV, pp 570, 572.
15. We know from Lieutenant-Colonel Frazer, who was also at the headquarters, that both he and Wellington had orderlies and it would have been very unusual had De Lancey not also had one. Frazer, *op cit*, p 572.
16. Frazer, *op cit*; p 572. Some of the papers were later found and returned to Wellington. Frazer, *op cit*, page 582. If Wellington's documents could disappear in the chaos for a week and then be found by chance, it seems scarcely surprising that De Lancey's documents were also lost.
17. Willoughby Gordon (the same man who served for such a short time as QMG in the Peninsula [see Chapter V]) was a well-known schemer and it is worth noting that none of the Outbooks covering his period as Military Secretary (1804–9) are to be found, although those of his predecessor and successor are both in the Public Record Office (WO 3/594 and 3/595, respectively). Thus, it is not only papers from the operational theatres that are missing. (See *Journal of the Society for Army Historical Research*, Volume XXI, p 60 f/n 1.)

18. Gurwood, *Dispatches*, 1852 edition, pp 142–3.
19. *Supplementary Dispatches*, Volume x, p 496.
20. Frazer, *Letters*, p 536.
21. Robinson, Major-General CW, 'Waterloo and the De Lancey Memorandum,' *Journal of the Royal United Services Institution*, Volume LIV, May 1910, p 590, footnote 3.
22. Letter Evans to Siborne dated 14 October (no year given), Siborne, *Letters*, pp 59–60.

BIBLIOGRAPHY
Books

Peninsular and Waterloo Campaigns

'A Near Observer,' *The Battle of Waterloo, Containing the Series of Accounts Published by Authority, British and Foreign, with Circumstantial Details,* Seventh Edition, John Booth, London, 1815.

'A Near Observer,' *Additional Particulars of the Battle of Waterloo, also of Ligny and Quatre Bras, with Circumstantial Details, by a Near Observer,* Volume II, John Booth, London, 1817.

'An Englishwoman' [Mrs Eaton, née Waldie], *Narrative of a Residence in Belgium during the Campaign of 1815 and of a Visit to the Field of Waterloo,* John Murray, London, 1817.

'An ex-Aide-de-Camp,' *Three Years with the Duke of Wellington in Private Life,* Saunders & Otley, London, 1853.

'A Staff Surgeon' [Dr Henry, 66th Foot], *Trifles from my Portfolio, or recollections of Scene and small Adventures during Twenty-Nine Years' Military Service,* 2 volumes, Quebec, 1839.

Browne, Thomas Henry, *The Napoleonic Journal of Captain Thomas Henry Browne: 1807–1816,* ed. RN Buckley, Bodley Head for the Army Records Society, 1987.

Dalton, Charles, *Waterloo Roll-Call,* William Clowes, London, 1890.

Esposito, Brig-Gen Vincent and Elting, Col John, *A Military History and Atlas of the Napoleonic Wars,* Greenhill Books, London, 1999.

Fraser, Edward, *The Soldiers Whom Wellington Led,* Methuen, London, 1913.

Fraser, Sir William Augustus, Bart, *Words on Wellington: The Duke – Waterloo – The Ball,* JC Nimmo, London, 1889.

Frazer, Sir Augustus, *Letters of Colonel Sir Augustus Simon Frazer, KCB, commanding the RHA in the army under the Duke of Wellington, written during the Peninsular and Waterloo campaigns,* Major-General Edward Sabine, RA ed., Longman, Brown, Green, Longmans & Roberts, London, 1859.

Gleig, Mary E (ed.), *Personal Reminiscences of the Duke of Wellington,* John Murray, London, 1904.

Gleig, Reverend R, *The Story of the Battle of Waterloo,* John Murray, London, 1907.

Gore, Captain Arthur, *Explanatory Notes on the Battle of Waterloo,* London, 1817.

Gronow, Captain RH, *Reminiscences and Recollections*, London, 1889.

Gurwood, Lt Col John, *The General Orders of Field Marshal The Duke of Wellington*, Clowes & Sons, London, 1837.

Gurwood, Lt Col John, *Dispatches of the Duke of Wellington*, John Murray, London, 2nd edition, Volumes III, V, VI, VIII, XII (1853–1859).

Hofschröer, Peter, *1815 The Waterloo Campaign, Wellington, his German Allies and the Battles of Ligny and Quatre Bras*, Greenhill Books, London, 1998.

Hofschröer, Peter, *1815 The Waterloo Campaign, The German Victory*, Greenhill Books, London, 1999.

Jackson, Col Basil, *Reminiscences of a Staff Officer*, London, 1903.

Larpent, F Seymour, *The Private Journal of F Seymour Larpent, Judge-Advocate General, Attached to the Head-Quarters of Lord Wellington during the Peninsular War, from 1812 to its Close* (two volumes), Sir George Larpent, Bart, ed., Richard Bentley, London, 2nd edition (revised), 1853.

Longford, Elizabeth, *Wellington: Volume 1. The Years of the Sword*, World Books (Weidenfeld & Nicolson), 1971.

Moore Smith, GC, *The Life of John Colborne, Field Marshal Lord Seaton*, John Murray, London, 1903

Moore Smith, GC (ed.), *Autobiography of Lieutenant-General Sir Harry Smith, Baronet of Aliwal on the Sutlej, GCB*, John Murray, London, 1901, Volume 1, 1853.

Müffling, Major-General Freiherr Friedrich Carl Ferdinand von, *Passages From My Life, Together with Memoirs of the Campaign of 1813 and 1814*, 2nd edition, revised, Richard Bentley, London.

Robinson, Major-General CW, CB, *Wellington's Campaigns – Peninsula – Waterloo 1808–1815*, Hugh Rees, London, 1907.

Ropes, John Codman, *The Campaign of Waterloo – A Military History*, New York, 1906.

Shaw Kennedy, General Sir James, *Notes on the Battle of Waterloo*, John Murray, London, 1865

Shearer, Maj Moyle, *Recollections of the Peninsula*, P Haythornthwaite, ed., Spellmount, Staplehurst, 1996.

Siborne, Major-General HT, *Waterloo Letters. A Selection from Original and Hitherto Unpublished Letters*, Cassell, London, 1891.

Siborne, Captain William, *History of the war in France and Belgium in 1815 covering minute details of the Battles of Quatre-Bras, Ligny, Wavre and Waterloo*, T&W Boone, London, 1844.

Smith, Digby, *The Greenhill Napoleonic Wars Data Book*, Greenhill Books, London, 1998.

Stafford, Alice Countess of (ed.), *Personal Reminiscences of the Duke of Wellington by Francis the First Earl of Ellesmere*, London, 1904.

Stanhope, Philip Henry, 5th Earl, *Notes of Conversations with the Duke of Wellington, 1831–1851*, London, 1888.

Swinton, The Honourable Mrs JR, *A Sketch of the life of Georgiana, Lady De Ros, with some reminiscences of her family and friends, including the Duke of Wellington*, John Murray, London, 1893.

Sweetman, John, *Raglan – From the Peninsula to the Crimea*, Arms & Armour Press, London, 1993.

Thomson, RH, *Scientific Soldier, A Life of General le Marchant, 1716–1812*, Oxford University Press, London, 1968.

Vale, Colonel WL, *History of the South Staffordshire Regiment*, Gale & Polden, Aldershot, 1969.

Wellington, 2nd Duke of, *Supplementary Despatches of Field Marshal Arthur, the Duke of Wellington*, John Murray, London, 1857–72, Volumes VIII, IX, X, XIV.

Yonge, Charles Duke, *The Life of Field-Marshal Arthur, Duke of Wellington*, Chapman & Hall, London, 1860, Volume I.

De Lancey Family

Appleton, *Cyclopedia of American Biography*

Archibald, Douglas, *Tobago Melancholy Isle, Volume Two 1770–1814*, University of the West Indies, St Augustine, 1995.

Calneck and Savory, *History of the County of Annapolis.*

Carmichael, Gertrude, *The History of the West Indian Islands of Trinidad and Tobago – 1498–1900*, Columbus Publishers Ltd, Port-of-Spain, Trinidad.

Forsyth, William, *History of the Captivity of Napoleon at St Helena*, 3 volumes, John Murray, London, 1853.

Laurence, KO, *Tobago in Wartime: 1793–1815*, University of the West Indies Press, Jamaica, 1995.

Pillans, T Dundas, *The Real Martyr of St Helena*, Andrew Melrose, London, 1913.

Spencer, Alfred (ed.), *Memoirs of William Hickey*, Volume IV (1709–1809), Hurst & Blackett, London, 1925, 5th edition.

Venn, John A, *Alumni Cantabriensis (Parts I and II)*, Cambridge University Press, London, England, 1922.

White, RJ, *Life in Regency England*, BT Batsford, London, 1963.

Hall Family

Becke, Major AF, *The Royal Regiment of Artillery at Le Cateau, Wednesday 26th August 1914*, Royal Artillery Institution, 1919.

Brown, Richard, *Society and Economy in Modern Britain 1700–1850*, Routledge, London, 1991.

Brown, Robert Lamont, *Robert Burns's Tour of the Borders 5 May – 1 June 1787*, The Boydell Press, Ipswich, 1972.

Cockayne, GE, *The Complete Baronetage*, Alan Sutton, London, 1823.

Constable, Thomas, *Archibald Constable and his Literary Correspondents, A*

Memorial by His Son, Edmonston & Douglas, Edinburgh, 1873 (Volume III).

Daiches, David; Jones, Peter; Jones, Jean, et al, *A Hotbed of Genius, The Scottish Enlightenment, 1730–1790*, The Saltire Society, Edinburgh, 1996.

Edgeworth, Maria, *Castle Rackrent*, 1800

Hall, Captain Basil, RN, *Account of a voyage of discovery to the West Coast of Corea, and the Great Loo-Choo Island, including an account of Captain Maxwell's attack on the batteries at Canton, and of an interview with Buonaparte at St Helena in August 1817*, John Murray, London, 1840

Hall, Captain Basil, RN, *Travels in India, Ceylon and Borneo*. Selected and edited with a biographical introduction by HG Rawlinson, George Routledge & Son, London, 1931

Scott, Sir Walter, edited and with introduction by Fiona Robinson, *Fiona, The Bride of Lammermoor*, 'World Classics', Oxford University Press, Oxford.

Smith, Sally: *Cockburnspath: A History of a People and a Place*: Dunglass Mill Press, 1999.

Thorne, RG, *The House of Commons: 1790–1820*, Secker & Warburg, London, 1986.

Williams, Captain Godfrey Trevelyan, *The Historical Records of the Eleventh Hussars, Prince Albert's Own*, George Newnes, London, 1908.

Lady De Lancey's Narrative

Grierson, Sir Herbert, *The Letters of Sir Walter Scott* (12 volumes), London 1932–37, (Volume IX [1825–1826]).

Hay, Captain William, CB, (edited by his daughter, Mrs SCI Wood) *Reminiscences 1808–1815 Under Wellington*, Simpkin, Marshall, Hamilton, Kent & Co, London, 1901.

Hills, Robert, *Sketches in Flanders and Holland*, 1819.

Robertson, J Logie, MA (ed.), *The Poetical Works of Sir Walter Scott*, Oxford University Press, 1901 (1951 edition).

Russell, Lord John (ed.), *Memoirs, Journal and Correspondence of Thomas Moore:* Volume IV.

Ward, Major BR, *A Week at Waterloo*, John Murray, London, 1906.

MANUSCRIPTS

Anon, *Traditions of Dunglass*, Notes Written for Mrs Basil Hall, 1883. Courtesy of JDH Hall, Esq.

Burns, Robert, *Journal of Tour of the Borders*. Courtesy of John Murray, Publishers

De Lancey, Lady Magdalene, *Lady De Lancey's Narrative*, Courtesy of her great-great-great grandson (her personal copy).

De Lancey, Lady Magdalene, *Lady De Lancey's Narrative*, Scottish Record Office, Edinburgh (GD 206/4/48)

MAGAZINE ARTICLES

'A Staff Officer' [Colonel Basil Jackson], 'Recollections of a Staff Officer,' *Colburn's United Service Magazine and Naval and Military Journal* (four parts: Sep, Oct, Nov 1847 and Jan 1848).

De Lancey, Lady Magdalene, 'Lady De Lancey: A Story of Waterloo,' *The Illustrated Naval and Military Magazine*, Volume VIII, No 48, June 1888, pp 414–16.

De Lancey, Lady Magdalene, 'A Week at Waterloo,' *The Century Magazine*, Apr 1906, Vol LXXI, No 6, New York.

Edmonds, Brig-Gen Sir James E, 'Wellington's Staff at Waterloo,' *Journal of the Society of Army Historical Research*, Vol XII, 1933, London.

Hall, Capt Basil RN: 'The First Englishman Napoleon Ever Saw' [original Ms of Hall's meeting with Napoleon, with an introduction by Lady Sophie Hall], ed. Lady Sophie Hall, *Nineteenth Century*, Oct 1912, pp 718–31.

Hussey, Christopher, 'Country Gardens Old and New: Dunglass, Haddington,' *Country Life*, 12 Sep 1925, pp 396–403.

Robinson, Maj-Gen CW, 'Waterloo and the De Lancey Memorandum,' *Journal of the Royal United Services Institution*, Vol LIV, May 1910, pp 582–96.

'Sportsman', 'Dunglass: The Home of Sir John Richard Hall,' *Scottish Field*, Dec 1918, pp 258–60.

Tipping, H Avray, 'Portraits and Reminiscences of the Halls of Dunglass,' *Country Life*, 10 Apr 1920, pp 483–85.

Ward, SGP, 'The Quartermaster-General's Department in the Peninsula' 1809–1814,' *Journal of the Society of Army Historical Research*, Vol XXIII, pp 133–54.

Children, John George, Letter to the Editor, *Illustrated London News*, Saturday 27th Nov 1852. Vol XXI, No 593, p 469.

OFFICIAL DOCUMENTS

Public Record Office, Kew. Many documents including:

> **PRO WO 25/745.** Statement of the Service of Lieutenant Colonel De Lancey, Permanent Assistant Quarter Master General. Headquarters Badajoz, 18 October 1809.
> **PRO ADM 51/4099.** HMS *Lyra*: Captain's Log.
> **PRO ADM 37/5903.** HMS *Lyra*: Muster Roll

British Library. Many documents, including:
> Indian Records **L/MIL/9/116, 257, 258** and **259**. Honourable East India Company military embarkation lists

DOCUMENTS OF RECORD

The Times
Gentleman's Magazine

BIRTHS, MARRIAGES, DEATHS

All stated births, marriages, deaths, Wills and Administrations (admon) in England and Scotland have been authenticated from original records in the Public Record Office, Kew, the Scottish National Record Office, Edinburgh, the Families Records Centre, London, and County Record Offices in Devonshire, Somerset and Wiltshire.

Index